Film and Television in Education

The Falmer Press Library on Aesthetic Education

Series Editor: Dr Peter Abbs, University of Sussex, Brighton

The aim of the series is to define and defend a comprehensive aesthetic, both theoretical and practical for the teaching of the arts.

The first three volumes provide a broad historic and philosophical framework for the understanding of the arts in education. The subsequent volumes elaborate the implications of this comprehensive aesthetic for each of the six major art disciplines and for the teaching of the arts in the primary school.

Setting the Frame

LIVING POWERS:
The Arts in Education
Edited by Peter Abbs (1987)

A IS FOR AESTHETIC:
Essays on Creative and Aesthetic Education
Peter Abbs (1988)

THE SYMBOLIC ORDER:
A Contemporary Reader on the Arts Debate
Edited by Peter Abbs (1989)

The Individual Studies

FILM AND TELEVISION IN EDUCATION:
An Aesthetic Approach to the Moving Image
Robert Watson

LITERATURE AND EDUCATION:
Encounter and Experience
Edwin Webb

DANCE AS EDUCATION:
Towards a National Dance Culture
Peter Brinson

THE VISUAL ARTS IN EDUCATION
Rod Taylor

THE ARTS IN THE PRIMARY SCHOOL
Glennis Andrews and Rod Taylor

MUSIC EDUCATION IN THEORY
AND PRACTICE
Charles Plummeridge

EDUCATION IN DRAMA:
Casting the Dramatic Curriculum
David Hornbrook

Work of Reference

KEY CONCEPTS:
A Guide to Aesthetics, Criticism and the Arts in Education
Trevor Pateman

Film and Television in Education: An Aesthetic Approach to the Moving Image

Robert Watson

The Falmer Press

(A member of the Taylor & Francis Group)
London • New York • Philadelphia

UK   The Falmer Press, Rankine Road, Basingstoke, Hampshire
         RG24 0PR

USA   The Falmer Press, Taylor & Francis Inc., 1900 Frost Road, Suite
         101, Bristol, PA 19007

© Robert Watson 1990

First published 1990

British Library Cataloguing in Publication Data
Watson, Robert
    Film and television in education: an aesthetic approach to the
    moving image. — (Falmer Press library on aesthetic education).
    1. Educational institutions. Curriculum subjects: Media studies
    I. Title
    372.8

    ISBN 1-85000-714-4
    ISBN 1-85000-715-2 pbk

Library of Congress Cataloging-in-Publication Data
Watson, Robert, 1947–
    Film and television in education: an aesthetic approach to the
    moving image/Robert Watson.
    p. cm. – (The Falmer Press library on aesthetic education)
    Includes bibliographical references.
    ISBN 1–85000–714–4: ISBN 1–85000–715–2 (pbk.):
    1. Motion pictures in education – Great Britain.   2. Television
    in education – Great Britain.   I. Title.   II. Series.
    LB1044.W36 1990
    371.3′ 35–dc20

Jacket design by Benedict Evans

Typeset in 11/13 Bembo by
Chapterhouse, The Cloisters, Formby L37 3PX

*Printed in Great Britain by Burgess Science Press, Basingstoke
on paper which has a specified pH value on final paper
manufacture of not less than 7.5 and is therefore 'acid free'.*

Contents

List of Figures   vi

Acknowledgments   vii

Series Editor's Preface   ix

Chapter 1   Education: The Legacy of the 1960s   1

Chapter 2 The Beginning of Film   11

Chapter 3 Conventional Narrative Sequence   17

Chapter 4 From Snapshots to the Long Take   43

Chapter 5 Language, Genres and Television   95

Chapter 6 Film in the Narrative Arts   131

Bibliography   151

Index   169

List of Figures

Figure 3.1:   A man being pursued by a car?   20

Figure 3.2.i: Camera positions – the visual impact of the close-up.   23

Figure 3.2.ii: Reading the frames – the importance of camera-to-subject position.   24

Frames 2.3 and 2.4: Camera position near the ground with its 'eyeline' level with the subject.   25

Frames 2.5 and 2.7: Low angle and high angle camera positions.   26

Figure 3.3:   Aerial view of a man and woman, with four possible camera positions and the close-ups they would frame.   31

Figure 3.4:   Shot/reverse shot patterns.   33

Figure 3.5:   Repetitious use of the shot/reverse shot pattern.   35

Figure 3.6:   The over-the-shoulder shot.   36

Figure 3.7:   The symmetrical pattern of a sequence of shots.   37

Figure 3.8:   Camera position 5 – duplicating the woman's point of view.   37

Figure 5:1   A simplified plan of the *Fawlty Towers'* stage set.   124

Figure 5.2:   A simplified plan of the *Fawlty Towers'* dining room set.   125

Acknowledgments

At The London School of Film Technique (The London International Film School), I received a vocational training which I have come to regard, over the last twenty years, as a model of disciplined creativity in education. My sense of the underlying significance of basic film conventions has evolved and been strengthened through a decade of teaching in comprehensive schools and, since 1986, my work at Bretton Hall. I should like to thank Carol Lorac for commenting so usefully on early versions of several chapters, and Dr Peter Abbs for involving me in this project initially, and inviting me to address open seminars at Sussex University. The questions and discussion following these talks helped to determine the areas explored in this book.

Robert Watson
Bretton Hall College
January 1990

Preface

There can be little doubt that of the six great arts which the Library of Aesthetic Education is committed to defending and defining, film has been the most ignored in the curriculum of our schools. There is a grand irony in this for film is not only the one unique art form developed in our own century but also the most unequivocally popular.

As Robert Watson shows in the first chapter of this book, it is symptomatic of the condition of film in education that most of the limited attempts to include it have failed to grasp its artistic nature and its expressive possibilities. For example, among the first serious attempts to include film in education must be listed F. R. Leavis' and Denys Thompson's *Culture and Environment* (1933); but, in that once highly influential book, film was virtually equated with cultural pathology whose dire influences had to be critically resisted at all costs. Subsequent initiatives, influenced by the Newsom Report (1963) were generally more positive in recommending film in the classroom but essentially as a kind of dramatic stimulus for discussion, or as illustrative material for project work; in other words, not as a profound art form requiring aesthetic response and creative engagement. Under more recent developments in Media Studies, film (along with television and video) continued to secure some space in the curriculum but, once again, the aims have been primarily ideological and discursive. Film was envisaged as part of a system of communications which had to be decoded in terms of ideology and contextualized in terms of power and control. The analysis may have had much to recommend it – we need to know who owns what and why, just as we need to be able to read the hidden messages of advertising – but, at the same time, the approach missed entirely the crucial aesthetic element, erased the difference between propaganda and art and failed to see the liberating creative powers of the camera when put in the hands of the learner.

Robert Watson's *Film and Television in Education* with its telling subtitle *An Aesthetic Approach to the Moving Image* sets out to remedy the neglect. It does so in a number of closely related ways.

First of all, the book advocates a highly practical aesthetic for the teaching of film, television and video. The author celebrates 'camera as eye, camera as pen, camera as accessible to everyone of whatever ability as an expressive tool to observe, record and create with'. This means that film in the curriculum ought to include the sustained experience of making film, and involve a purposeful and exacting apprenticeship with the medium itself. Part of the value of this book is that it provides the teacher with detailed guidance in this area. It suggests very specific ways of beginning and of developing artistic and creative work in film.

Secondly, the book calls for an unapologetic recognition of film as a great art form, as fully capable of exploring and representing the nature of human truth as any of the other traditionally established arts. This calls for an end to the peevish tradition of denial which is rooted in the polemic of F. R. Leavis, and which is not yet quite over. It calls also for radically new ways of envisaging the responsibilities of the arts teacher and the arts faculty. Any aesthetic education, worthy of the name, must now be seen to involve a profound initiation into the whole complex field of film, that vast international and interactive web of artistic traditions, of worthwhile attempts and actual triumphs. In this respect the teaching of film belongs to the teaching of all the other art forms and shares the same vital model. This model, which was outlined earlier in the first two volumes of the library (in *Living Powers* and *A is for Aesthetic*) insists on the dynamic relationship between the student's own expressive work and the field of achieved and inherited work in the same medium. Yet, strangely, this is a model which has not been developed in film.

Thirdly, Robert Watson suggests that we can and must extend the aesthetic of film to television and video. While certain differences can be noted between these modes of expression there would seem to be no fundamental discontinuity. They belong together and they all possess an aesthetic quality and potential, in the case of television and video, often pitifully undeveloped. In this study, the author is particularly concerned to demonstrate an analysis of popular entertainment through aesthetic, rather than ideological, categories. His unusual analysis of *Blind Date*, of the news, of commercials, of sit coms and pop videos is not only challenging, but also offers an example of the kind of analysis which can be developed in the classroom and studio. What is distinctive about the analysis is its emphasis on genre and its recognition of the reciprocal relationship between artistic convention and human meaning. Once again, it implicitly challenges some of the methods used in Media Studies and offers alternative ways of working closer to those used in sensitive literary and arts criticism.

Finally, the book calls for a literacy in film. One of the great problems of film lies in its transparency, its apparent naturalness, its seeming inevitability – as if it was merely an unobtrusive extension of the human eye. The seeming naturalness – the 'realism' – obscures the artifice. It is this characteristic which partly explains why for so long in the classroom film was used as a means to information and as a dramatic stimulus for discussion and why its art and artifice went unacknowledged. Our fundamental aim here must be to dissolve that illusion so as to disclose the underlying structures of the artifice and the intentionality which directs the movements of the camera. Every part of the programme advocated in this book: the making of film by students, the appreciation of film, the aesthetic and evaluative engagement with popular television programmes, depends on an understanding of what, a little imprecisely, can be called the grammar of film. This grammar includes an understanding of all the main structural elements of film and their complex interaction: of the variety of camera shots, of composition, of genre, of lighting, of music, of colour, of dialogue, of acting. An initiation into the field of film calls for an initiation into its aesthetic grammar. At one important level *Film and Television in Education* simply provides a dictionary of terms, of examples, of techniques, of titles, and in so doing provides much of the language which has been badly missing at least in the educational world. In providing the practical and aesthetic language of film, television and video this book, at once, illuminates the necessary practice and makes it thereby the more possible.

Now arts teachers know what, with regard to film, they are fighting for, how the discipline could be constituted aesthetically and why it matters.

Peter Abbs
Centre for Language, Literature and the Arts in Education
University of Sussex
January 1990

Chapter 1

Education: The Legacy of the 1960s

The film is *the* art form of the first half of our century.

Berger, J. (1965)

... film is by any standards today, of entirely marginal intellectual interest *per se*. It cannot possibly justify itself as the basis for a substantive discipline or field of study.

Garnham, N. (1981)

Media education ... seeks to increase children's critical understanding of the media – namely, television, film, video, radio, photography, popular music, printed materials, and computer software.

Bazalgette, C. (1989)[1]

Whatever became of *the* art form of the first half of our century over the last twenty-five years? It appears to have been mugged by the media.

> ... what we also did in the '70s was to jettison theories we never thought we'd have to rework. Aesthetics was élitist; production merely creative; pedagogy took care of itself. In fact, these never really had the status of theories anyway: part of the politics of that period was precisely to discard 'atheoretical' notions that were being used to justify a contempt for politics and for history. But just because we may have been right then, does not mean that aesthetics, production and pedagogy will never be needed, cannot be theorized. If we really want to make sense of the media, we need these theories too. (1986)[2]

I don't believe such a puritanical and philistine politics *was* right then; part of its legacy can be seen in the curious collocation of eight named media which, if not quite gratuitous, seems to be based on little more than the opportunist notion that if the word *Media* is repeated often and firmly enough it may be taken to constitute a subject area. I don't underestimate the importance of inculcating a 'critical understanding of the media', but they are not homogeneous; corralling them into an already crowded curriculum must result either in superficial study or in the selection of optional choices – that, of course, could mean that film, or television, or radio (any of them), might simply disappear. The assumption that all these media are equally important will not be questioned here, but the assumption that an education in any one must be comparable to, or even synonymous with, any others is false. How has the situation arisen in which '*the* art form of the first half of our century', in John Berger's words, has been assimilated into such a heterogeneous selection of media? A partial answer can be found in my essay in *Living Powers*, which includes a chronological account of significant educational developments, but I think the question is better served if we recall something of the mood of the time when Berger was writing.[3]

Film in the 1960s

The 1960s was, *inter alia*, the period of the French New Wave, when each new film by Godard was a cultural event that seemed to reshape the language in ways that dismayed some and exhilarated others. Conventions were being challenged, broken down and re-assembled. Part of the value of this process was that it helped those of us who were only just discovering the language to understand that it *was* in fact composed of conventions, evolved traditions and distinctive national, generic and individual styles. References to the cinema of the past, particularly to Hollywood, were sometimes affectionate, sometimes scathing, but either way called for revaluations – making it new meant recognizing the past in order to respond to the present. Retrospectives made, say, Renoir's films of the thirties as immediate as those of Godard, Truffaut, Resnais, Marker and the rest; young film makers from Eastern Europe were emerging – Jiri Menzel, Milos Forman – and from elsewhere established directors seemed to be joining the onward rush of the new wave – Bergman, Bunuel, Fellini, Antonioni, Kurosawa, Satyajit Ray. The veteran director, Fritz Lang, turned up in one of Godard's films, so did Samuel Fuller. It was an extraordinarily fraternal period and it didn't matter very much that England contributed little creatively, or was unable to sustain the impetus of directors like Lindsay Anderson, because England was at least very receptive.

In addition to *Sight and Sound* and *Films and Filming*, *Movie* magazine had started in the summer of 1962, blasting British cinema, praising American and giving some attention to the rest; Studio Vista started a series of *Movie* paperbacks; Lorrimer began publishing screenplays; Secker commenced their Cinema One series; Zwemmer and Tantivy also ran series of film books, and these publications were so profuse that the impression was of a single international film culture that was tangibly and vitally *present*, and this presence was of course reinforced by the range of old and new films available in cinemas, film societies and, to a lesser degree then, on television.

It was a period when Film was part of what it meant to be young and intellectually curious. Film was not an academic discipline, nor yet a forbidding zone where competing theoretical discourses were elaborated; it was, or appeared to be, part of a more generous and openly enthusiastic culture. Film was a vibrant source of energy, and it exemplified what the phrase 'a living art' is supposed to mean.

Film and Television in Education

Given the demonstrable surge of interest in the art it is not unreasonable to look for comparable new initiatives in film teaching. The main positive thrust in earlier decades had come from the theoretical work of Pudovkin and Eisenstein, and had centred on the art of editing, or montage, and that had been combined with the influence of Grierson and the Documentary movement of the thirties. That was fairly spartan stuff compared to the broader but more negative appeal of work such as Leavis and Thompson's *Culture and the Environment* (1933), much of which could be implemented within English teaching. As late as 1950, the Wheare Report (the report of the Home Office's Committee on Children and the Cinema) saw film much as Leavis and Thompson had, as a harmful influence:

> A large number of films are exposing children regularly to the suggestion
> that the highest values in life are riches, power, luxury and public adulation
> and that it does not matter very much how these are attained or used.
> According to these films, you can eat your cake and have it too.[4]

By implication, the only reason for teaching film would be to inoculate the young against it. But by 1963 the Newsom Report, *Half Our Future*, was, if not exactly endorsing film as a mature art at the centre of cultural discourse, at least acknowledging its power over the young without adding the customarily overt judgmental tone:

> The culture provided by all the mass media, but particularly by film and
> television, represents the most significant environmental factor that
> teachers have to take into account.[5]

So film and television were not to be ignored – they weren't going to go away – and yet the tone of the passage is not encouraging: an 'environmental factor', however significant, doesn't really convey the 'Bliss was it in that dawn to be alive' feeling which was not uncommon in the sixties. People whose job is 'to take into account' an 'environmental factor' are presumably unaffected by it themselves; instead of responding critically to a vital experience in their own lives, seeking ways of sharing their perceptions with pupils, they are detaching themselves from their culture and looking on from outside, or down from above, and with the best of intentions – often starting where the children are – they discard their own insights and intuitions and set about constructing a subject that is socially relevant. Intense as it may be, their commitment is to an abstraction, an ideology, and not to the concrete problems inherent in an education in art.

Newsom's terms of reference were in themselves significant – the remit was to consider the education of 13–16 year olds of average and less than average ability. The recognition that established subjects, conventionally taught, were not always appropriate to the needs of large number of pupils was to be welcomed, but the opening it helped to create for film, television and other media was limiting and clearly did not reflect the way that film was perceived in the world outside educational establishments. That these media could appeal usefully to less academic children is undeniable, but so could other subjects if taught more imaginatively; similarly, film and the other media could be taught to the *most* academic students without lowering their standards, but the Newsom Report helped fix the perception of film as one of the mass media, and of mass media as an environmental factor to which the young of average and less than average ability were particularly susceptible.

A year after Newsom, the British Film Institute (BFI) began what turned out to be a very short series of books by teachers describing their work in film and television studies. *Film Teaching* (1964), gave four accounts of work in Adult and Higher Education; *Talking about Television*, (1966), described work with secondary school pupils 'ranging in ability from far below to slightly above average'; *Talking about the Cinema* (1966), recorded courses taught in further education, while its supplement, *Film and General Studies*, summarized courses for students who were 'well within the Newsom Report's frame of reference. The great majority left school at fifteen. Many of the girls are telephonists, punch-board operators, file clerks; the boys, craft apprentices, dental technicians, office assistants'. All these publications were concerned with appreciation, tending towards a thematic approach and an interest in social problems. (Other influential books of the period that should be mentioned are Raymond Williams, *Communications* (1962), Denys Thompson (Ed), *Discrimination and Popular Culture* (1964), and Stuart Hall and Paddy Whannel, *The Popular Arts* (1964).) A quotation from the supplement to *Talking about the Cinema* reveals something of the way in which film appreciation was adapted for the children identified by Newsom:

> Occurring at the lowest level of abstraction of all the arts, film can provide a strong shared group experience. Given its illusion of actuality and its emotional powers, film can serve to stimulate discussion as perhaps no other medium can.[6]

These courses were certainly, and I'm sure usefully, about talking, and about writing, but because the 'illusion of actuality' was a largely unexplored, unquestioned phenomenon films could be used as virtually unmediated, or transparent, communications of attitudes, situations, themes – the discussion centred on dramatized social issues rather than the art that enabled them to find whatever distinctive expressive form and power they conveyed.

In 1966 the BFI also made available, in a somewhat cheaper format, *Film Making in Schools and Colleges*, but there seems to have been little attempt to make a connection between the development of practical and creative skills – the language in use – and studying the films made by professionals. Apart from Douglas Lowndes' excellent *Film Making in Schools* (1968) there was no further substantial contribution to film as an expressive art that children might articulate their own ideas in, at least not during this period (Keith Kennedy's *Film in Teaching* followed Lowndes in 1972 but was markedly inferior). Consequently, the dominant approach – 'film can serve to stimulate discussion . . . ' – failed to bring anything new to the curriculum.

One aspect of film was exploited, its immediacy of impact. It was 'at the lowest level of abstraction of all the arts', so easy to read that its language could be ignored. Film's contribution, then, was primarily as a substitute for English for those who had difficulties with the abstractions of the written word. By stimulating talk and writing, film was developing English skills, and English was at the same time moving away from literature towards theme and topic work, towards 'extracts' rather than works, chosen for their relevance to issues around which projects could be based. For this was also the period of the Dartmouth Seminar and the revaluation of language in use. Much of what emerged from that is still *in* use, of course, though the arguments are increasingly being questioned (see, for example, David Allen's *English Teaching since 1965* and Edwin Webb's chapter in *Living Powers*).

Questioning the 'sociolinguistic' approach which has characterized much English teaching since the late sixties, Webb writes, in defence of literature, that it provides, arguably,

> *significant* voices; *mature* voices which articulate experience in an *achieved form*; and which are grounded in that accumulation of *collective experience* which we call *culture*. Is literature to be provided because it offers opportunities for the study of 'language-situations'? or does some other purpose inform its use? Does literature have 'values' not necessarily shared by other language-productions?[7]

The same questions could be asked of film, other media, and other media productions, but they weren't being asked in schools in the sixties, and when television, radio and newspapers proved even easier to handle (cropping and captioning photographs, simulating radio broadcasts with tape recorders, making newspapers, and so on), such questions could hardly arise. Film was quietly marginalized. The subject had not been formulated on the basis of its aesthetic but according to its utility, and that was shared by most communications media. But in the next decade media teaching too became problematical for those who were in the business of offering guidance:

By 1970 it was generally recognized that it was impossible to write and teach coherently about a subject area – film – that didn't possess a rigorously theorized body of knowledge, hence *Screen*. The same is true about teaching and education – an analysis of education and the education system is required before it is possible to understand either the position the teacher currently has to adopt or to conceive of an alternative, more useful construction of that position. Having outlined possible areas for work within the constellation film/television/media/image studies over the past six years it has become increasingly clear to the editorial board of *Screen Education* that . . . it is difficult to offer even tentative strategies for teaching those areas.[8]

When one gets so far up an ideological cul de sac that it is impossible to proceed with any kind of education, the time has probably come to question the efficacy of the ideological framework; but the BFI's Educational Advisory Service *was* able to move ahead almost immediately, and almost as if ideology could be sidestepped:

Partly, we have felt it necessary to emphasize film and television as media rather than as merely 'arts' . . . along with this shift towards film and television as media among other media has been a complementary shift . . . towards a general concern with all communication through images. . . . But how *are* images understood? *What* do we understand and *how* is it that we do understand? If images are seen as *constructed* through the use of certain devices within the context of certain *conventions*, then our attention as educators is drawn towards the ways in which meanings are constructed and towards the uses to which the image is put in society. Who is saying what? to whom? how? why?[9]

These fine questions should have been asked by students *Talking about the Cinema* in the mid-sixties. Now they were being asked about 'all communication through images' but, curiously, they were being asked in a discourse that wanted to deny itself access to 'arts'.

By almost any standards one can apply, television is now at least as important as film: more people spend more time watching it, more people are involved in making it, its effects (insofar as they can be ascertained) are more pervasive. Only from the narrow perspective of artistic quality – a perspective which our January column indicated we did not think the most fruitful for media studies – is it possible to argue for the supremacy of film, and even this can hardly be argued in respect of current British production.[10]

Albeit grudgingly, film is granted its importance 'from the narrow perspective of artistic quality', but that perspective is not 'fruitful' – mass appeal is the criterion of *real* importance. But if that criterion is applied seriously it will not make television *per se* the main subject of study, for there are television programmes which neither seek nor achieve high ratings – it will dispense with such programmes and attend only to those which have the greatest appeal (as well as the predictable soaps, the most popular programmes would include first television screenings of popular films, coronations, and royal weddings). Applied to other media the same criterion would severely distort radio, make a nonsense of photography, and work pretty well, I suspect, with popular music – I've no idea how computer software would fare!

Film was pushed aside because, ostensibly, 'artistic quality' was no longer a criterion for determining what should be taught, though the evidence suggests that it hadn't been taught as an art in the sixties anyway. Some film theorists continued to struggle intelligently with the problem inherent in artworks that were of and yet not wholly contained or explained by the society that produced them. In fact, looking back over the last twenty-five years, it isn't hard to trace a powerful argument that starts with director-centred (or *auteurist*) criticism, then challenges both theories of authorship and impressionistic methods of criticism, and attempts to secure a sounder academic base for the whole discourse. At the same time the structuralists' approach really didn't need to confront aesthetic problems at all, and could look more convincing when applied to representative mass media products; similarly, at least part of the feminists' approach centred on gender issues in genre areas such as popular melodrama. A persuasive attack on the concept of 'the author', and a deflection of interest from the specific qualities of particular works to questions of representation in genres or across historic periods, could be combined with the practical difficulties of setting up film appreciation classes and the greater ease with which similar themes could be tackled in other media – against all this film had its 'narrow perspective of artistic quality'. And there were those for whom 'artistic quality' evoked a Pavlovian response: high art, élitism, the tradition of an inert but dominant class, and so on.

But by the late seventies the media *were* apparently to be explored as aesthetic forms ('the ways in which meanings are constructed', 'Who is saying what? to whom? how? why?'), only without acknowledging the presence of the arts. The analysis and discussion of 'images' was to function as a means of drawing attention 'towards the uses to which the image is put in society'. I take this to mean that media study was to be undertaken as a kind of lock-picking operation that would reveal the intricacies of contemporary society, and not because particular media products were of interest in themselves, might have the complexity, or the simplicity, or the truth of works of art, might criticize or transcend contemporary mores.

Tracing the 'who' in 'Who is saying what?' etc. meant going beyond identifying the voices of characters in the story, beyond authorial voices, towards the 'who' of institutions, the 'whom' of audiences, the 'how' of manipulative practices and the 'why' of economics, power and control. And that sounded very important, so long as no-one reflected that the answers to these questions would soon be numbingly predictable. Institutions impose restraints and to some extent control freedom of expression, in every age and society. Large audiences seem to enjoy entertainment that is profoundly familiar in most respects, and therefore easy and comforting to 'read'. In media terms this means that formulaic programming which is conventional and conservative is encouraged. It seems to me that what is really interesting is not that phenomenon, or the general run of programmes to which it gives rise, but the ways in which programme makers find expression and variation within those constraints. In short, it seems to me that the real voices are *not*, after all, those of the institutions but those of the artists, and that we locate those voices in their works, and that the most interesting works are not necessarily football matches, news broadcasts, sitcoms and soaps (the staples of so much research in recent years), but those which, as Edwin Webb said, 'articulate experience in an *achieved form*' – and that has to include personal, felt, poetic experience as well as another minor variation on a stereotype. And so it has to mean film, film as well as television and video, the *art* of film even if the media we explore it with are increasingly likely to be video camcorders and VCRs with television monitors. At its most banal, television imitates old film conventions; at its best it not only derives from but also extends the possibilities of film art.

The eight media mentioned at the head of this chapter were adduced as part of a strategy for the primary school curriculum, where one might expect most of them to be made use of anyway. They are not all directly concerned with 'communication through images', of course, so clearly the educational arm of the BFI has changed its policies again in the last decade. (It was formed, we might remember, in the 'belief that the cinema, a great contemporary art and one of the powerful media operating in society, must find its place in the curriculum'.[11] But that was way back in 1957.) And policies *should* change, only not perhaps so far. There are limits to what is expedient in any circumstances. The media net is cast across business studies and communication skills, several new and evolving technologies, several aspects of popular culture, and English (presumably 'printed materials' implies some English). There doesn't seem to be any particular reason, then, why it stops short of Dance, Drama and Art, or fails to include popular media like the telephone (with innovations such as 'chatlines'), but even so it covers more than enough ground and is certain of at least partial success. No doubt that's better than risking the loss of the media altogether, as far as education is concerned, except as mere resources or devices used to teach something else. In the current educational climate – and I'm drafting this before the National Curriculum has taken effect – this might be the best one should expect. There is no chance of Film becoming a foundation subject. As an optional choice among the media it may be a minor adjunct to English and could conceivably be adopted for various supporting roles in science, technology, art and 'a modern foreign language'.

If this bleak future were to be as immutable as it appears, in the short term, inevitable, there would be no point embarking on yet another book. Large popular, technical, critical and theoretical literatures of film exist, yet its existence as a discipline in schools and colleges is at best tentative. But I believe this failure is partially attributable to the ways in which film study has been implemented in the past. And change *is* possible. Resources that weren't available in the 1960s, and were scarcely available in the 1970s, were sufficiently widespread by the end of the 1980s for new approaches to be initiated. Films can be bought or hired cheaply anywhere in the country. Most schools, colleges and private homes have video recorders; many have video cameras. This does not only mean that audiences have more choice over what they watch on television, it also means that a fundamental change in the nature of viewing, and in the experience of film, has occurred. What was traditionally ephemeral, rather like a live performance in that it could not be repeated at the individual viewer's behest, has stabilized. It's true that some films lose a great deal when shown on television, but the losses are relative and the gains, educationally, have hardly begun to be exploited. Indeed, we may be entering a propitious time for Film, considered as a language and an art. Film, television and video have different technologies, but they share a common language, and in all essentials this language is ready to be used and developed by everyone. It differs from other media productions because it *can* be used as an expressive language by anyone, and because it *has* been used so well for a century already that we have a rich resource in artworks from many countries, to study in their own terms and to draw on as we learn to articulate our ideas and feelings in film, on video, and through television.

The essential language does not require students to learn about organizations and institutions, finance and commercial operations, ownership, statutory obligations, scheduling, market research into audiences, and so forth – that belongs to media studies. It does not require classrooms to be turned into poor imitation television studios, and students into as full an imitation of a studio crew as can be assembled, so that a simulated news broadcast can be essayed – that too belongs to media studies. A better model was provided by the earliest film makers – Le Prince, the Lumière brothers, Paul, Acres, Méliès – or by Dziga Vertov with his 'camera-eye', or Astruc's 'camera-stylo': camera as eye, camera as pen, camera accessible to anyone, of whatever ability, as an expressive tool to observe, record and create with. You learn how to use it by using it, and by studying the uses others have made of it – sometimes mediocre uses, but sometimes extraordinary uses too. Film deserves its centrality not as a medium but as a great language whose finest, and ultimately most useful, expressions depend on its aesthetic form.

To learn to read this language, and write it, and understand who is really saying what, and what it is they're really saying, we must learn to read camera positions, angles and movements, compositions, lighting, and how all these elements are built up for the duration of a narrative; the choice of colour or the tonal range of black and white photography; the way music and other kinds of sounds are used; the actors, their acting, and the dialogue – whose effects can be subtly modified by all the preceding elements. And we can learn this language by reading films from Buster Keaton to Andrei Tarkovsky, including a good deal of television. And we can learn it, and our pupils can learn it, by the equivalent of speaking it, writing it, painting it, sculpting it, composing it, dancing it – by picking up a camera and using it to make stories.

Notes and References

1 Berger, J. (1965) *Success and Failure of Picasso*, London, Penguin Books, p. 70; Garnham, N. (1981) in Christine Gledhill (Ed) *Film and Media Studies in Higher Education*, London, BFI Education, pp. 3–4; Bazalgette, C. (1989) *Primary Media Education: A Curriculum Statement*, London, BFI Education.
2 Bazalgette, C. (1986) 'Making Sense for Whom?', *Screen*, **27**, 5, p. 36.
3 Robert Watson (1987) 'Film is Dead: The Case for Resurrection' in Abbs, P. (Ed) (1987) *Living Powers*, Lewes, Falmer Press, pp. 119–139.
4 The Wheare Report (1950) quoted in Lovell, A. (1971) 'The BFI and Film Education', *Screen*, **12**, 3, p. 14.
5 The Newsom Report (1963) *Half Our Future*, quoted in Butler, I. (1971) *To Encourage the Art of the Film*, London, Robert Hale, p. 17.
6 Kitses, J. (1966) *Film and General Studies*, London, BFI Education, p. 2.
7 Webb, E. (1987) 'English as Aesthetic Initiative', in Abbs, P. (Ed) *Living Powers*, Lewes, Falmer Press. p. 79.
8 Editorial in *Screen Education* (1977/78) **25**, p. 1.
9 BFI Educational Advisory Service (January 1978) *Visual Education*, London, BFI Education, p. 17.
10 BFI Educational Advisory Service, (April 1978) *Visual Education*, London, BFI Education, p. 21.
11 Quoted in Butler, I. (1971) *To Encourage the Art of the Film*, London, Robert Hale, p. 17.

Chapter 2

The Beginning of Film

I am in the National Museum of Photography, Film and Television at Bradford, which is close to where I live and work, and close to the city of Leeds where, some historians argue, film was born.

I am looking at a short film on a small screen. The film consists of one shot, made over a hundred years ago. It may be the first film to be shot anywhere in the world. No other art, unless we include photography, has such a compact history. But what I am looking at is not the original, nor is it a straight copy; it has become a demonstration of what film is.

Each time it finishes the screen goes dark for a few moments and then the shot is repeated. What it depicts is a street scene taken from above, from a second floor window perhaps. There are several people in the lower foreground, on a pavement, and just beyond them a horse-drawn carriage approaches. There are other people in diminishing perspective, and other horse-drawn carriages, but my attention is taken by the legs of the approaching horse, because that is where the movement is most apparent. Each movement indicates the passage of time between one photograph and the next. There are about eighteen photographs in all and if they were run at 'normal' speed the shot – little more than a fragment – would be over in about a second. But it takes longer. This shot is privileged: each frame has been printed several times, extending duration until the shot is watchable both as a sequence of filmed but still photographic images *and* as a recording of movement: analysis and synthesis of movement can be observed together.

It would be impossible to see this in real life. The tension I feel as I wait watchfully for that precise moment of transition is generated by something wholly artificial. I know there cannot be a surprise in store; the next part of the step is inevitable, can only confirm what I know and take for granted. And yet this unnatural retardation of movement somehow transforms it into a fresh discovery. Here is movement as it is being constituted, something constructed out of the flow of visible life. I see clearly, for example, that unlike real life this movement is discontinuous: between one frame and the next parts of the action have occurred which are *not* recorded. Illusion is involved. I am looking at something of the technology that makes film possible, and I have an emotional reaction of a sort, but I don't think I'm responding to a work of art. On the other hand, how can I be sure? This technique of step-printing to slow down the images, for example, could be used with considered creative intent, could be more than a technique, then – part of the expressive language. But in that case it isn't the film that Louis Le Prince made, which would run by in less than a second. I am looking at a film which is over a hundred years old and which has just been made.

What I feel is akin to the astonishment and delight registered by the first audiences when films were projected by the Lumière brothers in 1895. They marvelled at the accuracy and diversity of the movements which the camera was capable of recording – smoke rising from chimneys, waves lapping, people and animals walking. This childlike sense of wonder at the capacity to capture, fix, something as intangible as light and movement is no longer part of our gaze when we go to the cinema or watch television. The contemporary gaze *knows* that already, and it isn't enough, the novelty has gone. Our gaze is no longer awed with 'How can that be so?' but rather, that being so and beyond question, it asks 'What next? What follows?'.

We want film images to *do* something, to add up to more than a brief animated snapshot, depicting a scene from a single viewpoint. Le Prince's demonstration of what his single-lens camera could do its like an unfinished sentence, the first few words uttered in October 1888 towards a new language. His assistant, James Longley, described the film:

> Leeds Bridge – where the tram horses were seen moving over it and all the other traffic as if you was on the bridge yourself. I could even see the smoke coming out of a man's pipe, who was lounging on the bridge.[1]

By chance the naiveté of the expression here is happily appropriate. Le Prince's film cannot tell us what is to follow; it is being born and doesn't yet know what it is or will be – Look, a photograph, a black and white photograph that *moves*! Look at the horse drawing the carriage, how its legs carry that weight forward! Now it's gone. Wait. Here it is again, and exactly as it was last time! Precisely the same movements, picked out of time and space, framed in film and repeatable forever – nothing quite like this has existed in the world before. But what is the value of this image, or these images? As a photograph the street scene is not particularly beautiful, or unusually informative. And the images are not the images of rhetoric. They record an actual scene, inaccurately and imperfectly, to be sure, but nonetheless directly. Is this film a tribute to an extraordinary scientific and technological achievement, or is it valuable because it heralds a great new art? Perhaps there is no separation, no art without its technology. Look again.

The film is not projected on Le Prince's apparatus or on a modern film projector. I am watching a video on a monitor. Instead of being set up vertically for group viewing, as domestic sets are – like scaled down versions of cinema – this screen is set back nearly horizontally in a desk, for the individual spectator. It is a curiously suggestive conflation of film history, nearly a return to the kinetoscope viewer, the peepshow, developed by Dickson and Edison. That used film too, but the images weren't projected onto a screen. You peered down into the box, alone, excluding the world around you. Perhaps it's worth remembering that the invention of television, too, closely parallels the inventions of photography and film.

> ... in 1842 Alexander Bain ... first proposed a device to send pictures from one place to another by electric wires ... In 1862, Abbe Caselli transmitted the first electric picture from Amiens to Paris ... In 1880, Leblanc developed the complete principle of scanning wherein a picture is divided into lines and each line into tiny segments ... 1884 ... the rotating scanning disk ... In 1890 ... a system for a television receiver ... [2]

Like film, television was concerned with the production of pictures and with the dislocating of space (finding a way of transmitting what can only be seen *here* across a distance to the receiver *there*), but instead of photography television used radio as its medium, and so instead of recording it was able to communicate instantaneously. But this clear distinction between the media began to blur almost as soon as television became operative. Several methods of recording were attempted in the 1920s, including the conventional use of film in the first instance, which would then be scanned for transmission. And today video is beginning to be used extensively in film making.

The technology between my gaze and Le Prince's original street scene does more than suggest a confluence of media, does more than relate some of the earliest ways of watching films to some of the latest, and it marks more than a return from the spectacle of cinema to the intimacy of home-viewing. This modest screen, endlessly showing its modest film, serves as a reminder that the massive international film and television industries grew out of and, as far as we the viewers and potential makers are concerned, can ultimately be returned to something this tentative, this *possible*.

For a moment forget those intimidating credits that top and tail the modern commercial product – producers, directors, camera crews, sound crews, electricians, set designers, wardrobe, make-up, costume, colour consultants, caterers, actors, writers – they are all necessary, they all perform important functions, but the functions they perform do not always need such a broad division of labour. For a moment, think of a film as a diary, or any personal expression. After all, anyone can point a camera out of an upstairs window and record a scene as effective as Le Prince's. But you won't be a pioneer in quite the same sense – you won't have devised and built your own cameras, working by trial and error towards the equipment that will succeed in the task most efficiently. Your equipment will be sophisticated. Your results will be more realistic, inasmuch as the images will resolve more detail and be in plausible colour. If you only point your camera through a window and record a short street scene your satisfaction will probably be short-lived, because that's all you will have done. Some movement, some sound. What was once a difficult concept, finally and marvellously realized, is now an exercise that can be fairly effortlessly carried through, signifying – apparently – nothing much. The initial motivating concept has gone inert. We rarely, or never, watch films simply to be amazed by their capacity to *record*, at least not consciously, because they do that all the time. There has to be something more, in effect another concept, a concept at least as new and remarkable as that which led to the inventions of photography and film.

The new concept does inhere in the invention and the fact of recording, but not as a logical inevitability. The invention itself could be predicted, but not the art it made possible – we see that it was inherent retrospectively. An easy way to reinforce this point is by an analogy with recorded music. When we buy records or tapes we may concern ourselves with the quality of the recordings, but usually only to the extent that the sounds we want to hear are reproduced as clearly as possibly, without detectable creative interference from the sound engineers. Clear recordings depend on sophisticated technology and a high level of skill in the manipulation of equipment, but these do not result in an aesthetic of disc or tape. What matters is the quality of the music which is reproduced, the interpretation it is given by particular musicians. The adequacy with which that interpretation is reproduced is all that reminds us that the recording is not absolutely neutral or transparent. It is conceivable that film could have remained a mere medium in this sense, with comparable technological advances and the development of trained image-engineers.

All films, videos, and most television programmes are, before they become anything else, recordings. Most films, videos and live television broadcasts show us elements of a world that we recognize already from outside the boundaries of technology and art – landscapes, rooms, people walking, driving, talking. These media are, therefore, easier to *dis*regard than to regard closely, especially since much of their art conspires with transparency to involve us with the illusion, to 'take us in' willingly. On Le Prince's film are impressed the images that realize the initial concept of fixing movement and reproducing that impression. The concept may have gone inert or grown banal with familiarity, but that doesn't mean it has become disposable. It is what we register first, without having to think about it or respond consciously to it, and it is what encourages us to believe that everything of interest resides, as with recorded music, in the subjects or events being recorded.

However, even in Le Prince's film I can see there is something beyond a neutral, objective recording, an older concept already assimilated: the photographic view of the street is reasonably attractive to look at. That says something about the concepts *I* have assimilated too, of course; it connects me, not with the actual street, but with the sensibility of the cameraman. The connection may seem slight – there were many *better* images of streets prior to this one, by architectural, sociological or aesthetic criteria –

but it is nonetheless of crucial significance. I cannot know what considerations occasioned the choice of where to position the camera, only that the resulting shot is 'well-composed', that is, it conforms to acceptable compositional standards derived from the visual arts, with a strong diagonal adding its dynamism to the central feature of the traffic of the street. The camera records in the way that the pen writes, the brush paints, the chisel sculpts: it is an instrument. To see how this instrument would soon be used to re-compose our perceptions of what streets look like, contrast Le Prince's received aesthetic (received of course from photography, and from painting since the Renaissance, an aesthetic based on monocular perspective, a single, fixed viewpoint, and a framed, two-dimensional image) with the work of Karl Freund in Ruttmann's *Berlin* and in sequences of Murnau's *The Last Laugh*. These, too, are 'old' films, from the last decade of the 'silent' cinema, but they are also modernist works of art. The camera is moved *through* these streets, it doesn't just record the movement *on* them; it is being repositioned continually and rhythmically, shooting by day and by night, and adopting superimpositions.

The bulkiness and weight of Le Prince's camera, the shortness of the strip of film, and preconceptions about how to look, secure his achievement in the nineteenth century, but already then, as something new was being born almost simultaneously on several continents, three features were discernible:

1   The immediate documentary goal – the recording and reproduction of human and animal movements in realistic synthesis (as well as the accurate recording of various artefacts which have no apparent volition – the buildings – but might in due course fall down. The historical record).

2   A reliance on existing pictorial conventions in framing and composing these recordings, that is, a tentative concern with expression – how the scene is to be seen.

3   Out of the combination of these two features, the potential for the third – freer expressiveness in the act of recording; the modification of neutrality by selectivity; the mediating presence of whoever directs the camera.

Most of the pioneers had abandoned film long before the new concept was sufficiently established for anyone to begin considering film as an art form. (The first American theory of film was Vachel Lindsay's *The Art of the Moving Picture*, (1916). In the same year Hugo Munsterberg's *The Photoplay: A Psychological Study* was published. The latter is generally regarded as the first major film theory[3].) New to film and also new in the world, the concept involves moving from a form capable of recording received images as *impressions* to a form capable of transforming what it receives into its own *expressions*.

The expressiveness of the form – choosing *what* to record as well as *how*, *where* and *when* to record it, then rearranging the *duration* and *sequence* of the recorded pieces to form a pattern or a narrative – will give film affinities to other arts such as painting, drama, music and literature, as well as its own characteristics. In the following pages I will introduce some of the most widely used conventions. Even those that have become hackneyed through over-use need to be identified so that students can develop and articulate appropriate critical responses in 'reading' films, and acquire a kind of loose syntax to use or transcend in film making.

Notes and References

1   Kilburn Scott, E. (1931) 'Career of L. A. A. Le Prince', reprinted in Fielding, R. (1983) *A Technological History of Motion Pictures and Television*, Berkeley, University of California Press.
2   Lankes, L. R. (1948) 'Historical Sketch of Television's Progress' reprinted in Fielding, R. (1983) *A Technological History of Motion Pictures and Television*, Berkeley, University of California Press.
3   See Dudley Andrew, J. (1976) *The Major Film Theories*, An Introduction, Oxford, Oxford University Press.

Chapter 3

Conventional Narrative Sequence

The narratives of the world are numberless. Narrative is first and foremost a prodigious variety of genres, themselves distributed amongst different substances – as though any material were fit to receive man's stories. Able to be carried by articulated language, spoken or written, fixed or moving images, gestures, and the ordered mixture of all these substances; narrative is present in myth, legend, fable, tale, novella, epic, history, tragedy, drama, comedy, mime, painting... stained glass windows, cinema, comics, news item, conversation... Caring nothing for the division between good and bad literature, narrative is international, transhistorical, transcultural: it is simply there, like life itself. Barthes, R. (1977)[1]

Every narrative must have its language, not just that which channels it or conveys it (the medium), but that which more actively communicates it. The language of film narrative has no *precise* equivalents for phrases, clauses, sentences, paragraphs and chapters, or for nouns, pronouns, verbs and adjectives, or for figures of speech, or for colons, semi-colons, hyphens and full stops, but it is capable of producing the kinds of effects gained by some of these devices, as it is of producing effects like those gained in the theatre by act and scene divisions. It uses a language of conventions but it is also, 'like life itself', excessive, in that it is always using and often being understood in terms of elements which cannot be contained within any single system of conventions. The excess includes that which we register common-sensically as 'real-life', that which is usually the essential subject matter, that which is likely to appear autonomous – recorded but not significantly interfered with by the recording medium – that which may appear to elude systematic appraisal.

Going back to Le Prince's street scene, for instance, none of the recorded elements belongs obviously to film art: the buildings, the street, the parapet of the bridge, the strolling people, the horse-drawn traffic – these are what we see, what we want to see, in this narrative of a second or so of movement, extracted from an October day in Leeds in 1888. At any given moment in any film, a large part of what commands our attention is likely to belong to this irreducible excess which resides prior to, inside, and still beyond the art's conventions. But that does not mean that only the film which *subdues* excess by imposing unusual camera angles, extreme forms of lighting, disorientating cuts from shot to shot, and so on is the 'true' art-film. In the 1960s there was a fashion for this kind of flashiness. The film of *The Ipcress File*, (1965), directed by Sidney J. Furie, was a deliberately downbeat story of espionage; its spies were civil servants without glamour, and their world was ordinary and a bit seedy. It was filmed in colour and widescreen, compositions serving the screen shape rather than the story, so that quite irrelevant foreground props would frame scenes elegantly but distractingly, and there were high angles, low angles, even a shot from inside a refrigerator, all of which created a separate visual plot that was pretentious and laughable. One was aware of the mediating gaze of the film makers, but that did not improve the film. So we must be careful, when considering narrative conventions without the context of a full film, to remember that they are only expressive *possibilities*, ways of shaping that excess which will sometimes be the very heart of what we wish to communicate.

So far I have written of the excess as 'real life', because I think that is an aspect of film and television everyone recognizes and many would use to distinguish film from the other arts – its relation to the existing human world is simply so much more evident. To understand the basic structuring of film narrative, however, it will be useful to localize the excess as *story*. Here I am not so much concerned with the way film fills its *space* with visual representations of the physical characteristics of people, places and things, as with how it handles events or actions in *time*.

This excess, *story*, is the raw material. For example, everything that happens to you, or that you make happen, today, in full chronological sequence, may stand as your story of today. But if you want to re-tell it there will be parts that don't fit, parts you may wish to re-arrange, emphases you will make to highlight what is most typical or significant. This shaped narrative is the *plot*. The plot may well include revelatory flashbacks at appropriate moments but, at least in the classical account by Aristotle, it will remain fundamentally chronological, with a beginning to introduce the action, a middle to develop it, and an end to conclude it. The *story* is artless and important because it constitutes 'what really happened'. The *plot* is artful and only important if it selects and orders what happened so skilfully that that 'truth' is conveyed convincingly, even though it is now represented, say, on a stage, with actors, and has a specific duration. Some of Chaucer's tales were already well known as myths, legends, allegories, folk-tales; Shakespeare worked on chronicles, lives, prose romances, other plays. Their versions became authoritative and supplanted earlier ones because their plotting brought these stories to their final, most convincing, most truthful, shape.

If you switch on the television and catch a live discussion, the narrative is the progress of the conversation, the action and reaction of the participants. Story, raw material, will be dominant, and plot minimal. This may appear to be the case with more obviously constructed programmes too, because in most commercial cinema and television the plotting conventions (which include lighting, camera, sound and editing as well as dialogue and descriptions of action) are designed to further the illusion of realism. This almost makes film a perfect Aristotelian model, with plot not drawing attention to itself but merely serving to arrange the salient features of the story in their proper order and with exemplary clarity. Only for Aristotle the story, to be worth plotting in the first place, dealt with actions of tragic or epic significance. *EastEnders* and *Neighbours* move, distract or irritate us with commonplaces, and encourage us to escape from any troubling confrontation with what, in Plato's sense, is *really* real.

For Russian Formalist critics like Shklovsky the story (or *fabula*) didn't really matter; it was no more than a pretext for the plot. The story *could* be completely trivial, could even be abandoned. The plot (or *sjuzet*) included digression and all the other rhetorical devices Chaucer ever played with and alone constituted the art and the scope of one's interest in it. *The Ipcress File* would become a fascinating subject for study precisely because of its mismatching of styles and confused purposes. Most twentieth century critical analysis has gone some way towards the formalist position, to uncover *how* a thing is said, but without losing Aristotle's sense that *what* is said still matters, so that evaluation finally combines plot and story in something like *how well has this artist dealt with this story?* It is Aristotle's meaning of plot that we follow when we ask someone to tell us the plot (or, indeed, story) of a play or film and expect to be given a summary of the sequence of events. However, I am going to use the word in its slightly less familiar sense to illustrate how one of the simplest stories is plotted to make a narrative sequence. The conventions I shall use evolved unsystematically over a number of years but had gained widespread acceptance by the 1920s and are still in use – which doesn't mean they cannot, or should not be challenged, but, rather, that they have become normalized. A convention works rather like a 'grammatical' sentence, as a coherent normative base around which variant forms can take effect, not as an absolute criterion of value. Just as there are writers who compose nothing but beautifully-turned sentences in books that are lifeless, so there are film makers whose works are perfectly well constructed and tedious from beginning to end. A convention is an accepted standard procedure, comprehensible, well used, efficient. It can serve, but not create a personal style.

The simple story I want to tell has something to do with a man and a car. The plot is suggested in the pictures for *Figure 3.1*. Such simple sketches, incidentally, can be put on a blackboard quickly, then as easily rubbed out and replaced in discussion; they may also help to persuade students that telling stories in pictures requires little skill in drawing.

In *Figure 3.1* there are eight frames, corresponding to eight 'shots' from a film. One frame is blank, four include a vehicle, three a figure. The frames are not numbered and I've found that whether the sketches are done before the students arrive or in random order while they watch it makes no difference to the majority reading of the plot: when asked what is happening here, most students reply that a man is being

Figure 3.1 A man being pursued by a car?

pursued by a car (or a van, whichever is easier to draw), which runs him down and continues on its way.

The Sequence

Does the story have to be about a man getting run over? Couldn't it also be the story of a man who sees a car, chases after it, and then lies down exhausted as it speeds away? Couldn't it also be the case that there is *no* story, there there is no connection between car and man?

The information is ambiguous, partly because it doesn't tell us enough of the story. The plot lacks a beginning; it is a sequence, in bare outline. Most students will read the regularly spaced frames according to the convention for reading print and strip cartoons, starting with the car at top left and ending with the car bottom right. Within the sequence is a simple pattern of repetitions according to whose logic the blank frame should be occupied by the figure; then that pattern is reversed in the last pair of frames. Thus, a rhythmic pattern encourages anticipation, prediction, regardless of the shot *content*, the action being described. A plot will sometimes confirm expectations, sometimes confound or defer them. Because the car occupies the first frame it is natural to presume that it pursues the man – the sequence prompts that interpretation. But already several assumptions are being made.

One is that this sequence is complete. But if the first frame were eliminated, or preceded by another shot of the man, then the 'man chases car' story would have more credence. If we assume the sequence to be complete, and to run in the logical order we have given it, there is still a conceptual leap from these frames to the experience of a *film* sequence, where images replace each other at a standard speed, at least since the twenties, of twenty-four frames per second (twenty-five on television). The drawn frames represent shots, but no indication is given of the *duration* of each shot, or the duration of the whole sequence. And we have to assume, for example, that the car is not stationary. That most students do so testifies to the familiarly hackneyed nature of the plot, but also to the power sequencing has on the imagination. The horizontal line (a kerb?) is common to all seven sketches, as is the *implied* movement given by *direction* – car and man face screen right throughout – and the alternating frames do nothing to contradict or disrupt this implication (this notion can be played with by having car or man face screen left in a couple of frames – 'man runs towards car'? 'two cars trap man'? 'man panics, loses sense of direction, and faints'?).

So far, students will have established that there could have been several original stories. Interpretation is deduced from the sequence of the plot. Car and man have not appeared together in the same shot but a relationship has been strongly implied by *cutting* them together in alternate shots. Duration has also been suggested, albeit weakly, by the changes in the three drawings of the man – walking, running, prostrate. Nevertheless, if these drawings were to be used as a *storyboard* (a visual blueprint for the camera to imitate) the resulting film would lack something in dramatic interest. It is visually monotonous. Why? Each shot is seen from the same position, angle, height and distance. Each shot is a *long shot*, maintaining the strong horizontal line, as well as the same camera-to-subject line – level and parallel with the ground. Le Prince's street scene had a much stronger dynamic, although it too was a long shot, because he used a *high angle* and a *diagonal* rather than horizontal composition. Even so an effective sequence could be made from *Figure 3.1*, particularly if there was fast movement along that horizontal, and if that movement was emphasized by a lateral camera movement – tracking or panning with the car and the man (extraordinary examples can be found in Kurosawa's *Throne of Blood*, (1957) and *Seven Samurai*, (1954)). But some of the alternatives are probably better. Steven Spielberg's small-budget *Duel*, (1972), uses the conventions with great versatility. The film was made for television, but released theatrically in this country. There is little dialogue and the plot seems not much more elaborate than *Figure 3.1* here: a salesman is menaced by a truck. But the film is witty, perceptive and exciting. Spielberg said he tried to avoid, in his television apprenticeship, 'the television formula of closeup, two-shot, over-the-shoulder, and master shot',[2] but in fact he made extensive use of it, as do most directors, only he used other, less predictable combinations as well. In television these conventions *are* often formulaic, which is why reading television as film language is often like reading 'Janet and John' books, which do, of course, have their uses.

What should go into the empty frame in *Figure 3.1*? Logically, the car hitting the man, the scene's climax and the one moment when we expect both elements to meet in one shot. This image can be presented at first in the same way as the others, with no change in camera position. The man will probably be placed on the bonnet, under the wheels, or in flight over the car like some Minoan bull-leaper. But if this is a separate shot how do we get *to* it from the preceding shot of the car, and *from* it to the succeeding shot of the fallen man? If we stay with the car until it hits the man then perhaps this shot should be a continuation of the preceding one, not a new shot at all – it isn't different enough. If, as the pattern of repetition suggests, we start this new shot on the man, then the *next* shot is really a continuation – we just stay on him where he falls.

Any alternative requires a change of camera position and, possibly, a multiplication of shots of shorter duration, which might well affect the temporal sequence in relation to *story* time. If we cut from the car to a *close-up* of the man's face – turning, realizing he is about to be hit – then we'll still need something more before we can cut to his prostrate body. And if we want to *suggest* the collision, rather than have our actor actually knocked down by a fast car, how can we do that? What selection of *details*, rapidly cut together (or, to take another convention, done in slow motion), would imply that impact? Would it be feasible to use an analogy – something hard hitting something soft? An egg breaking on the floor, a hammer smashing a melon? Such specific images may be either absurd or excessive. A consideration of their potential would involve some discussion of the narrative context beyond the sequence itself, as well as perhaps the beginnings of a discussion of style and intent. Justification would depend on the *tone* of the sequence, the way characters, motivation and action have been built up, whether or not largely gratuitous imagery would fit, whether or not to establish similar referents earlier. The blank frame, then, could open a discussion leading to a reconsideration of the way the whole sequence has been plotted so far. How could it be made more vivid?

Camera positions

The first five frames of *Figure 3.2* could be read as direct substitutes for the corresponding frames of *Figure 3.1*, each *long shot* being replaced by a *close-up* – the alternating pattern of subjects stays the same, but the visual impact is quite different. The selection of significant dramatic detail literally brings the viewer closer, within the larger action of the sequence, which is no longer so clearly visible, perhaps, but is experienced rather than observed. As a general rule, *long shots* allow greater

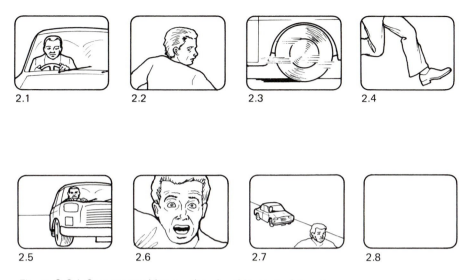

Figure 3.2.i Camera positions – the visual impact of the close-up.

detachment while *close-ups* encourage involvement. Necessarily, then, the director's choice of where to position the camera will radically affect the plot.

Another point worth noting is that it is now the eighth frame which is blank because the collision has not yet occurred. The closer details increase dramatic involvement, movement, and the sense of speed, but more shots are liable to be required to complete the sequence – it is becoming a descriptive passage, and as it does so the distinction between *story* and *plot* should become clearer. The kinds of excess mentioned earlier are still apparent, but so is the element of creative control or manipulation. One begins to read film not just as a chronological statement of the action but with some attention to the *the way* it is presented, and that attention is informed by the extent to which one may bring to a reading an awareness of the way this type of sequence is *generally* described, and of the many *other* ways it might have been presented, an awareness that can concentrate attention on what is really being said here, what is meant by *these* camera positions rather than others, by *this* particular combination of shots rather than another.

In the following account of a sequence from *The Quiet Man*, (1952), for instance, Joseph McBride and Michael Wilmington perceive the elaboration of a major theme of the film, not in terms of dialogue but camera placement:

> When the fight finally occurs, it has become the nexus of so many points of communal conflict that it ranges all over the countryside, surrounded by a horde of spectators. Ford shoots it repeatedly in long-shot to emphasize its communal, dance-like aspects, and gives us a score of vignettes within the

action. The dramatic crisis is rooted in Sean's private conflicts, but it finally affects the whole community. To enter the community, he must understand and accept the rules and traditions of its basic unit, the family. It is his refusal of his public role (his standing in the community) which prompts Mary Kate to refuse her private role. The film ends in consummate harmony, with all the villagers gathering to give tribute to a visiting Anglican prelate (the parish priest hides his collar and urges the crowd to 'cheer like Prostestants'), and Sean and Mary Kate running into their cottage to complete their marriage. But before we see the couple, Ford gives us a long series of 'curtain call' shots of the other characters. Individual harmony is a condition of communal harmony. (1974)[3]

I don't altogether agree with this interpretation, but I do find it a productive illustration of the principle that the camera-to-subject position can be crucial to a critical reading, affecting atmosphere and pace and, potentially, deepening the psychological insight that may be read out of the work.

Returning to the humbler narrative in *Figure 3.2*, it may be noticed that there is something 'wrong' before the final shot: 2.7 appears to be out of sequence after the big close up in 2.6. Reading the frames from 2.3 to 2.6 we expect the car to be much nearer than it is in 2.7. Any sequence is predictive. Logically, playing to expectation, 2.7 *should* be either an extreme close-up of the car (or its driver), or show the moment of impact. On the storyboard at least, 2.7 looks as if it would 'fit' better if it preceded 2.1. Which other shots in this sequence could be rearranged, or used more than once?

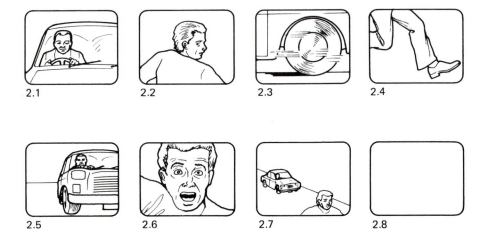

Figure 3.2.ii Reading the frames – the importance of camera-to-subject position.

Instead of reading *Figure 3.2* as a second complete narrative sequence, its frames may be taken as a group of suggestions – the sorts of shots we could interpolate with some of those in *Figure 3.1* (another example would be a shot of the approaching road taken from inside the car, perhaps over the driver's shoulder). Students will throw out most of these ideas, and more, very quickly, so that the blackboard soon accumulates enough sketchy material for the standard camera positions to be named and seen to emerge from a language already familiar. These positions are relative, not exact:

A *long shot* usually means one that will include its subjects comfortably within the frame; if the subjects are tiny and move across a vast landscape it may be called an *extreme long shot*.

A *medium shot*, or *medium close-up* of a figure is usually from above the knees to just above the head.

A *close-up* could include head and shoulders, or only the head; an *extreme* or *big close-up* could be any significant feature: the eyes, lips, a bead of sweat on a forehead, a hand gesturing.

If such specific description is indicated in the screenplay (and not all directors want such direction from writers) the terms are generally abbreviated to their initial letters: ELS, LS, MCU, BCU, etc.

I would say all the shots in *Figure 3.1* are long shots, and all in *Figure 3.2* (except 2.7) are close-ups, but I wouldn't argue if another reader said 2.1 is a medium shot or a medium close-up.

Having communicated some of the expressive story-making possibilities derived from the juxtaposition of standard camera positions – and so far these have all assumed a fixed camera and, for the most part, average camera height of about five feet – selected frames from *Figure 3.2* can also suggest the potential of deviations from the norm. In 2.3 and 2.4. the camera is positioned nearer the ground, but its 'eyeline' is still level with the subject.

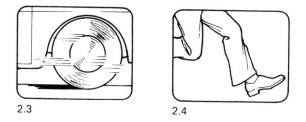

2.3   2.4

Frames 2.3 and 2.4 Camera position near the ground with its 'eyeline' level with the subject.

2.5 and 2.7 show two alternatives: in the first the camera is positioned near the ground and tilted *up* slightly, while in the second it is positioned above standard tripod height and tilted *down*. These positions are known respectively as *low angle* and *high angle*.

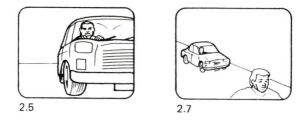

2.5   2.7

Frames 2.5 and 2.7 Low angle and high angle camera positions.

Angled shots (shots which deviate from the horizontal camera-to-subject axis) tend to distort perspective and scale, and can be used deliberately to exaggerate the size or proportions of a figure or an object. In the low angle, 2.5, the front of the car looms large in the frame and thus appears more threatening, powerful and thematically important (this is the part that will cause most damage to the victim!). A shot like this will often employ a lens that deviates from standard, too. The standard lens is 40mm or 50mm. A wide angle lens, appropriate here, may be anything from 30mm to 14mm – the smaller number gives the wider field of vision and greater distortion. The low angle shot also used to be called the 'hero' angle. Shooting the hero in medium close-up from a slight low angle could make him more imposing, authoritative, strong in the frame – especially if that angle was not used indiscriminately elsewhere. Using it for the villain as well would diminish its subliminal moral effect, though one may well want to do that or, indeed, subvert the code and humanize the hero by showing him from standard camera height (more or less at eye level), or even from a slight high angle. The high angle shot, as in 2.7, from above looking down, tends to diminish stature, compressing rather than extending a figure. It is an effective way of suggesting vulnerability or isolation, especially if combined with a long shot.

The last reel of Sam Peckinpah's beautiful film, *Guns in the Afternoon*, (1961), is a perfect statement of the conventions addressed in this chapter. Despite the fact that it conforms to the conventions of its genre, the Western, by ending with a climactic shoot-out, and despite the fact that this is filmed in the classical style, the sequence is not mechanical or formulaic because plot and story are in accord. The graduated low angle shots of Joel McCrea do not merely 'place' him as hero, though by increasing the angle subtly they do have the effect of glorifying and regenerating him as he enters the confrontation that both justifies and ends his life. The low angle makes possible a strong diagonal, with his gun-arm extended and crossing the frame bottom to top in the simplest and most powerfully balanced visual composition. Particularly in contrast to the shots of the other figures, relatively disorganized and exemplifying uncontrolled forces of violence, the shots of McCrea valorize a life based on a simplistic chivalric ideal of righteous virtue, justified honour. He *appears* to be indomitable within a fully controlled image that emphasizes economy and directness of action. But the composition also has the limitations of its strength: as an emblem of a human life it is inflexible, rigid as his philosophy, unyielding to nuance and frailty. The Hammonds, the enemy, in their awkward stances, seem despite their manifest wickedness, helpless before this superhuman retributive force.

The sequence also builds on contrasting visual and aural *rhythms*. McCrea and his partner, Randolph Scott, begin their walk towards the showdown and as they get into step a quiet march rhythm begins on the soundtrack. They are strengthened into an harmonious, unstoppable forward movement, while the loose line formed by the Hammonds has no ordered rhythm of its own.

But rhythm really needs to be explored separately, with study film extracts, because a storyboard can only suggest limited tonal and compositional rhythms within and between static frames. Rhythm includes the *duration* of each shot and the pattern set up by editing together shots of varying lengths, the movements that occur *within* each shot and their relation to the internal movements in preceding and succeeding shots; rhythm also includes dialogue, sound and music, the larger structural features of day and night, interior and exterior, repetitions of images and sounds, and so on.

Camera movements are as much a part of the plot and experience of a film as the static camera positions I have been describing, but they are not always used in a disciplined way in commercial films and television, and inexperienced students, especially if working with lightweight cameras hand-held, have a tendency to move the camera almost indiscriminately. I think it is important to impress anyone being introduced to film as an art with the discipline of intelligent preparation, and consideration of what will be gained by a camera movement, or what *kind* of movement will be appropriately expressive, is preferable to ill-informed experimentation whose results cannot be evaluated against creative intentions. I know it can be fun to pick up a camera and play around with it, and some will learn quickly in this way, but time and resources are usually limited, so some instruction – including the imposition of constraints – is a practical necessity, and it is unlikely to preclude mistakes or stifle imagination anyway.

The discipline of plotting for a static camera in a fixed position is well worth practising. Its antecedents would include the great majority of short films made in the formative years of cinema, and it has also formed a sturdy backbone for most commercial feature-length films; latterly it has become almost a fetish with avant-garde film makers, much as the mindlessly mobile camera was for a time in the 1960s. Used intelligently, as in *The Chronicle of Anna Magdalena Bach*, (1968), the predominantly static camera, with occasional discreet and minimal movements, concentrates attention on Bach's music and the tableaux, and intensifies emotional restraint into a profoundly moving aesthetic experience. (Interestingly, Straub has said that a direct influence on this film was his viewing of several films by the great silent director, D. W. Griffith.) Used as little more than a fashionable style, a short-cut to significance, as in several of Peter Greenaway's films, it loses seriousness and becomes an exercise in pretty but repetitive composition, intellectually vacuous and emotionally DOA.

With the camera positions and angles already sufficiently noted there is ample material for storyboarding a sequence far better than that originally shown as *Figure 3.1*. Partially contradicting the advice in the paragraphs above, I've sometimes encouraged students to practise the skills of making storyboards as if they had been given an unlimited budget and shooting schedule – the resulting work would often be impossible to film with the facilities available to most schools and colleges, but the process helps to develop confidence. One of the most effective sequences I've seen was made by a boy in a supposedly 'low ability' secondary school class. He showed a hawk in the sky, at first as seen from the ground, tiny in the frame, then in close-ups from above and from the side, showing head and eye. There followed bird's-eye views of the fields below, then a close up of a mouse. The sequence moved towards its climax as the hawk swooped, its shadow falling across the creature. There was a big close-up from the mouse's point of view of the enormous talons, then a long shot of the hawk flying away, in silhouette, the creature held in its claws. The boy knew in advance that this was not a practicable subject for filming in class (though with more time he might have attempted animating it in 8mm), but his pleasure came from his discovery of a descriptive narrative power he hadn't been aware of, and which had not been evident in his written work. Subsequently there have been several wildlife documentaries on television, containing a similar range of extraordinarily intimate shots, edited so cleverly that the wild animals and birds seem to become actors in a fictional (and as narrative, deeply conventional) drama, but this boy hadn't seen them. He was working from observation (he lived on a farm), memory, imagination and the opportunity of the slight stimulus of a brief introductory discussion about storyboarding.

An alternative exercise for reinforcing the basic conventions is to provide a story outline verbally, almost as a puzzle: a certain amount of information is given, now it has to be conveyed entirely through pictures. For example, the sequence may begin with a man setting the timer on a bomb and placing it in the boot of a car, and end when the bomb explodes. Two couples have to be introduced, the couple in the car and another couple out walking. There is a busy street scene. The car and the walking couple must arrive at a border checkpoint at the same time. These elements occur in the opening sequence of *Touch of Evil*, (1958), and when the students have had fifteen minutes or so to make eight or twelve quick sketches they can compare the film sequence with the shots they've selected. Usually several frames will match closely, and there'll be a few ingenious variations. The fact that Welles' sequence is an elaborate crane shot lasting just over three minutes inspires awe but does not deter students from picking up the camera positions located within it (see Hitchcock's comment, p. 86), and giving them an example with an exuberantly moving camera seems to make them more alert and critical when they check the frequent and often mundane use of similar but static set-ups on television at home.

Some of the differences between film and television, and the practical differences of using film or video when film-making, will be discussed in a later chapter, but one characteristic of film stock has had such a fundamental influence on the development of the art that it has to be dealt with here. Unlike the electronic medium of television, which is capable of transmitting a 'live' picture without interruption for any length of time, film stock has a physical bulk which necessarily enforces a durational limit upon any shot. The early films of the Lumière brothers ran for a little under a minute, because that was the time it took to crank the length of film available through the camera. By 1898 a magazine capable of holding 400 feet of film had been designed by J. A. Prestwich. By 1948, when Hitchcock made *Rope*, magazines holding 1000 feet were in use; this meant that with the camera running at normal speed a maximum shot length of ten minutes was possible (though no one but Hitchcock utilized it, and the *average* shot length for feature films has always been well under a minute, and usually under a quarter of a minute).[5] With a video camera plugged into a mains supply it is possible to film a continuous shot lasting several hours, and there are occasions when this recording facility is invaluable. I've filmed school plays, for example, when there was no opportunity for a camera rehearsal, no place to cut without losing part of someone's performance, and only the lighting blackouts between scenes to work like fades out and in; students sometimes make filmed records of drama rehearsals or fashion shows in much the same way.

But in all such uses the camera is subordinated to the event. The ingenuity of the operator should afford it *some* expressiveness, but it is limited – as if a writer were *only* allowed to write journalistic coverage of party political conferences. With greater scope for freedom of expression comes a greater awareness of the need for discipline, a sense of tradition, a suppler language to explore. In film terms, one has to consider how to get from shot A, however long that lasts, to shot B. Should the transition be disguised, or is it important enough for its visibility to be insisted upon? How do the professionals handle space and time, how do they keep the story going so that your interest doesn't flag during long dialogue scenes, so that you are unaware of their manipulations, so that you seem to be watching precisely what you want to watch at a given moment? It is time to learn the 180 degree rule.

Never Cross the Line

The 180 degree rule is observed in virtually every edited film which attempts to preserve narrative continuity. It is also broken with impunity – without even being noticed – in so many circumstances that I am inclined to qualify its importance by adding that it doesn't always matter. The best practical advice is when in doubt, use it, because even if it doesn't always matter it *does* always work – it is based on common-sense observation. When in a situation where it is difficult to implement, and where you have to work fast or lose the shoot, then risk breaking it. Only during the projection of rushes afterwards, or when you look at a rough-cut (the first editing together of the sequence in an approximation of its intended form) will you be able to see whether or not continuity has been seriously damaged. In many location, interior and studio situations, however, it will be found that the rule is easier to observe than to break, for reasons that will become obvious.

When we watch performers on a stage we have no difficulty following their movements: we can see the whole set, and which directions actors enter and leave it from. Our attention may shift from one speaker to another, or wander to some detail elsewhere, but we don't risk losing our orientation because our viewing position is fixed and we have the whole area of the action before us. Edited camera movements and positions alter the environment, and relations within the environment, in ways that are filmic rather than theatrical. There is a similarity to the way our attention shifts in the theatre, but only as long as the plot parallels our desires, as long as we keep seeing what we expect, or half-expect, to see. If the shots are joined randomly we will quickly lose that orientation. The visual information contained in a close-up omits to tells us where that person is in a particular space, and in relation to the other actors.

Theoretically, the camera could be situated *anywhere* in relation to its subject: if the subject is imagined at the core of a globe, and the transparent skin of the globe can shrink until it touches the subject or expand until the subject is barely visible, the camera *could* be anywhere on that circumference for the first shot, and anywhere else for the second, and so on, infinitely. Nobody in the history of cinema has exploited that range because nobody is that daft. And also because most film makers have wanted to tell a story rather than make audiences nauseous. So for practical purposes the range of camera positions is drastically reduced. You can place your camera wherever you like on that pulsing globe for one shot, but that placing will have to explain or be explained by your next choice. For example, an extreme high angle long shot of a figure in a street will be saying something different from an eye-level long shot at the same distance of the same figure. It may be saying something dramatically significant: 'This figure is about to shake hands with a Martian'; or it may be struggling to pile on a symbolic significance that the eye level shot couldn't reveal. At the end of Stuart Rosenberg's *Cool Hand Luke*, (1967), the camera draws away from the prisoners/disciples of the deceased Luke in a helicopter shot that seems to be poignantly evoking our relation to their plight: we have been involved with their lives but now the film is ending and we're leaving them in their world, confined to the landscape where they work out their sentences. But as the helicopter gets further away we are obliged to see that the roads where the men work form a cross (and if this point is missed, a photograph of Luke is superimposed over the cross of the roads; the photography had been torn up, but the pieces have been reconstituted and the tears form another cross. Are we part of his ascension too?).

For most purposes, then, the freedom of the camera is restricted by the need for consonance with the narrative context, and that is usually dependent to some extent on the conventions we have come to recognize. By cutting together shots from two camera positions we could easily make a couple standing face-to-face *appear* to be back-to-back, or someone walking left to right *appear* to be walking right to left. These are not so much tricks as games with the relativity of direction and position. We perceive a movement as left to right because of our position in relation to it. By taking up the diametrically opposite position, thus looking back directly at the space we have vacated, we would register the same movement as right to left. Which is why the 180 degree rule is observed. There may be times when you would *want* to disorient the audience, but if you do not want to confuse anybody you may model your sequence on the classical Hollywood paradigm: an *establishing* or *master* shot, which gives the set and performances in long shot, followed by an appropriate selection of two-shots, shot/reverse shot exchanges, close-ups, etc. in accordance with the 180 degree rule.

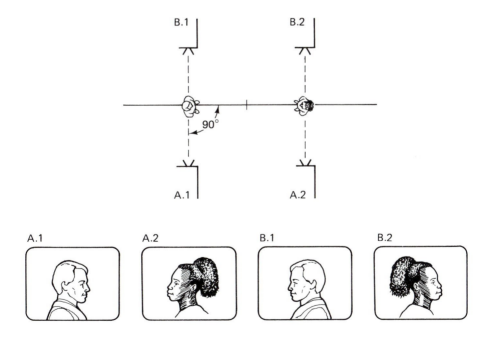

Figure 3.3 Aerial view of a man and woman, with four possible camera positions and the close-ups they would frame.

The top sketch in *Figure 3.3* overleaf is an aerial view of a man and woman facing each other. Four possible camera positions are marked as A.1, A.2, B.1 and B.2, and the close-ups they would frame are shown below. Frames A.1 and B.1 depict the same subject, who has not moved. *Screen direction* has changed by 180 degrees, but if he were running and we cut from A.1 to B.1 his 'rhythm' would be lost immediately; he would appear to have made a magical change of direction and *we* would notice the jolt even if he didn't (and he wouldn't, because it didn't occur in 'real life'). In short, this is *not* the 180 degree rule; we have chosen the wrong *axis*. It should not run across his shoulders and through his ears, but should follow his direction – more specifically, it should follow the direction of his gaze, especially if the shot is going to be paired with one of what he is gazing at or moving towards.

If we stay with the man for the moment, A.1 is now at 90 degrees to the axis formed by his directional gaze, and so is B.1. But these positions *reverse* his gaze. Effectively, then, the 'line' divides the field into discrete halves, and a continuity sequence would be composed *either* in A *or* in B. An apparent exception to this rule occurs if the camera moves in the course of a shot, beginning, say, at A.1 and tracking around the man to end at B.1. But because we can see this change as it is happening our sense of direction is not confused. We would expect the *next* shot in continuity to be situated in field B. So the line may be crossed *within* a shot, the appropriate field for subsequent shots being determined by the siting of the camera at the *end* of its movement (similarly, if the actors move about within a shot then the directional line will move with them). Confusion for the viewer is only likely to occur in a direct cut from field A to field B, but if the disposition of the actors has been clearly established such a cut need not be particularly disturbing. We have become habituated to sequences that make no attempt to create or maintain narrative continuity – in many pop videos, for example – and in television coverage of football matches and track events occasional reversals of direction occur without necessarily 'losing' us. But that isn't really the point. The 180 degree rule works quite fundamentally because it derives from ordinary habits of perception: any creature with eyes sees and makes sense of what it sees from its own subjective point of view. If we are watching a spectacle from a position in field A we can adapt quickly to a new position in the same field, less quickly to the opposite field.

The value of the 180 degree rule lies in its efficacy as a device to ensure straightforward narrative continuity, but also in the potential it releases for effective *disruption*. By breaking the rule with care, rather than through ignorance, we can hope to emphasize a particular visual or dramatic point (one of the most facetious ways of making an instantly recognizable parody of the European 'art-film', for instance, is to mimic Bergman's beautiful framing of close-ups and two-shots with the characters facing the camera, sometimes with little definable space around them and no sense from shot to shot of whether or not any time has elapsed. There is a continuity of faces and psychology and anguish, but *narrative* continuity in place and time has become ambiguous).

Figure 3.4 Shot/reverse shot patterns.

The plotting in *Figure 3.3* is of course very wooden. There would not be many circumstances when one would choose to shoot a scene between two people from such rigidly defined axes. The conventional centre around which to plot camera positions for a dialogue sequence would be the mid-point of the directional line between the participants. The paired frames in *Figure 3.3* might be appropriate for a direct confrontation, one profile against another, and as such they give a graphic illustration of why not to cross the line, but the 180 degree rule is employed most frequently for the shot/reverse shot patterns shown in *Figure 3.4*.

Shot/Reverse Shot

Figure 3.4 represents the couple in a slightly more intimate situation – dinner in a restaurant, or, with little modification, an interview or late-night television discussion. All camera positions are on the same side of the line, and numbered to match the frames below, which already plot a coherent conventional sequence. We can examine each of these shots in numerical order.

1 Long Shot

This locates the couple in a specific setting – brightly-lit studio set, bustling boulevard café, low-lit restaurant – which can be adequately described in the space around them. Framing ensures that they retain our interest and the setting adds atmosphere. The camera is positioned at about 75 or 80 degrees to the mid-point of the axis. In the first drawing I've also tried to indicate a high angle, though it shouldn't be immediately noticeable. It just seems more 'natural' because the couple are seated and if we were going to move closer we would probably be standing. A camera level with them at this point would imply that we too were seated and *could* therefore imply a deliberate subjective viewpoint. If the scene is a bustling café, with people passing to and fro in front of the camera, we should expect to hear the sounds of the place even with our attention on the couple; but even if this establishing shot describes an empty studio the distance and slightly elevated camera position would imply lowered voices (just as a low angle, with its visual distortions suggesting power, etc., would more readily be associated with raised voices). So the first shot primes expectation of a conversation that will begin at a restrained, intimate level.

2 Medium Shot

This brings us into comfortable proximity to the couple. Any background noise will usually be faded down now because it has literally become part of the background (some of it, as it were, behind *us*, because we have moved in closer). We are close enough to hear what they say – the visual and aural scales more or less matching – if they speak naturalistically. The camera has moved along its axis, and is still at 75 or 80 degrees. A cut from the first to second camera position is sometimes called an *analytical* cut, but a reversal of this movement along the axis is not, as far as I know, called a synthesizing cut and the term seems to me misleading in most practical instances. In getting closer to the significant area of the emerging drama the camera is itself actively a part of the context of that drama. Taking *any* shot out of its context for examination would be analytical, as would examining any sequence, but a movement towards or away from the subject is just that, a function of the plot. The image always analyzes, duration always synthesizes, and the reverse is at least sometimes true too – film does not have to function like a micro-biologist's slide just because the *camera* uses an optical system.

In this case frames 1 and 2 could be the starting and finishing positions of a single tracking shot in towards the subject, the 'information' in the finishing position obviously having accrued something from the starting position. The mood of such a movement would be related to its speed. Done quickly it would set up expectations of urgent dialogue, or something secretive, which would probably be accompanied by rapid cutting in subsequent shots. Done slowly, the track would prepare us for gentle romance. In Martin Scorsese's segment of the three-part film, *New York Stories*, (1989), there is a slow track-in on Rosanna Arquette as she watches a painting being made and her mood changes from anger with the artist to a kind of rapture at the work he is creating. According to Terri Minsky this shot was tried at four different speeds – twenty three, thirty, forty and fifty seconds – before Scorsese selected the slowest as the most appropriate.[6]

From position 2 it would be quite possible to cut directly to 6 and initiate the shot/reverse shot pattern, as it would be possible to use these positions repeatedly in conjunction with the pair I've placed next. Frames 2 and 6 are close enough to set up or imply the pairs that follow. In a lengthy dialogue these repetitions would almost certainly be employed, as they are, for example, unimaginatively but with mechanical efficiency, in so many television interviews (see *Figure 3.5*).

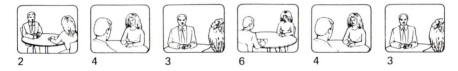

| 2 | 4 | 3 | 6 | 4 | 3 |

Figure 3.5 Repetitious use of the shot/reverse shot pattern.

3 and 4 Shot/Reverse Shot in Medium Close Up

This framing is known as an over-the-shoulder shot, and the paired shots can be alternated for however long the scene lasts. Even when this rather unadventurous procedure is followed, however, it is not simply a response to the dialogue (i.e., when the man in 3 stops speaking, cut to the woman in 4 or 6, and so on). That creates a very stilted visual pattern, drawing unwanted attention to pauses and the unnaturalness of the construction. Instead, some shots will be held to show the subject listening, and when a cut *does* come it will usually be made on the last word of a phrase or a sentence, not on the pause that follows. In this way the changes of viewpoint give us the impression that we are following the logic of the dialogue or the relationship, our attention being drawn from one speaker or listener to the other by what *seems* to be our own curiosity. (The quality of video equipment currently available for amateur or low-budget school work is not such as to make such precise editing – to the frame – at all easy. Positions perhaps slightly further back than in 2 and 6 – where lip movements would not be closely detected – would allow a reasonable compromise, but skill with the soundtrack would still be needed. An alternative is to use longer takes and move the camera intelligently, that is, with an intuitive and sensitive grasp of the rhythms of the unfolding situation.)

If the couple are equally interesting characters we might expect the paired shots to balance in duration and number, but the director may decide to upset this balance, even if in the 'real' situation neither party is emphasized. By maintaining shots from position 4 longer than those from 3 our visual attention would naturally be on the woman. The effect would either be to strengthen whatever she says, making her dominate the conversation, or to involve us with her plight by making the man (seen only partially, from behind) more mysterious and interrogative. If an interview is shot in this way we see more of the interviewee, as we would normally want to, but the interviewer may still be the controlling presence, visually diffident (almost absent), but directing our gaze. A variety of nuances and changes of emphasis can be gained without altering the dialogue or the tones in which it is delivered, so the importance of camera positions in an edited sequence becomes clear – the camera does not merely record a primarily aural encounter, it comments, and can counterpoint, add irony, and in many ways manipulate the 'reality' it interprets. Shot/reverse shot exchanges are not always so strongly directive, and on chatshows and so on they do often seem to aspire to neutrality. Louis Malle's *My Dinner with André* is a feature-length conversation between two men in a restaurant, and exploits the convention as thoroughly and imaginatively as any film I can think of (except perhaps Ozu's steady and profoundly human *Tokyo Story*, (1953)).

The over-the-shoulder shot is sometimes referred to as a point of view (POV) shot, and although that's often reasonable it isn't quite accurate. Frame 3 is *close* to the woman's POV, but not as close as 5, which is an exact duplication of her POV (see *Figure 3.6*).

3   5

Figure 3.6 The over-the-shoulder shot.

5 Close-up

In the numerical sequence of shots this would be a privileged close-up of the man, because I haven't matched it with the corresponding reverse shot of the woman. Its singularity gives it prominence. In terms of the camera plot for the whole sequence it represents a kind of apex – the camera, having approached along one axis of a V shape, will now withdraw along the other axis, making the close shot the climax of this particular visual narrative. Shots 6 and 7 complete the movement and give the sequence a near-symmetrical pattern (which would be quite symmetrical if the close-up were inserted between the shot/reverse shot pair of 3 and 4 as in *Figure 3.7*).

Figure 3.7 The symmetrical pattern of a sequence of shots.

For shot 5 the camera is actually positioned on the line, but as it doesn't *cross* the line the visual continuity is maintained. A glance at the plot will also show that setting up the camera in this position it not straightforward – it can't readily be done during a live transmission: the woman has to move out of the way for her POV to be duplicated (see *Figure 3.8*).

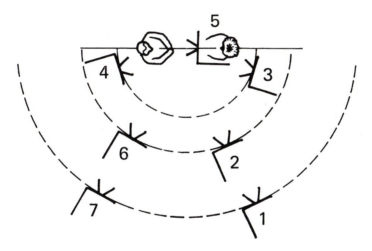

Figure 3.8 Camera position 5 – duplicating the woman's point of view.

In television studio filming there would probably be at least two cameras operating simultaneously from, roughly, positions 3 and 4; if used, a third camera would be on the outer arc, positions 1 and 7, for cuts to the long shot. But location shooting is often done with a single camera, procedures differing between a scripted and an unscripted film.

If the film is scripted and filmed conventionally, then the whole sequence will be shot as a *master* shot (that is, the *establishing*, or *long* shot) so that the whole action is covered; then the closer two-shots, over-the-shoulder, close up and reaction shots will be taken (many of these requiring more than one 'take', of course, because of faulty delivery of the lines to be spoken, problems with lighting, problems with sound, problems with the camera). The sequence is then reconstructed from this mass of material by the editor.

In an unscripted interview this procedure is not practicable, so the interview will usually be filmed in a single over-the-shoulder shot (shot 4 if the woman is the subject), which may be combined with a track or zoom in towards close up and back again. Sometimes the camera tries to cover both sides of the interview in the single take, positioning somewhere between 2 and 6 and then *panning* from interviewer to interviewee. The obvious disadvantage of this is that an unexpectedly important comment or reaction could be missed. An inexperienced camera operator might then instinctively pan back too quickly (zip-pan) in the hope of catching the remnant of the moment; the effect, unfortunately, is to make the viewer visually conscious of an error – mostly it's better to stay put and maintain the initial camera rhythm. This medium close-up, with a stable or a moving camera, then becomes the equivalent for the master shot, and unless the interview is being transmitted instantaneously it will be covered by a long shot, filmed 'wild' – that is, without synchronized sound – which can be cut into the sequence later. (It may be shot before or after the interview takes place, but can of course be edited to occur at the start *and* conclusion if that looks appropriate.) Similarly, reaction shots of the interviewer nodding wisely in understanding or grinning gently will also be shot wild; he might be filmed in close-up asking certain questions again, even if the interviewee has left by this time.

The final frame of *Figure 3.4* was left blank. Would any of the preceding set-ups fit it? To some extent that would depend on the internal rhythms of the scene. The camera may have drawn away in 6 and 7 during a period of calm. If the couple have been arguing and have reached an impasse which is suddenly broken, shot 8 might well return to a big close-up. If the scene has reached a natural conclusion it could signal the start of a new scene, with an exterior, for example.

What I hope has become obvious is the fact that even within a routine sequence, conventionally plotted for camera, considerable latitude for inflection is possible simply by varying the shot/reverse shot pattern, the duration of individual shots and the movement of the camera. The rule about not crossing the line has been observed throughout, partly because it is easier to observe than to break – lighting rigs, electric cables, booms and other sound equipment, various technicians and assistants, would all have to be moved to set up on the far side of the line, so the rule not only conforms to the acceptable parameters of our habits of perception, but also emerges out of efficient practice and is therefore economical as well.

But that doesn't explain why the convention has become so hackneyed in television interviews, which could, as I have suggested, be shot from a single position in a single take, with both participants on screen (a *two-shot*). The explanation is aesthetic, however mundane the actual results. The television interview technique has derived from a sequencing pattern for narrative continuity in film; we have become so habituated to the convention that it appears natural. Shot/reverse shot exchanges, even if we don't really notice them, continually provide a minimal visual variety, and there is a widely held yet largely untried assumption that without that variety we should get bored and switch channels. But when the convention is used dully, as a formula, *it* becomes boringly predictable as well as irritating. If someone is interesting enough to listen to, then he or she will be interesting enough to watch. Fred Astaire's objection to interpolated close-ups during dance routines is at times equally applicable to dramatic sequences, dialogues and monologues – there may be more to be gained from *less* editing, from respecting the *continuity* of a performance.

What I have illustrated in *Figure 3.4* is a very simple set-up – just a couple seated at a table – where the line is easily established and then remains constant. Such scenes occur frequently enough, but the rule still applies in more complex situations where it is rather more difficult to implement. If there are several actors, and they move about, then the line will also move; indeed, there could be a number of lines in the course of a scene. Continuity is then best maintained by *eyeline-matching*, where the reverse shot of a pair follows the directional gaze we have just left. If, for example, the woman in frame 4 were to look *away* from the man and off frame *right*, we would normally expect the next shot in the sequence to be more or less from her new POV, showing us whatever it is she addresses – if what she sees is someone looking back at *her*, then *that* look would be directed slightly off frame *left*, and so the eyelines would be matched.

The 180 degree rule extends beyond shot/reverse shot and eyeline matching, beyond the sequence contained in one location, because narrative continuity is not necessarily confined to one sequence – characters may leave the scene and need to be picked up in the next scene: so there is a convention about leaving and re-entering the frame.

Imagine a door to the right of the frame. The man gets up, crosses the room, and exits frame right. If at any point he re-enters the same scene we would expect him to come from the right. If, on the other hand, the next shot depicts a *new* scene (say, whatever is beyond that door), he should enter it frame left. This is quite logical if we extend his directional line or simply imagine the two scenes side by side, like connecting rooms or the drawings in a cartoon strip, but the adjoining room will not necessarily adjoin the film set, and storyboarding is only another convention. It isn't difficult to find in the early films of D. W. Griffith jarring examples where a character leaves one scene frame right and enters the next shot frame right. They jar now, but maybe they didn't when they were made. Early directors were discovering the cinema as they went along, as were their audiences. Deliberate mismatches, where narrative continuity is disrupted, can be found in some Japanese films (and the critic Noel Burch[7] elaborates a fascinating but not, I think, wholly convincing argument about their significance *vis à vis* Western cinema), and are also part of a peculiarly British approach to humour, where calculated incompetence is used as a facile pseudo-satirical weapon in television revues.

There is sufficient material in this chapter for several introductory workshop sessions. To recapitulate: we've looked at ways of constructing a narrative sequence in images derived from various camera positions (long shot, medium shot, close-up;

standard height, low angle, high angle); we've plotted out camera positions with reference to the 180 degree rule, considering shot/reverse shot, directional gaze, eyeline matching and the convention for entering and leaving the frame. I assume that if a sequence of lessons along these lines is planned, then students will have gained some experience of storyboarding and shooting material on video or Super 8. It is also essential that films are studied, and if it isn't feasible to have BFI film extracts available during the sessions, then students should at least be encouraged to watch television at home. I've been struck by the number who return to class surprised, even offended, by the extensive reliance of the medium on devices they hadn't previously taken note of. What students discover, in sitcoms and soaps and gameshows and chatshows, is the previously unseen banality of *camera* expression, the failure to *do* anything with the material beyond repeating its most mechanical formulations. What they may also begin to discover is that popular programmes which seem essentially televisual, at least in the sense that one couldn't imagine them gaining from a cinema screening, rely on a filmic mode of expression for much of their effect. Even so, random sampling from the schedules is not the most satisfactory method of study, and worthwhile texts should be recommended. In addition to the films already mentioned I'd suggest *The Birds*, (1963) and *Rio Grande* (1950), both available on video.

The Birds

Find the long sequence which is sandwiched between two more famous sequences, the gathering of the birds behind Melanie Daniels, which leads to the attack on the children as they race down the road, and the next attack on the town. In between is a 'quiet' sequence in a diner, involving a number of customers and staff. There is a lot of talk. Several characters are introduced for the first time and have to be characterized economically: each will have a different interpretation of what the birds represent (e.g. a rational ornithologist, a drunk quoting scripture, a practical fisherman, a scared parent, a slick salesman and variously bemused others). In terms of the quantity of expository and speculative dialogue it is a complex scene, likely to be static and 'stagey' in the worst sense. Watch it for the obviously pre-planned but nonetheless effective way Hitchcock groups his actors and manipulates shot/reverse shot through subtly changing compositions that make full use of screen space. Two characters will be talking in the foreground when a third enters in long shot between them, apparently inconsequentially. The third character approaches, then moves to set up a new diagonal composition in three-shot. Each cut to a new camera position is part of a logical and precise choreography, even when the camera does not move during a shot, so that formally balanced compositions are continually re-made on actors' movements and our attention is smoothly redirected towards each new dramatic point. Look at the use of perspective, the drunk at the end of the bar being slightly looked down on, literally, and the people from his POV being slightly looked up to. Having studied this sequence once or twice, imagine how it might be played on a stage. The dialogue and acting are of course effective and essential components, but what gives this sequence its aesthetic form is its cinematic structure, the composition of its visual elements. As it comes to an end, for instance, Melanie, who had fallen silent and occupies a minor position in a three-shot, standing a little behind the two dominant speakers, retains some of our attention simply because of her position in the frame. We may or may not notice the first time her gaze slips momentarily from the hero. Gradually her head turns away, and then she begins a movement to unbalance the composition. And we are quite delicately led to anticipate the next attack, the next sequence.

Rio Grande

Look at the opening sequence, a cavalry troupe returning to their fort. Ford likes shots where riders emerge into che frame from bottom left to right, making a strong diagonal movement into long shot somewhere near centre frame, disappearing into the distance. Consequently as one shot is succeeded by another there is sometimes an ambiguity about whether or not the line has been crossed. Over a sequence of shots there will often have occurred a transition, riders initially moving right to left now moving left to right, but it never seems to be confusing. The rule can be broken (in fact the first ten minutes of *Stagecoach*, (1939), would give students of the 180 degree rule a field day). After the shots under the opening titles a group of riders gallop from right to left to meet the returning troupe. The gates of the fort open and there is a brief track in towards them as the cavalry emerge through the dust. The dominant movement now is, appropriately, left to right, a movement into the fort. When we see the riders and their loved ones in the same shot the dominant movement is maintained and we are some way behind the wives, children, etc. A couple of static shots do cross the line, showing us the anxious faces of the women and the others, but these are not at all disruptive, and every shot of the returning men retains directional continuity. Movements, music and looks all express the weary nobility of the soldiers and the anxiety of their wives that any might be injured (in contrast to the initially more exuberant movements of the small escort party galloping out and the rush of children in the same direction – I haven't attempted to describe the whole sequence).

The first of the wounded men comes by on a stretcher drawn behind a horse. Cut to a two-shot, the figure on the right of the frame turning his head and yelling off frame left, 'Sick call!'. Immediately after this shot we cut to the horses and men, but this time the dominant movement is reversed. It is particularly noticeable because the cut is abrupt and starts on one of the horses, very big in the frame, its movement impossible to ignore. This horse is also drawing a wounded man. Why the blatant crossing of the line? It is a transitional moment, and the tone of the music becomes more sombre. The next shot, with the dominant direction left to right regained, shows the first of the captured Indians. Without needing to show any close-ups of how anyone reacts to these men, without any crude stereotyping or loss of the dignity and gravity of the situation, Ford just modulates the tone slightly, signalling it with one directional change, and deepens its sobriety. The Indian prisoners are not singled out as villains, even though there is no doubt that in this context they are the enemy; on the contrary, they are included in the dominant group movement, integrated into the dominant tones of the sequence.

Lindsay Anderson, trying to define the elusive but distinctive quality of Ford's work, used the phrase, 'some kind of moral poetry',[8] and that, I think, is what sequences like this exemplify. It's also why it's worth spending the time to learn how to recognize basic conventions, so that one is able to respond when they are transcended. Peckinpah, Hitchcock and Ford all use them, in the sequences I have summarized, and all have a strong sense of visual composition. Ford's sequence looks freer, more spontaneous than Peckinpah's or Hitchcock's, and yet his compositions are if anything more beautiful in the way they suggest the relationship of man and the environment. The conventions have not imposed a formulaic style on the three sequences; each expresses its own vision.

Towards the end of the nineteenth century, film started with the single, static shot, lasting well under a minute. Instead of extending the duration of that shot, the principle of film construction became to add a second shot, then a third, and so on. Repositioning the camera from shot to shot, then editing together the resulting pieces of film, meant that a narrative could be assembled using actors, but not in quite the way they would be used in the theatre. Between script and continuous performance a crucial intervention occurred, which was in effect both a new script and a new performer: film.

Notes and References

1 Barthes, R. (1977) *Image–Music–Text*, London, Fontana/Collins, p. 79.
2 Spielberg, S. (1984) quoted in Smith, D. G. (1984) *American Film Makers Today*, London, Blandford Press, p. 134.
3 McBride, J. and Wilmington, M. (1974) *John Ford*, London, Secker and Warburg, p. 115.
4 Roud, R. (1971) *Straub*, London, Secker and Warburg, p. 72.
5 Salt, B. (1983) *Film Style and Technology: History and Analysis*, London, Starword, p. 252.
6 Minsky, T. (1989) 'New York Stories: Martin Scorsese', *Premiere*, (April), 2, 8, p. 112.
7 See Burch, N. (1979) *To the Distant Observer*, London, Scolar, passim.
8 Anderson, L. (1981) *About John Ford*, London, Plexus, p. 14.

Chapter 4

From Snapshots to the Long Take

The Aesthetic Field of Film

In this introductory section I shall consider how film developed by borrowing from existing forms of popular entertainment to become a distinctive but hybrid art. The confusion of 'realism' with reality is examined with reference to 'live' television and the technique of multiple-camera shooting, and the essentially filmic methods of reconstructing reality are revealed. These provide the basis for the seven succeeding sections of the chapter: Continuity Editing, Script, Dialogue Styles, Use of Sound, Lighting, Deep Focus and The Long Take.

> Cinema did not only develop technically out of the magic lantern, the Daguerreotype, the phenakistoscope and similar devices – its history of Realism – but also out of strip cartoons, Wild West shows, automata, pulp novels, barn-storming melodramas, magic – its history of the narrative and the marvellous. Lumière and Méliès are not like Cain and Abel; there is no need for one to eliminate the other. It is quite misleading to validate one dimension of the cinema unilaterally at the expense of all the others. There is no pure cinema, grounded on a single essence, hermetically sealed from contamination.
>
> Wollen, P. (1969)[1]

That the evolution of a filmic language should be related to other forms of popular entertainment is not surprising: no medium can set proprietary boundaries around spectacle or narrative, and any medium exploiting these properties is likely to borrow from, or simply discover contingent affinities with, other media. Many single-shot films of the 1890s, whether or not one regards them as precursors of documentary and realism, can be seen as inevitable inheritors of the snapshot. Eastman's first Kodak cameras were introduced in 1898 and 1899 ('You press the button – we do the rest!').

What films added was of course movement, but what they provided had an interest already in some measure created by photography and by journalism. And already by 1898, when R. W. Paul made a sixty-five foot silent version of Lord Lytton's *Last Days of Pompeii*, film makers were beginning to attempt adaptations from contemporary novels and plays (and from the classics: at least from 1908 onwards, Shakespeare and Dickens were frequently resorted to wherever films were being made). Other, and perhaps more appropriate, subjects were found in contemporary vaudeville, or music-hall; short comic 'turns' adapted well to the new medium, and for many years film comedies retained their origins not only in slapstick routines but also in duration: melodramas were gradually extended to one reel (1000 feet, or ten minutes) and more, while a comedy would still fill only half a reel. Comedies began to grow longer, not by deepening characterization but by adding more turns.

The early systems for synchronizing sound on disc were generally used for recording songs, again tending to make the film experience an equivalent to music hall. Throughout the 'silent' period musical accompaniment, verbal commentary and sound effects must have added excitement and verisimilitude to the visual spectacle, and these additions would also have been familiar within the theatrical experience. As early as 1896, R. W. Paul was hand-colouring some of his short films, but tinting was more widely used (night sequences tinted blue, for instance), and this effect too would have been familiar to audiences from magic lantern shows and plays. John L. Fell has even argued that specific camera movements, such as the tilt or the tracking shot, are in essence similar to stage effects gained by moving scenery and sets.[2]

It might seem, then, that since film has always been such a hybrid form any claims that it is an art in its own right must founder on close examination: the sequential narratives of strip cartoons are plotted through 'edited' images, using long shots, close-ups, high and low angles, and strip cartoons have often been far more adventurous than films in their dramatic use of a varying frame size and shape; stage plays are plotted throught acts and scene changes, and the actors can use their bodies and voices in a continuous, live performance; novels can fuse dialogue, atmosphere, pictorial description, inward states of mind, can move backwards or forwards in time, and so on. But if film has gone to popular literature, drama and other sources for stories and for some of its modes of expression, these other arts and media too have been embedded in the cultural forms of the age.

Eisenstein has described how D. W. Griffith discovered *montage*, the 'principle of building and construction', in Dickens;[3] subsequently film has influenced other arts (as has photography since the mid-nineteenth century). The sentence from John Berger used as an epigraph for Chapter One opens a paragraph in which the development of film is paralleled with the preoccupations of cubism:

> Artistically, the film is the medium which, by its nature, can accommodate most easily *a simultaneity of viewpoints*, and demonstrate most clearly *the indivisibility of events*.[4]

The Newsreel sections of John Dos Passos's *USA* are an overt reference to the influence of film, as are the Screen sections of Solzhenitsyn's *August, 1914*, but the impact has been more pervasive. The contemporary American novelist Cormac McCarthy, for example, is often compared to Faulkner and Melville, even to Mark Twain, Poe and Crane; with *Blood Meridian* (1985) the comparisons extended to Conrad, Milton, Shakespeare, Hieronymus Bosch and, significantly, Sam Peckinpah. The novel does actually bear these comparisons surprisingly well; an intense poetry of harshly beautiful landscape and human atrocities is combined with a curiously detached tone to render a very American heart of darkness. *Blood Meridian* is a sophisticated literary 'text', but one feels behind it, as necessary as its literary antecedents, Peckinpah's *Major Dundee*, (1965) and *The Wild Bunch*, (1969), Dick Richards' *The Culpepper Cattle Company*, (1972), Robert Benton's *Bad Company*, (1972) and Arthur Penn's *Little Big Man*, (1970) (though admittedly here the influence could have come from Thomas Berger's novel). In an earlier novel, *Child of God*, (1973) comparison with Faulkner is unavoidable, but the way that McCarthy makes plausible his protagonist's actions, makes him both humanly pathetic and horrifically inexplicable, seems to me to connect this fiction with Crabbe's *Peter Grimes* and Hitchcock's *Psycho*, (1960).

What I am suggesting is that literature too is a hybrid form; indeed, that each art will nourish and be nourished by other arts; that this is a natural and desirable process. Verdi's *Otello* and *Macbeth*, Prokofiev's *Romeo and Juliet*, Kurosawa's *Throne of Blood* and *Ran*, (1985), are not imitations of or homages to Shakespeare, but interpretative acts which become transformations of narrative into the new art. I would like to suggest that where modern and contemporary literature is studied, film should be studied also; the corollary of this is that when we study film we should be open to literature and whichever arts bear on the discourse. I am welcoming the fact that film *is* a hybrid art whose origins can be fruitfully sought but probably not satisfactorily isolated, and whose aesthetic should not be narrowly defined. Part of the value and richness of film is that it *does* continually cross over into other provinces and challenge the efficacy of exclusive disciplines.

However, if film is to be given the weight it merits in arts education, either as a self-contained subject or as a co-partner in an ideal arts-centred environment, we still need to build further on our vocabulary of its conventions and possibilities, to take up some of the implications of editing and camera movement within the dominant mode (in mainstream cinema and television) of 'realism'. I'm not sure how serviceable this term is, but I mean it to include melodrama, the thriller, science fiction and various kinds of dream-worlds whose operative principle is the delineation of plausible human behaviour.

We know that many of the expressive devices used in film and television today were beginning to be used in the first decades of film's history. Recent research, particularly in America, is making it more difficult to ascribe particular inventions, or evolving conventions, to strokes of individual genius; isolated uses of the close-up, the sequential use of a location exterior and a studio interior, parallel plotting and so on, are no longer quite so isolated. Nevertheless, I think one may still say that although a number of 'filmic' qualities were in use by 1908, (and by that I mean that they had achieved some sort of recognition and repetition/development), they were not yet completely normalized. Many more films imitated theatrical structure, as Robert M. Henderson notes:

> The motion picture was, in large part, merely a photographic record of a stage play. The length of a shot was synonymous with the scene in a play. If a play had twelve scenes, the motion picture corresponding to the play contained twelve shots. Each shot was made with the camera in a fixed position, approximately center-orchestra, and both the actors and the setting were photographed in their entirety.[5]

The mysteries of light, lenses and emulsions were the province of the cameraman; the director's job was to elicit adequate performances from his actors. As late as 1914, when Karl Brown went to work as assistant to D. W. Griffith's cameraman, Billy Bitzer, the affinity with stage production was still apparent. Brown describes his first job, of 'putting down the lines' – a literal marking out on the set of the framelines of the camera:

> Next, drive a broad-headed nail – a roofing nail was ideal – into each mark. Then stretch strong white cord from nail to nail, beginning at the back, progressing to the front and across, and then back to the nail at the other edge of the set. Tie off. Now everyone knew exactly the stage area covered by the camera, which was not only never to be moved but which was sometimes even anchored to the floor with strong lash-line secured by a stage screw. Actors could then walk carelessly down toward the camera, secure in the knowledge that as long as they stayed inside that white cord, their feet would not be cut off and audiences would not wonder how people could walk around without feet.[6]

Audiences today accept that on film people can 'walk around without feet', and that acceptance may become a kind of blindness to the question 'Why should we want them to?'. Griffith was treating the framelines of the image as a stage proscenium, presumably because the stage mediated real life acceptably; the device was both theatrical and realistic, yet film could transcend that theatricality and that realism. We don't, after all, see people in their entirety at all times, but once the film begins to approximate to the ways in which we do see people, fragmenting the gaze, it becomes itself subjective, particular, in a way the stage cannot. It adopts another kind of realism and precisely as it does so depends upon a convention which is *unreal*, because it obliges the audience to *share* that subjective mimicry: crudely, we learn to see through someone else's eyes, with their emphases, their repetitions, their exclusions, their sense of duration and change, their rhythm and timing. When people 'walk around without feet' we are accepting them within an art that has moved from theatre closer to literature, an art which has the potential to attain what Karl Brown understood to be Griffith's 'highest objective', 'to photograph thought'.[7]

Some correspondence should be maintained between current practice and historical development. Having started with an examination of a chase sequence – or anything that illustrates and exaggerates the range of camera positions – and having given students opportunities to storyboard fairly freely, they may be encouraged to question the expressiveness of some of these devices (which come to mind so readily one might risk the suggestion that there is a clichéd flavour about them). A consideration of the *minimal* resources needed to make a narrative could now prove effective: Why do we want these people to walk around without feet? Why go for a close up here? What alternatives exist? How long should this shot be held? Why not take a story and break it down into a half dozen static scenes, each scene complete in itself and consisting of a single shot? This would reduce editing problems. Would the result be film or theatre?

The theatrical scenic structure is still the basis of many film narratives (though one might as easily refer to it as the novelistic chapter structure), only it is disguised and likely to appear more naturalisitic. We may cut away to follow some parallel action, but even if the scene is sustained changes of camera position, combined with camera movement, usually occur, so that the shot/scene equivalence is replaced by the sequence/scene. An exercise which invites students to return to the single shot per scene will hardly be a pointless task of historical imitation. In the context of a growing awareness of current conventional practice it is a means of refreshing the past and bringing something of its openness to the present; it is a means of questioning and coming to recognize the aesthetic, and that will involve questioning simplistic assumptions about progress.

Even if we accept the general validity of Henderson's collocation of Biograph films circa. 1908 with the stage, the *differences* should also be evident. The films were short, usually anything from three or four minutes to about ten minutes, so the shot to scene correspondence would be purely a matter of numerical sequence, with no durational similarity. And the films were silent, even though a range of sounds could be added at the exhibiting stage. The actors would translate the play into gesture, expression, movement, simplifying and heightening their mimes to communicate the maximum emotional charge in the minimum time. But aside from brevity and silence, the films were *films*, two-dimensional, framed, and usually greyish images projected to larger than life-size onto a screen. However strong the urge may have been to duplicate a stage play, no duplication was strictly possible. A static camera trained on actors on a set still becomes something other than 'a photographic record of a stage play', if only because each element is a choice, not a limit. Particularly now. Why accept current practice as more real than what has gone before? Only habituation to a convention makes it seem easier or more inevitable that when we pick up a video camera we record synchronized sound. It may be more interesting to eliminate dialogue and explore mime, and to dub something quite different on to the soundtrack (most video cameras currently available for amateur use have an in-built facility for over-dubbing): a spoken commentary, music, collected sounds – the sound can be built up separately from tape recordings, mastered on to one tape and then simply transferred onto the video tape. Quite painlessly, then, we can begin to move beyond an automatic reliance on mainstream television practice and take imaginative possession of the equipment.

I am recommending an a-historical spirit of creative inquiry, much as the great soviet film teacher Lev Kuleshov seemed to be doing in one of the last pieces he wrote:

> ...I don't want the artistic properties of film to be lost in the process of technical advancement but *to return with a difference* on each new level and compensate for everything that was lost. At present we can already see signs of a *revival* in the best films everywhere, but it is not happening fast enough.
> ... there is one thing I want, and that is for the future cinema to integrate the artistic qualities and features it possessed in its various phases with the newly discovered means of expression.[8]

One very obvious 'difference' of returning to the single shot per scene model has been noted above: synchronized sound is recorded directly on to the tape of the video camera. But, as I have suggested, we don't have to use the facility just because it is there. It is a fact of the technology, but only a factor in our aesthetic: reference to the past encourages us to question it.

In the decades prior to the successful demonstration of film apparatus, inventors speculated about what the future would bring. The barrister, Wordsworth Donisthorpe, writing to *Nature* early in 1878, made these predictions:

> ... the life-size photograph shall itself move and gesticulate precisely as he did when making the speech, the words and gestures corresponding as in real life.
> ... by this means a drama acted by daylight or magnesium light may be recorded and re-acted on the screen of a magic lantern, and with the assistance of the photograph the dialogues may be repeated in the very voices of the actors.
> When this is actually accomplished the photography of colours will alone be wanting to render the representation absolutely complete, and for this, we shall not, I trust, have long to wait.[9]

Experiments with synchronized sound and colour were under way well before the turn of the century, but the sound was recorded on separate machinery. 'Marrying' sound and image, by whatever system, was a subsequent process, and this initial disjunction was, surely, crucial. The necessary division of labour, separation of functions, meant that different solutions to the representation of real life had to be found, visually and aurally. The visual language developed largely without sound, and sound was gradually accommodated to it.

If you watch films on television you may notice an occasional jump, where the film has been damaged and a few frames are lost; you may also notice that the corresponding jump on the soundtrack occurs slightly later, and will sometimes throw dialogue out of lip-synchronization. The soundtrack has been married to the film – its optical or magnetic stripe running alongside the images – but is always a short distance beyond the frame it relates to. This doesn't matter when the film has been edited *before* the sound stripe is added, and that has always tended to be the case in professional film making, but video cameras provide direct sound recording on tape. The resulting problem is similar to that of direct sound recording on film, in that precise editing, to the 'frame', becomes very difficult.

It is relatively easy to obtain a picture that looks and sounds as good as anything on television, but unless you have access to very expensive editing suites, the similarity may end at the moment your shot ends, the edit being noticeable either because of interference visually or because it has inadvertently cut out a necessary phrase. The advantage of having direct sound on film can seem a disadvantage in editing, because the conventions we are looking at evolved for continuity editing with *silent* film. It could be argued, of course, that 'messy' edits have an authenticity that shouldn't be disguised but, rather, advertised, until they too become conventionalized – isn't it legitimate to say that the limitations of the tools at one's disposal constitute a reality affecting the work one produces?

'Return with a difference', then, whether with a video camera or Super 8, sound or silent, and reconsider the question of film as theatre, film as film, and film as realism.

It isn't necessary to go to minimalist cinema or the late films of Resnais to find creative play with the tensions of film and theatre. For nearly a hundred years film makers have been adapting stories, novels and stage plays, sometimes doing everything in their power to conceal their stories' origins, sometimes, apparently, drawn by the technical and artistic challenges of *not* 'opening-out' the drama. Alfred Hitchcock deliberately restricted himself on several occasions to a small company of actors in a small space. *Rope* will be mentioned shortly, when I discuss the long take, but there's also *Dial M for Murder*, (1954), nearly all filmed in an apartment set, *Lifeboat*, (1944), which explains itself, and *Rear Window*, (1954). Sets and actors in these films are restricted, as on a stage, but camera movements and editing to different positions alter the environment, and relations within the environment, in ways that are manifestly filmic, not theatrical. But the camera doesn't have to move either: Ozu's *Tokyo Story*, already mentioned, is one of the loveliest, stillest, and most gently moving films ever made, and there's hardly a pan, tilt or tracking shot to be found in its quiet, orderly unfolding of undramatic sequences. In fact I remember one movement, when the elderly couple take a tram or a bus ride and the camera – still stationary – is on board with them. The movement is provided by the mode of transport. I saw the film at least twenty years ago, then more recently on television, and that brief hint of movement still retained its delicate dramatic beauty, like a sigh when the sun breaks over clouded walls.

Film and theatre, film and realism. I want to introduce another pairing, film and television, to help clarify what is distinctive about film whenever we experience it.

As we've established, film has always had to record and re-present its images, and sound has had to be recorded, mixed and married to the final print. Television can relay live pictures and sounds instantaneously. Film makers were obliged to create a language in the assembly of shots of different lengths. This language enabled them to tell stories and, as its devices and experiments gained acceptance and became conventions, it became self-effacing, transparent, imparting an illusion of reality or continuous story-time. Ostensibly, television already *had* a closer approximation to reality, and didn't need to take over that way of seeing and telling in order to create that illusion. Yet it did, and it does. Television, whether live, taped or filmed is always filmic in its aesthetic.

The paradox, or confusion, is neatly adverted to in the announcements that often accompany American sitcoms: 'This show was taped/filmed before a live studio audience'. How does that statement affect the artistic mode of the show? Does it mean that the show was recorded once through in its entirety, and hence 'live', or that the studio audience sat through all the re-takes and filmed inserts? At best it means that the laughter was not pre-recorded elsewhere and edited in at appropriate moments. Studio response gives a better illusion of the atmosphere of a live performance, but no guarantee that the performance is actually live. What matters finally is the plausibility of the constructed illusion, and in that sense a filmed performance from the 1920s is as live as tonight's news bulletin.

Characteristically, television provides a mixture of live and pre-recorded programmes. Many of the live programmes are being recorded simultaneously, so we can get almost instant playback, in slow motion and freeze frame, of significant moments. Distinctions between live and recorded, and, I think, between reality and fiction, become blurred, but those who wish to separate film and television, either to claim the superiority of the former as art or to claim that the latter is an art in its own right, argue that what distinguishes television is its live-ness. Some, Colin MacCabe, for example, locate a 'Golden Age' of television in the 1960s, so we might expect to find the medium diverging markedly from film in this period.[10] Some of the most memorable programmes of this period – MacCabe regards them as masterpieces of television – were *Steptoe and Son*, *Till Death Us Do Part*, the Tony Hancock series, *Z Cars*, and plays by David Mercer, John Hopkins, Dennis Potter and John Osborne. English television, at about the same time as English cinema, had discovered the themes, and often the writers, of the English theatre and the English novel of a few years earlier. The practice which seemed initially its strength, the live television drama, was superseded by the heightened realism of 'documentary-style' filming on location. In some ways the period culminated in the powerful emotional didacticism of *Cathy Come Home*, (1966), whose legacy would include *The Price of Coal* and *Days of Hope* in the seventies, and *The Boys from the Blackstuff* in the eighties. The live television drama has left no substantial legacy, though sitcoms and gameshows have continued to be predominantly studio-based, with an audience and at least an element of live-ness. With few exceptions (the director, Ken Loach, cameramen like Tony Imie and Chris Menges) most creative contributions to the Golden Age came from actors and writers.

In fact, it seems to me that instead of being at its zenith, English television in the sixties had entered a phase of lively uncertainty, comparable to film before the First World War. In retrospect at least, the writing of these class-conscious, realist comedies and dramas sounds very mannered, literary and theatrical, and 'live' transmission goes some way towards the edgy immediacy of a stage performance. But at the same time there is a consciousness of recording, screen, the distanced audience – a consciousness of television as a *filmic* medium. So even live drama was unmistakably *constructed*. The ingenious but cumbersome solution was to use several cameras. Each camera could run continuously, and while one was moving into position for the next choreographed shot the producer would be watching the images of all the cameras, ready to cut on cue from camera one to camera two or three. The intention was to make a live play look less like a window on a stage production, more like reality. The model of reality was the edited film. And even the simultaneous use of multiple cameras was not an invention of television.

In the first decade of the century two film cameras would sometimes be run side by side, though mainly, it seems, to cover the action in case one broke down. By the second decade there were instances where up to twenty cameras were deployed to cover spectacular action. The purpose was largely economic – it would cost so much to stampede the cattle or race the wagons repeatedly – but the edited effect was aesthetic, an immediate, vivid physical reality was captured. It was recorded, but full of dynamic movement and life – not live, like theatre, but real, like life.

In the 1920s Cecil B. De Mille more precisely anticipated the film/theatre/live/realism nexus of television drama's Golden Age:

> De Mille chose during the 1920s to shoot a film in its dramatic order so that the actors would build up characterization and psychological intensity as they would in a stage play . . . First he prepared a story in continuity form so that only three or four sets would be needed at a time, and subsequent sets would replace these as the staff progressed through the story. Then he used multiple cameras, some for long shots and others for close-ups. Descriptions of this vary but it appears that he set up one camera at a long shot, a second one right next to it with a longer focal length lens for a close-up, and several

other cameras at angles for more close-ups and two-shots. Thus, the scene could be played through, the various shots could be edited together to provide the classical establishing shots and cut-ins, and the action would match.[11]

De Mille's practice differed from that of live television in two obvious respects: first, it could only be applied to a scene or sequence, duration being limited by the available maximum length of film in the magazines; second, although implied by the disposition of the cameras, the editing occurred *after* principal shooting and, because there might be a need for re-shooting or re-selecting from out-takes, and re-editing after responses to previews were analyzed, editing the film could be a staggered rather than a concentrated process. In live television the *whole* drama would be shot 'in its dramatic' order as 'in a stage play', and editing would be done as the programme was unfolding and being transmitted. Under De Mille's direction the actors' performances might take days or weeks to complete, rather than the hour or two of the live drama, or the exhibited film. But what do the differences really amount to? There is disjunction in the momentum of performance, but scene for scene the aims and procedures are closely matched; an unscripted, felicitous gesture could be caught by the film as easily as by the television cameras, and that element of spontaneity is part of what one hopes to experience in a live production. However, the film cameras will also pick up, and the film editors probably eliminate, various kinds of mistakes: actors missing their cues, corpsing, being in the wrong place at the wrong time. And these would be transmitted on television, as they would be evident on stage.

It is impossible to calculate the extent to which an audience, albeit unconsciously, desires to see something go wrong. The possibility of encountering a bad performance is part of the pleasurable tension one brings to the series of anticipations that help constitute the theatrical experience. For the most part, film removes that possibility, and television drama soon followed film. But what is being removed is only one kind of accident, or breakage, in the continuity of the dramatic illusion of reality. Happier accidents can be retained, along with most of the spontaneity of a rehearsed, but for the moment, live performance; most importantly, realism *as a style* can be retained. The advantage of the live and sustained television drama, then, becomes more dubious, if what distinguishes it from film is primarily the sensed risk of unintended disaster. Its other qualities, as I remember, consisted largely of a certain roughness and an occasional clumsiness in camera movements, a certain tension probably related to remembering and reaching the marks on time, to sustaining the complex choreography of the piece. And most of these qualities can be filmed if one wishes to adapt them for conscious artistic effect.

I am not suggesting that television, whether recorded or live, is identical to film, nor am I hinting that it is inferior. I am suggesting that its procedures are so similar as to belong to the same aesthetic, so that the art of film embraces and can be extended by television. That there will still be forms of television that 'work' only on the small screen is as obvious as the perception that some films only 'work' in cinemas; the fact remains that although the media can be differentiated institutionally and in specific technologies, their forms of realism and their handling of spectacle and narrative encourage us to read them as essentially the same kinds of texts. This does not mean that a study of television alone will suffice, though eventually, and if we had no historical curiosity, I suppose it might. Much of what is most impressive and creatively stimulating in the language and the art still resides in film. Television continues to undervalue its visual potential and, quite understandably, to emphasize, at its best, acting and dialogue.

The use of multiple cameras, in film and television, developed in the service of veracity, and out of a belief that the key to realism lay in sustained performance. Paradoxically, the multiplication of viewpoints inevitably broke down the very performance it sought to capture whole. At issue here is a conflict between reality and representation, and between stage realism and film realism. At one pole is *continuity editing*, assembling the narrative from hundreds of long shots, medium shots and close-ups; at the other pole are *deep focus* compositions, which enable us to see actors, action and environment interacting on various planes within one shot, and the *long take*, whose steady gaze does allow us to witness a sustained performance. Between these poles are acting techniques, scripts, dialogue styles, lighting and various uses of sound. The multiple camera paradox can, I believe, be used to explore most of the constituent elements of the art of narrative film.

Continuity Editing

Narrative developed by cementing relatively short lengths of film together to suggest continuity rather than interruption. The conventions outlined in Chapter Three exemplify this on the small scale of the sequence. A feature film might be composed of hundreds of shots, dozens of sequences, numerous locations. Some of these might require the building of elaborate sets, or location filming in different countries, but whether the physical shift from shot 1 to shot 2 moves the camera thousands of miles or the distance between a medium shot and a close up, narrative continuity is gained by the same principle, of joining shots necessarily filmed at different times.

With the exception of the very short, single shot subjects made in the first few years of the medium's history, *all* films adopted this principle of shot by shot construction, whose *aim* was to produce the illusion of steady progression, despite spatial and temporal shifts, and the illusion of continuous action, event and performance, but whose *method* soon revealed the plasticity of the film itself. Continuity editing *constructed* the dramatic event from its discrete shot elements, and had to do so because the technology did not exist for recording a drama of, say, ninety minutes' duration in real time.

A shot can be made shorter, or repositioned elsewhere in the narrative, or even copied and repeated (and by adjusting the speed of the camera, or by optical printing in the laboratory, it can be speeded up or slowed down); an editing rhythm can be created which has little or no reference to any ostensible event being recorded. The opportunities for manipulation at this plastic level are extensive, and can place the burden of narrative continuity on the medium itself rather than the actors or the script.

Some films are essentially 'made' at the editing table. During the Second World War, for example, there were documentaries produced by the National Film Board of Canada without a foot of film being shot by them. They sorted through footage from disparate sources and, by editing it and adding commentaries, made original films that the original camera operators would have had no idea they were contributing to.

But in most cases the editing phase is anticipated by the continuity script and throughout shooting, and perhaps the most significant consequence of this is that films can therefore be shot out of sequence. On a large scale this means that a second unit can be dispatched to a distant location to film, say, charging gorillas, while the main unit may be filming an actor's reaction shots in the studio; it means that all the scenes in a given location or set can be filmed one after another, and edited into their allotted place in the narrative later; on a small scale it means that the master shot of a sequence can be filmed in one take, followed by two-shots and close-ups. Everything can be, and frequently has been, done with a single camera. Griffith would view the rushes of his master shots, decide then which close-ups to use and where they would be needed, and film them subsequently against a neutral background.

Against this procedure, De Mille's use of multiple cameras seems anachronistic: continuity editing evolved as the solution to a peculiarly filmic problem, that of prolonging a dramatic narrative beyond the physical capacity of the medium to record it as it occurred. The need for simultaneity was obviated by the established realist conventions (shot/reverse shot patterns, etc.) linked to editing procedures.

Multiple camera shooting both acknowledges continuity editing (film at its furthest from stage acting conventions) and seeks to transcend it by retaining more of the integrity of a performance. The method is a fascinating conflation of opposed views of where the art of film resides (or of what realism consists in, or of the function of the director). Is it in montage, which subordinates the shot to the whole, and can so manipulate the pieces of film that any reality inscribed on them may be wilfully distorted, or rendered inert until re-animated through juxtaposition and collision? Or is it in the integrity of the performances, the reality unfolding before the camera, which the camera should reveal as fully as possible, and editing tamper with as little as possible?

With live television broadcasting, and with filming on video tape, it is of course possible to do away with editing altogether, and respect the reality of the event more or less completely (never absolutely, because the camera's field of vision is restricted and has to represent a degree of selectivity in its positioning). In practice no one goes to this extreme, I think because it is assumed it would be dull – that is, not filmic, not televisual. I don't see why this should necessarily be so; nevertheless, by incorporating the structural principle of continuity editing, the multiple camera shooting of live television drama ensured that television, while absorbing something of the theatre, developed as an expressive medium under the aegis of film.

Acting Techniques

The Camera Man kept holding up one, two or three fingers at different intervals. Another code system, this one related to lenses. One finger equaled a wide shot. Two, a medium shot and Three, a tight shot. He tried not to look at the fingers. For him, one finger meant 'fairly relaxed'; two equaled 'fairly tense'; three – 'extremely tense'. He wished they hadn't told him what the fingers meant. It didn't do him any good to know. He wasn't doing anything different no matter what lens they were using, no matter how many fingers they held up. So why even tell him? What he needed to know was why did his Character want to kill her Character in the first place?[12]

This is from a short piece written in 1979 and published in *Motel Chronicles*. Evidently it is an autobiographical anecdote derived from Sam Shepard's experience on the film *Resurrection*, which starred Ellen Burstyn, but it could have been written sixty years before. The actor is new to film: 'He wasn't doing anything different no matter what lens they were using', except that the close-up made him tense, and what he 'needed' to know was his character's motivation. But how much motivation do we read from the actor's face (acting), and how much do we read *into* his face from the cumulative context of that shot in that narrative (montage)? The following passage was written by Lev Kuleshov in 1920:

1. A man receives a letter, opens and reads it. Cut to the text of the letter, which says that the woman he loves has been unfaithful to him. Next we see a close up of the actor's face registering grief.
2. A man receives a letter, opens and reads it. Cut to the text of the letter, which says that he has lost his entire fortune. Next we see a close-up of the actor's face registering grief. If you ask any actor whether he will play the same emotion (expression) for a man who has lost the woman he loves and for a man who has lost his money, he will certainly say no, the emotions will be different. Now if, having filmed the two scenes, we insert the last piece (man grieving) of the first scene into the second scene, we shall get absolutely the same screen impression of the actor's emotion as with all the right pieces. Thus montage proves that the actor can just as well be

unaware of the causes that have plunged him into grief, occasioned his joy, etc., for in the cinema the expression of an emotion by the actor does not depend on the cause of that emotion.[13]

Evidence that this kind of manipulation of shots works (even with sound) can easily be found in, for example, the well-executed series of television commercials where comedian Griff Rhys Jones 'acted' with Jack Hawkins in *The Cruel Sea*, (1954), Marilyn Monroe in *Some Like It Hot*, (1959), Gary Cooper in *High Noon*, (1952), John Wayne in *Without Reservations*, (1946) and Steve McQueen in *The Great Escape*, (1963), (no doubt there were further examples and the series obviously derived from Reiner's *Dead Men Don't Wear Plaid* and Allen's *Zelig*, (1983)). For the purpose of the exercise, observe not the comic interpolation but the extent to which the original footage seems to respond to it.

Interestingly, although this implies that the film is made in editing, and that a consistently developed performance is therefore not strictly necessary, Kuleshov takes pains to stress that 'montage is subordinate to shooting, and only pieces that have been shot correctly can be edited'.[14] Correct shooting is concerned with lighting, composition and movement – movement within the shot, as well as movement from this shot to the next in sequence – and so it is concerned with a new kind of acting. The Russian directors studied as much American work as they could get hold of, and Griffith was particularly celebrated for his expressive innovations (the intelligent *use* he made of various narrative devices rather than his invention of them), and the concomitant quality of the acting in his films. He understood, for example, that the close-up required a less histrionic, more naturalistic style, and that the movements of hands and arms could be isolated into evocations of mood. If the static, theatrical long shot had encouraged actors to enlarge gesture in keeping with the broad strokes of melodrama and keeping the attention of the audience near the back of the stalls, the fluency of continuity editing began to encourage the delicate intensities of restraint, the slighter gesture, the gentler glance. The camera seemed capable of revealing qualities of thought, feeling and radiance that had little to do with stage acting techniques, and some of Griffith's most popular actresses were relatively inexperienced when they began working with him.

In Kuleshov's workshops the actor, now referred to as the 'model', was given an extraordinary training in preparation for film work. Eisenstein went further, in the interests of realism, and used non-professional actors, or non-actors, chosen according to his principle of 'typage' – that is, having the right *look* for the part. There is a danger of sterotyping and caricaturing in this (and Eisenstein was a skilful cartoonist), but non-actors can contribute a subtle range of expression and an authenticity quite outside the conventional spectrum of 'fine' acting. When I see a Meryl Streep performance I'm always conscious that I'm responding to a persuasive set of skills – I may even be marvelling at how real the character seems, how different from the last one she played, and so on. When I see Robert Bresson's *Mouchette*, (1967), there is no acting, but rather a sense of being in an exact yet mysterious world, an ordinary world with no star performances and no big dramatic moments, but where the least gesture can be imbued with the disturbance of the spiritual, and where the culmination of all gestures seems pre-ordained.

So no, we don't need multiple cameras for heightened realism; there are other ways of obtaining something more cinematically true than a skilled performance. There's no reason why students beginning to make films should limit their subjects to attempts to imitate the stock-realism of acting in most television plays and most contemporary films. Consider the restrictions placed on the cast of *EastEnders*: they are given no opportunity to coordinate movement and gesture with camera movement and cutting rhythm; their vocal range is rarely allowed to shift beyond dyspeptic grumbling and aggressive, confrontational dialogue; ratiocination is suggested by a sourer frown than usual – small wonder that large audiences have turned to the bright sets and cheery banalities of *Neighbours*, where at least some of the whimsical absurdities are intentional. Why not consider instead some of the more pretentious but occasionally inspiring experimental work in *Dance on 4*? Here you may see dancers who are not dancing, and not acting, but executing movements which are repeated serially in various combinations. Or consider Stephen Berkoff's *Metamorphosis*, (1989), where the acting is expressionistic, funny and scary, and where the set and the lighting are appropriate to the acting.

In other words, consider the question of realism: Griffith's realism, Eisenstein's realism, Murnau's expressionistic realism in *The Last Laugh*, the realism of post-war Italian cinema, of English documentary in the thirties, of contemporary documentary (the differences between, say, *Beirut – The Last Home Movie*, (1988) and *Four Hours in My Lai*, (1989) – both based on estensive interviews, the former lush and operatic and vaguely decadent, like a Visconti movie, the latter unadorned, plain and almost unbearable); and against these realisms, consider *Cathy Come Home*, (1966), Ford's *They Were Expendable*, (1945), Anderson's *This Sporting Life*, (1963), Tarkovsky's *Nostalghia*, (1983), *News at Ten*, *EastEnders*. What *is* realism? Is there only one sort of acting and filming available? Why not use an actor whose face you never see? Why not use a *voice over* narration? Make a film on people's feet, approaching, meeting, departing? Hands? Shopping bags? Film is not theatre. The actor may not need to know what is in her character's mind, or how she is going to sustain the tempo of a mood or a movement. Think of acting as an element of montage, and of montage as the careful study of minute relationships; think, if only to dismiss the idea shortly, of Kuleshov's notion that film can take 'down-to-earth reality' and transform it 'into an amazing heroic legend!'[15]

What is good film acting? Victor McLaglen played the eponymous, barely articulate Gypo Nolan in John Ford's *The Informer*, in 1934. The film looks, and sounds, mannered now – not one of the director's major works – but MacLaglen won one of the film's four Academy Awards for his interpretation. According to Ford's grandson, this is how the performance was achieved:

> John did everything he could to keep McLaglen off balance and thus
> inadvertently in character. He juggled the schedule without telling his
> leading man, so that McLaglen, a slow study under the best of
> circumstances, would have to learn new lines when he arrived in the
> morning. As the day progressed, John hurried McLaglen on and off the set
> at dizzying speed, showering him with abuse if he dared to slow down. In
> the afternoons, under the pretext of a rehearsal, John ran McLaglen
> through his 'next day's' scenes, while the cameras rolled away. McLaglen's
> tentative efforts with the unfamiliar dialogue resulted in some of his best
> takes.[16]

It's a cruel anecdote, which obliges me to add that to the stories of Ford's irascible temper could be added as many of his gentleness and quiet generosity, but it reminds us that the recorded performances we see on film may be painfully 'live' for the actors. Throughout his long career Ford also showed a preference for using the first take of a scene, before his actors lost spontaneity. He was also inclined to tear out pages of dialogue at short notice, make up new business on the spot, and to use what his actors thought were improvisatory rehearsals. Again, multiple camera shooting is not the only way of getting the breath of life into a film performance. It may not be a good idea, however, for students to become all-powerful creators on the first day of filming.

Script

> A scenario need not have any literary value. It can read like rubbish in terms
> of literature but translate into perfect filmic compositions, i.e., bring about
> a highly artistic result. To regard the scenario as a finished piece with its
> own value rather than an integral part of the production process is a sure
> way to doom it to incomplete cinematic embodiment.[17]

With the advent of synchronous sound the literary quality of the script may have improved somewhat, but Kuleshov's 1920 comment remains accurate regarding its status relative to the completed film. Samuel Beckett, applying for admission to the Moscow State School of Cinematography in 1936, expresses its value more succinctly: ' . . . the script is function of its means of realization . . . '[18]

The first films, being not very much more than snapshots expanded in time with movement, were unscripted. Later, directors like Chaplin and Griffith worked from an *outline*, which would not specify camera positions and continuity notes. In many of his silent films John Ford would make up the script in collaboration with his star,

Harry Carey, while on location, and get George Hively to write it afterwards. Some of the late-silent directors favoured the script *synopsis*, more detailed than a script outline in that it gave a scene by scene account of the plot. But the fully detailed *continuity script* was also much used, particularly once films had become longer and more complex, that is, after about 1914.

The continuity script was a blueprint which numbered and described each shot, indicated where intertitles (the explanatory titles, often with dialogue, that became redundant with sound on film) should go, and reduced the creative role of the director. Understandably, directors following Griffith and Chaplin would prefer the outline or synopsis, but the continuity script was an efficient part of the studio system, popular with producers.

Multiple camera shooting helped to establish the method of shooting the master shot of an entire scene in one long take, with briefer close-ups and reactions which would subsequently be inserted into it. This method became standard practice, though multiple camera shooting didn't, partly because of the difficulties of providing adequate lighting for the close-ups within a full-set lighting pattern, partly because of similar difficulties when recording sound. Shooting scripts tended to follow the master scene in the sound period, and were thus closer to the script synopsis than the continuity script (i.e., describing scenes, but not every shot).

As a general rule, then, we can consider the shooting script as less than a blueprint but more than an outline. It may provide brief character descriptions and a plot synopsis at the outset, and will probably proceed by numbering each scene in chronological order, giving spare details of time and place (Exterior, Night, the Road), descriptions of characters' movements or feelings, and the dialogue.

Commercially published screenplays are usually derived either from the final version of the *shooting script* (sometimes collated with the release print of the film – there may be wide divergences between the two), or from the *cutting continuity* (the detailed record of the finished film). In *The Citizen Kane Book*, (1971), both shooting script and cutting continuity are printed for comparison, but the determinedly unacademic and antagonistic Pauline Kael, after struggling to make the case that the film's main writer, Herman J. Mankiewicz, deserved more authorial credit than he'd received, completely failed to grasp what the cutting continuity (or, indeed, another viewing of the film) plainly indicated.

> Cutting continuities tend to be impersonal and rather boring to read, and if one examines only the cutting continuity, it is difficult to perceive the writer's contribution. Shooting scripts are much more readable, since they usually indicate the moods and intentions.[19]

No doubt this is true, if one wants a literary experience, but if one wants to understand more about a film and the weighting to give to its various elements in any critical analysis, then the shooting script is only useful insofar as it can be compared to a print of the film, or to the cutting continuity. In her next paragraph Ms Kael naïvely registers the difference that effectively demolishes her argument, only she is too set on demonstrating that *this* shooting script 'violates the old theory that movie scripts make poor reading' to notice:

> And it is particularly difficult to judge the script of a movie as famous as *Citizen Kane*. Inevitably while reading it one fills in with the actors' faces, the look of the shots – the whole feeling of the completed film.[20]

As it happens the shooting script was not solely the work of Mankiewicz anyway (Robert L. Carringer, in *The Making of Citizen Kane*, offers the most thoroughly researched account, and the fairest evaluation, of this celebrated issue that I've read). But the salient point is, I believe, that 'the actor's faces, the look of the shots – the whole feeling of the completed film' constitute its real 'writing', and these reflect the contributions of scriptwriters, actors, art directors, lighting, camera crews, composers – dozens of skilled artists and technicians whose work is coordinated by the director. The director may not always be the main creative influence on a film, and is never the only begetter of a film, but the director does usually deserve credit for the responsible job implied by the title, *directing*. The function is not synonymous with literary authorship, but then neither is writing a script. If one refers to a film *by* Ford, Welles, Hitchcock, Hawks and so on, it is with the understanding that many others have collaborated but, nevertheless, the director has finally shaped the vision in a particularly distinctive way. There are as many competent, anonymous directors as there are competent, anonymous scriptwriters, and there are many excellent films which seem to result from a happy combination of accidents (and an efficient studio system) rather than from any outstanding individual effort, but that does not affect the status of the script or the function of the director.

Film, as is often said, is a director's medium. That is not to say it can dispense with good writers, only that it needs writers who understand film. There is a sense in which film can be read like literature, but is has nothing to do with reading the screenplay; it has to do with attending to the moving image, spatial and temporal relationships, and dialogue, of course, and music, and other uses of sound.

One of the reasons why a fine shooting script may well make 'poor reading' is that it will only *suggest* the tenor and direction of those passages which, when fully embodied on the screen, will move us; its dialogue, though probably more pared down and more vivid, will have roughly the importance we would attach to dialogue as a separable element in a novel – it carries less of the narrative, less explicatory matter, than the dialogue in a play. Finally, its formulations are likely to be in one of the characteristic modes of realism, discouraging rhetorical flourishes in the interests of a plausible simulacrum of every-day speech patterns.

The particular value of scripting exercises is not so much to extend students' English skills in handling written dialogue, as to reinforce an understanding of narrative structure, of alternative ways of reconstituting the world as art. Practically, the synopsis or master-scene form of shooting script is the most useful model, detailing each scene but not each shot, except where a close-up or a particular camera movement is integral to the writer's concept.

Adaptation from a literary original – a novel, novel extract, or short story – helps to clarify similarities and differences between forms and brings out the critical discipline that inheres in creative expression. Mediating between written narrative and its potential transformation into film narrative, students ask 'How does this work in film?', but also, 'What is its function in the novel?' The process of selection, deletion and addition of material is analytical and evaluative.

An exercise which groups of my English undergraduates have found useful is in hypothetical scriptwriting (exigencies of time and the constraints of the syllabus mean that no film is actually made; neither is the shooting script ever completed). They are studying mid-nineteenth century novels which relate to The Condition of England question, and considering the position and attitude of author and reader *vis-à-vis* that question. With Mrs Gaskell's *Mary Barton* I ask them, instead of preparing papers for seminars or writing essays, to look at the novel as a vehicle for a four or six part television dramatization. In fact one of their tasks is to determine the number of episodes, and this leads to a careful examination of the dramatic structure of the novel. Are sufficiently strong dramatic or melodramatic moments spaced in the existing framework? Then, is there a clean, continuous narrative with a strong central focus? Should the curious shifts from powerful, 'documentary' realism to melodrama and romance be accommodated, or could the adaptation stress one or another of these as representing the 'real' *Mary Barton*?

Some students are angered by the living conditions suffered by these working people, and the contrast with the conditions in which their employers thrive, and so want to concentrate on the earlier parts of the novel, often moving John Barton to the centre of attention (as had apparently been Mrs Gaskell's original intention); they then have the problem of how to treat the rather novelettish infatuation of Mary for the rich young scoundrel whose murder will spiral the plot away from social analysis into cliff-hanging melodrama and the resolutions of last minute reversals, sentiment, and creaky coincidence. Other students feel that the latter elements are what could make *Mary Barton* a riveting period drama; they want to build up the poor but honest (and beautiful) Mary, and the misunderstood but constant lad who finally wins her; they also feel that Mrs Gaskell probably had the same motives they have – by involving the audience emotionally the social criticism can be made and felt without the risk of dullness or offence to gentle sensibilities. Both interpretations leave students with the problem of all the minor characters and what they contribute to the plot and the description of a particular place and period. Are all of them equally necessary, or could some be combined to make a smaller cast?

The discussion remains close to the novel and the kind of criticism that would emerge more tentatively, and I think with less commitment, from the more conventional address of current theoretical approaches, so the exercise needs no special pleading to be undertaken in English. At the same time it *could* be used to raise a number of subsidiary questions that might go beyond subject boundaries to some extent, questions about historical reconstructions and how seriously to take them, for example. With the possible exception of Ford Madox Ford's *The Fifth Queen* trilogy, written in the first decade of the century, modern literature has tended to exclude historical novels from serious consideration, or at least to classify them as a subspecies and something of a sport (along with bodies of work in other genres). Historical plays seem to have fared rather better, critically, especially if allegorical (e.g., *The Crucible*). In film and television serious historical and period reconstructions have relied heavily on adaptation rather than original material (in general – one could cite *Ivan the Terrible*, (1944), *The Seven Samurai*, *Andrei Rublev*, (1966) and a number of Westerns as notable exceptions). Yet separation of contemporary work into *genres* is, however convenient and sensible for some purposes, misleading when it leads to lacunae in critical discourses, and in the selection (and necessarily the exclusions) of set texts.

Students creatively involved in the adaptation of works from the past will be quick to realize how concerned with the present their engagement actually is, structurally, intellectually and emotionally. And if they turn aside from *Mary Barton*, or whatever text they have been using, and turn aside from the specific matter of direct adaptation to look at the uses made of the past in contemporary popular culture, they may discern a trend towards humour of various kinds (in literary fiction, from John Barth to Jeanette Winterson; in such films as *Jabber-wocky*, *Time Bandits*, *Life of Brian* and the *Blackadder* series on television). The humour in the novels is often bawdy, but more distinctively literary, a humour of fiction about the nature of fiction (we should include Umberto Eco and Italo Calvino, and perhaps some of the better known, if less intelligent, British writers). In the films and television series the humour tends to be more puerile, but at its most fascinating derives from the clash between a painstakingly authentic visual world (and we might ask by what criteria we judge these realistically lived-in costumes and locations to *be* authentic) and a manifestly late-twentieth century idiomatic environment. The reliance on genital jokes in the Elizabethan *Blackadder*, for instance, has an initial shock value because the care taken with costumes and sets makes us expect a different kind of language; unfortunately the writers have proved incapable of using that rupture with any imaginative force, so one is left with work that seems frustratingly incomplete – beautifully designed and acted, well lit, adequately directed, trembling with the potential to be one of the more memorable comedies produced in Britain, but crucially let down by the writers' lavatorial indiscipline.

The films by Terry Gilliam and other members of the Monty Python team have a similar visual splendour, similarly set against a mocking pattern of vernacular exchanges. The dialogue is probably weaker than in *Blackadder*, though sometimes witty, and the filmic narrative energy and imagination are far stronger. Nevertheless, the films work best by sequences, and moments within sequences, lacking an overall sense of purposeful direction. I don't know about students, but my own feeling is that these film makers could profit from a study of pacing and purpose in the nineteenth-century novel – but should this criticism be aimed at the scriptwriters or the directors? I will let Kuleshov suggest the grounds for an answer.

> Let us consider the various technical types of scenario:
> 1. The bare story, i.e., a literary exposé of the plot, basically cinematic but devoid of any detailed delineation of scenes or characters. The director fashions this scenario into a shooting script, which he uses for filming. This is an ideal scenario for a knowledgeable director, since men of letters do not know the first thing about pure film anyway.
> 2. A rough treatment, which elaborates the plot expression-wise, delineates the scenes and hints at the essential pattern of montage. Such a scenario constrains the director somewhat, for much of the imagery is forced on him by the writer.
>
> Note that in our interpretation the screen-writer is a representative of the alien art of literature who tries to impose something of his own literary element on our art.
> 3. Finally, a precise scenario with a montage-wise description of scenes and key moments, a 'pre-edited' script, a kind of sheet music for the director. In such a scenario each scene need not be narrated in a literary manner, it must only serve as a sign for the director, both in space (shot) and time (montage). This kind of scenario ought never to be written by men of letters but should be created by the director himself, for a writer can hardly be imagined to take up editing and directing without actually becoming a director. What the director needs from the screen-writer is the basic evolution of the story; then it is up to the director, i.e., the person who physically makes the picture, to turn this story technically and artistically into cinematic images and actions.
>
> In truth is is inconceivable that somebody should force their creative approach on the director. It is like trying to help a painter by advising him to apply paint here and there, disregarding the painter's obvious resentment of such advice.[21]

Undoubtedly, the director is, or should be, responsible for weakness in the script, and in any other narrative element of the film. The director should be able to alter the script, either personally or by delegating the task. However, the matter is complicated in several ways. Directors too are employees, and control may be vested in a producer who will over-ride the director's wishes; the budget may be too small to pay for re-writes (or better actors); the shooting schedule may be too tight for the luxury of re-takes. Some directors are also producers and script-writers, so, even if they have the freedom of a measure of independence from creative interference, who will tell them that the script is poorly structured, or times its effects badly, or can't be spoken without weakening characterization or mood? Separating various contributions to a film is rarely as simple a matter as reading its list of credits, which may have more to do with contractual agreements than who actually did what. Script credits are only the most notorious instance where successive writers may make substantial contributions without formal acknowledgment (other than pecuniary); sometimes the credit given to the director of photography is really due to the camera operator; the writer may be credited where the director should be, and vice versa; or the director for the work of the editor. Even so, a film can be broken down into its functional elements and individuals can be given responsibility for each of them; but it is reasonable to allow for the nature of collaboration, which includes discussion, compromise and some overlapping of roles.

Student or professional, the writer whose shooting script cannot be tampered with, perhaps extensively, will feel much abused and under-valued. The script provides a crucial set of references, but may also be the site for several points of departure.

Dialogue Styles

So also I cut myself off from the use of *ere, o'er, wellnigh, what time, say not* (for *do not say*), because, though dignified, they neither belong to nor ever could arise from, or to be the elevation of, ordinary modern speech. For it seems to me that the poetical language of an age should be the current language heightened, to any degree heightened and unlike itself, but not (I mean normally: passing freaks and graces are another thing) an obsolete one.[22]

Hopkins, in this well-known passage from a letter to Bridges, clearly distinguishes poetic language from ordinary modern speech; just as clearly he states their relationship so that the former is a concentration or a heightening of the latter. He is not against the maintenance of a living tradition, and mentions Shakespeare and Milton as exemplary precedents. What he objects to is the kind of obsolete poetic diction that popularly, and erroneously, identifies a wad of writing as an indulgent thing called poetry. Such tics should be instantly recognizable because they form no part of 'ordinary modern speech'; they arise from a desire to say something poetic rather than to say something definite. Of course, Hopkins was deploring a tendency in the current poetry of his age, and no one today – not even bad poets – would use *ere* and *o'er*, but does that mean that the relation between poetic language and current language is what Hopkins thought it should be?

It seems to me that the relation can be broadened without much distortion, so that poetic language, like Lawrence's art-speech, is the language of art. How is that language related to, and different from, ordinary modern speech, everyday life? If we eschew evaluative criteria and take as representative of popular contemporary drama something like *EastEnders*, the question may appear, at first, anyway, very difficult to answer. The sets and props are realistic (or even really real), the actors are recognizably ordinary and, if not quite like us, then at least like people we know, and as we suppose people we don't know to be; most of the things that happen to them could happen to anybody; the issues they confront are confronted by many of us; finally, the language they use sounds, to those of us who are not from the East End, just like ordinary modern speech. Unsurprisingly, we are likely to conclude that nothing has been heightened here, that there is nothing of poetry. We may even suppose that what *EastEnders* (and many more dramas) gives us is preferable to poetic language, that it gives us the real thing, life itself, without the *eres* and *o'ers*.

I would contend, on the contrary, that such programmes give us *too many eres* and *o'ers* in the reliance of their visual and aural language on conventional situations, stale devices, routine and predictable treatments. As an indication of the kind of thing I mean, consider the extensive use of a shuffled or rotated narrative. This can be traced back to its emergence in film as cross-cutting between parallel actions, in the first decade of the century. Used mainly for suspense, the device exploited tempo, with relatively long shots initially, then, as the danger increased, briefer shots, more rapid cutting between the victim and the approaching threat. But as a way of keeping several aspects of a complex story going simultaneously, it goes back much further. Here, for example, is one of Chaucer's transitions, in *The Knight's Tale*:

> Now wol I stynte of Palamon a lite,
> And lete him in his prison stille dwelle,
> And of Arcita forth I wol yow telle.

Shakespeare too, of course, cuts from one group of characters to another, between scenes, and sometimes years pass in those few unscripted moments. But all too often in soap operas the device is not integral to the dramatic fabric and the separated threads could be run continuously without loss or gain. You cut from what's being said in the pub/laundrette/café to what's being said in someone's flat/waiting room/market stall, and back again so that you keep in touch with the usually low-key stories of as many characters as possible, and so you are continually distracted from registering the banality of the writing, and you are even tricked into wanting to know what happens next (although another convention ensures that resolutions will be deferred). This has nothing to do with unmediated reality, obviously; it is an expressive, or poetic, use of the language, only here it's so mechanical, formulaic, that it's an *ere* or an *o'er*. If you think this is the poetry of reality you won't notice it; if you have experienced that poetry elsewhere it will try your patience.

Just as the poetic language, the film language, of soap operas like *EastEnders* tends to render certain terms obsolete and then perpetuate them, so, too, the dialogue and the way it is spoken conform to a somewhat jaded style, which is neither quite 'the current language' nor 'the current language heightened', but an attempt at the former through a kind of semi-skilled use of the latter. I've already implied that what seems to me the dominant tone of *EastEnders* is irritation. Within individual scenes this can have a certain power: most of the actors are at least competent, comfortable in their roles, and capable of delivering their lines at what seems the correct emotional pitch. But the accumulation of scenes of varying emotional intensity, varying dramatic significance, delivered *without* sufficient varying of pitch seriously undermines the modest aesthetic experience. The commitment to this particular formal style of realism, evoked with some consistency in sets, lighting, sound, camera set ups, and dialogue, as well as the way the dialogue is delivered, becomes a constraint that hampers character and plot development; the soap gets stagnant.

There is no easy solution to this problem. It isn't a matter of substituting a 'better' style, or of avoiding stylistic consistency; the problem is endemic to the serial form, and can only be controlled if closure is not deferred indefinitely. However, it is the formal style rather than the serial problem that I wish to draw attention to. Students should be aware that there are alternative ways of dealing creatively with ordinary modern speech.

Most modern stage, film and television drama observes the courteous convention which was stated visually in the shot/reverse shot pairings in Chapter Three: the man speaks while the woman listens; the woman speaks while the man listens. The pattern may be interrupted by scripted impatience, but actors rarely talk over each other's lines repeatedly. However realistic the dialogue is supposed to be, every word is usually audible. This convention is unlikely to change, but nevertheless it *is* a convention and may be effectively subverted.

In Howard Hawks' *His Girl Friday*, (1940), the pace is made frenetic, not be rapid camera movements, rapid cutting or rapid changes of scene, but because the actors deliver their lines at speed, and the lines overlap so much that you sometimes have to strain to catch them, and miss. Hawks observed modern ordinary speech.

> If you'll ever listen to some people who are talking, especially in a scene of any excitement, they all talk at the same time. All it needs is a little extra work on the dialogue. You put a few words in front of somebody's speech and put a few words at the end, and they can overlap it. It gives you a sense of speed that actually doesn't exist. And then you make the people talk a little faster.[23]

Ben Hecht and Charles MacArthur's successful and influential play, *The Front Page*, had already been filmed by Lewis Milestone in 1931, and the cynical, fast-paced wisecracking style was celebrated long before the story, significantly altered, became

His Girl Friday: one can't say that Hawks *invented* the technique of overlapping and speeding up the delivery of dialogue, but one can observe that he and Hecht collaborated on a number of scripts from the 1920s to the 1950s. It is evident in some of these films (*Twentieth Century*, (1934), *The Thing*, (1951), *Monkey Business*, (1952)), but is at least as evident in some of those Hawks' films that Hecht was not involved with (*Bringing Up Baby*, (1938), *Ball of Fire*, (1942), *Rio Bravo*, (1959)). Something of the effect is present in films Hecht scripted for William Wellman (*Nothing Sacred*, (1937) and *Roxie Hart*, (1942) – Hecht was uncredited for his work on the latter), but the scripts, credited and uncredited, that he worked on for Alfred Hitchcock (*Foreign Correspondent*, (1940), *Spellbound*, (1945), *Notorious*, (1946), *The Paradine Case*, (1947) and *Rope*, (1948)) can hardly be said to be characterized by this technique – their style is Hitchcock's. In any case, although the rhythms of written dialogue can suggest that a reading be slower or faster than normal, it is inevitably the director's decision, in working with the actors, to determine the precise pitch and pace, and whether or not to make of that a distinctive stylistic feature. Fast, overlapping dialogue is used extensively in *His Girl Friday*, not merely to depict reporters in a perpetual rush, but to bewilder and browbeat opponents, to deceive, to get away with callousness. It is both amusing and disturbing, and it is still exhausting, and that may be why it has never become a convention of mainstream cinema or television. (It's there, without the acerbity or insight, in *What's Up, Doc?*, which was Peter Bogdanovitch's hectic and overt attempt at Hawksian comedy in 1972, and to a lesser degree it's there, with some of the underlying paranoia and anguish, in *Fawlty Towers*, though John Cleese's performance seems, to confuse matters, to owe more to the Cary Grant of *Arsenic and Old Lace* than the Cary Grant of the Hawks comedies.) In *His Girl Friday*, and a number of films made in the thirties and forties, the approach is manifestly poetic: this is the current language heightened (as Hopkins added, 'to any degree heightened and unlike itself', but not obsolete), and because it is heightened it can say things which ordinary modern speech cannot. We register the relationship and the difference, and in that recognition respond to the art.

It is an element of film rather than stage art because we need the visual precision of two-shots and close-ups to retain our orientation; as a practical undertaking, it is an approach that can most effectively be accomplished by multiple camera shooting. Even so, students working with a single film or video camera should at least attempt it, or consider the possible alternatives to a straightforward, normal-speed, 'realistic' delivery of dialogue. What creative use could be made, for example, of the hesitations that occur in most conversations – the pauses, the ums and errs, the repetition of syntactically redundant words and phrases, the sentences that cease unexpectedly or become labyrinthine? There are so many facets of language which the film maker, perhaps more than any other artist, could observe and transform through use into a style and meaning previously not perceived, that it would be a shame to constrain students at the outset to the conventions of mainstream television 'realism'. More than a shame – it seems to me that until those conventions are shown to *be* conventions (whether by comparisons with Hawks, or with playwrights like Beckett or Pinter, or any mannered but not necessarily clichéd use of current speech) students are inclined to assume that they are as complete as tape recordings of spontaneous conversations. In fact, discussing and transcribing such recordings can be in itself a useful listening discipline, and may lead to freer kinds of scriptwriting.

Another potentially useful observation about language is that one hears it differently, according to circumstances. An audience for a stage, film or television performance occupies a position analogous to that of an eavesdropper, but is conventionally written-for: the audience is treated, like a participant, to conversations that can be heard in their entirety; the eavesdropper *may* occupy that position, but may also simply overhear fragments by chance (on a bus, for example, or passing amongst a crowd). These fragments may be random and meaningless, or the inadvertent listener may construct a purely personal meaning from them. Could such apparently casual, but nonetheless real, encounters with language be absorbed into the poetics of film?

Consider Robert Altman's *M*A*S*H*, (1970), (or, indeed, *The Long Goodbye*, (1973), *Nashville*, (1975), *A Wedding*, (1978), *Health*, (1980) or *Popeye*, (1980)). Much of the dialogue is inaudible, deliberately, or caught in passing as if by chance, but by design. The screen becomes a kind of audio-visual tapestry through which a narrative is woven, or through which a number of narratives are woven; conventional narrative linearity is, however, often obscured in the sensual simultaneity of the experience. Where it works, this technique gives an extraordinary sense of immersion in a particular social world, whose minute details have a cumulative impact to which 'plot' seems secondary; characters seem real because of their involvement in and extension through the convincing dimensions of their environment – we can feel that they are 'there' even when off-screen. The popular television spin-off from *M*A*S*H* jettisoned this crucial stylistic element and retained little more than the situation, conventionally filmed, along with tidied-up, insufferably self-righteous versions of the main characters.

Altman's technique, again more appropriate for multiple camera shooting and multiple sound recording (that is, again, appropriate for, yet hardly ever exploited by television), relies on complex technology, especially for mixing the sound tracks, but there's no reason why students shouldn't adapt the idea, at least to the extent of trying out different ways of delivering lines to take advantage of ensemble playing. He encourages actors to develop their own characters and improvise dialogue. He wants an audience to have a 'sense of the dialogue, the emotional feeling rather than the literal word; that's the way sound is in real life'.[24]

> I don't consider the dialogue, in most cases, part of the writing. I consider that part of the acting . . . To me, the writing – the authorship – is in the concept of the film.[25]

Somewhere between Hawks and Altman is the treatment of dialogue in several sequences of David Drury's *Defence of the Realm*, (1985). The characters in this film are mostly journalists, as in *His Girl Friday*, but it is less concerned with their venality than with the other stereotype of the profession, crusading for truth. Not quite working as a serious exposé of high level duplicity in the secret state (its revelations were already the stuff of yesterday's headlines – depressing but hardly startling), or as a thriller (there's an excellent Hitchcock-like sequence near the end, but so isolated it reads like a compromise), *Defence of the Realm* is still one of the few British films of the eighties to have a real sense of film's possibilities working through it. The ambient sounds of a newspaper office, a pub and a restaurant are foregrounded only a little more than they would need to be to create a realistic atmosphere *behind* the drama, but then the notion of ambience, with its implications of distortion, fragmentation, interference is exploited creatively as a narrative and thematic device.

The film is about concealment and the protagonist's efforts to gather, and then deduce the real meaning of, information. A sequence may start with one character in a private telephone conversaton, which he is recording and which we can overhear; but as we move across the office to the protagonist we lose, like him, this privilege and share his helpless curiosity. Another sequence: he is in a pub being noisily congratulated on the story he has broken when further details of the same story begin to come over the television news broadcast; again, he struggles to pick up more information, as we do; we cut to the same broadcast continuing in his boss's office, hear a little more, but also wonder what we are going to learn from his boss's interest in this story. We are frequently positioned as eavesdroppers just too far away to catch clues that may or may not be vital, while being obliged to listen to patches of close-up dialogue that get in our way. The verbal plot is scattered across numerous characters, telephone conversations, television news broadcasts, newspaper clippings and tape recordings until we have a sense of being almost as actively involved as the protagonist in sifting, deducing and discovering the sense of what is going on. This is filmic, poetic language, based on observation of real language 'situations', but it is rarely exploited dramatically; instead we are surrounded by dramas in which the actors speak clearly, one after another, with every sentence contributing its little bit to the development of the story, and we mistake this convention, sensible as it often is, for reality.

Use of Sound

I was talking to an old friend, a BBC film cameraman, recently; most of his work is in film, but he sometimes uses video cameras, so I was asking what differences he found in lighting, filtration, and so on. Later, casually, he threw out the remark that if video technology had come first, everyone now would be talking about the advantages of shooting with film instead. A similar hypothesis might be advanced with regard to sound: if direct recording of sound on film had always been possible – or, indeed, unavoidable – would everyone now be exploring the advantages of *separate* sound recording? It is easy to dismiss such questions, since technological developments did occur in a particular order, and even if it were possible to reverse that order we could not predict the sequence of applications; but that is not the point. The questions are not idle if they help us to look askance at current practice and the assumptions that support it.

If video had come first, everyone would now be excited about film because of its extraordinary image quality, which allows images to be projected on to huge screens; because of the sensitivities of film stocks and their manipulation during processing, which allow many subtle gradations of colour, tone and balance; and because the image is visibly present on the strip of film, so that you can make a cut exactly at the frame you want, just with a pair of scissors – so simple, so precise, such an obvious advance on all that equipment needed to edit video so accurately!

And if sound had been, from the beginning, the mere recording of voices to correspond with images recorded at the same time, what creative freedom there would be in a new system that enabled us to get away from the prosaic naturalism of synchronization!

But just as continuity editing was the evolution of a perceived limitation into a transparent realist convention, so sound recording evolved as an attempt to bury its separation from the image and become integrated with it until. To keep the same example, not as the apotheosis of contemporary film making, but simply as representative of widespread practice, we have the dull realism of *EastEnders*. All that technology, just to record dialogue realistically, just to catch the background noises which usually do no more than confirm what the visual backgrounds are also saying!

But we tend to take sound as much for granted as the image, as if the recording mechanism was no more than a switch. Video cameras *can* give us sound with image more or less as simply as that but, as I said at the beginning of this chapters, this facility is deceptive, and students realize it as soon as they try to imitate even the reality of a straight-forward soap opera. Sound is as carefully constructed as image, and can be developed as imaginatively, if we train ourselves to *listen* to films.

England's second talkie, *Blackmail*, (1929), sounds primitive and tentative now, even in what is probably its most famous sequence, but our responses are primed by our expectations. If, instead of looking for the details that confirm it as an old movie, we approach it as one of the earliest films to affect the transformation from silent to sound, we may be more likely to find a freshness, subsequently lost, that we may want to adapt and use today. The heroine has stabbed her would-be seducer to death. Next morning she is at breakfast with her parents, about to slice a loaf of bread. A gossipy neighbour enters and starts talking about the killing. Her voice fades until only the one repeated word, *knife*, can be heard, louder each time until the girl screams and drops the bread knife. Hitchcock's attempts at psychological realism, the world as it sounds inside the guilty girl's head, may be crudely conceived, even clumsily executed, but it is also a more imaginative use of the medium than can easily be found in contemporary mainstream cinema or television, where the human voice is rarely distorted for effects that could extend our definitions of realism. This example is particularly apt because early sound recording had one thing in common with amateur Super 8 cameras in the mid-seventies and video cameras currently available: it occurred at the moment of filming; there was little or no post-synchronization.

The following passage by Hitchcock's biographer, John Russell Taylor, sufficiently indicates the challenges students might care to set themselves; it is an account of the shooting of one scene in *Juno and the Paycock*, (1930):

> There is a scene . . . in which the family is talking in the living room, gathered excitedly round the new phonograph, oblivious of the fact that the son is crouched in anguish by the fireplace. Their conversation is interrupted by a funeral passing in the street outside, and then by gunfire, and meanwhile the camera moves in from a general view of the room and the family, past them to a close up of the guilty boy by the fire and his reactions.
>
> Easy enough, one would say, in terms of modern film-making. But what one forgets is that at the time the film was made all the sound had to be produced and recorded on the spot. So there had to be a phonograph playing 'If You're Irish, Come into the Parlour', and the sound of the Marian hymn being sung by the funeral procession as it passes, and the gunfire, and the conversation all created on one tiny stage. Unfortunately, to complicate matters, they could not find a suitable recording of the required song, so that too had to be done on the stage. Consequently, as well as the actors and the camera crew, there were present a small orchestra without basses to simulate the right tinny, distant sound, a prop man singing the song while holding his nose to sound as though it was coming from a phonograph, an effects man at the ready with the machine-gun effect, and a choir of abut twenty people to represent the funeral. All to be synchronized with the dialogue and fluctuating in relative volume and intensity as the window is opened and closed.[26]

A modest example of slight distortion of a naturalistic soundtrack can be found quite near the beginning of Ford's *Rio Grande*. The lieutenant colonel in command of the post is indoors, silent, with two of his officers when the new recruits arrive. We cross-cut briefly between the sobriety of the interior scene and the levity of the sergeant outside welcoming the recruits, who answer a roll call. On the first cut to the interior the sound drops almost imperceptibly and, naturally, it rises again as we return to its source outside, but then, while the exterior sequence of the roll call continues, the sound level changes oddly, gaining a hollowness, almost an echo, for which there seems no reason. It's too slight and brief a moment to be registered as anything more than a possible flaw, yet it does register in the sense that it brings about a delicate shift in the kind of attention one is paying. The next recruit to answer his name is Trooper Yorke, and the hollowness, as it were, reverberates to the interior as the commander of the fort hears his son's name. Music immediately underlines the dramatic significance of this moment, and helps to colour our emotional response, but that simple mechanical manipulation of the voices has already, with tact and restraint, begun to involve us in the relationship that will be explored as the film proceeds. Here it is not so much the actor's delivery of his line as the distortion in its recording that serves the dramatic texture, but even without being distorted the recorded voice can be subtly manipulated.

In Fritz Lang's *M*, shot in 1931, the voice is used as an expressive structural element in a way that has been absorbed into the convention and thus rendered virtually imperceptible. *M*, a child-murderer, has been cornered in an office block by a gang of underworld figures. They manage to capture and bundle him away just before the police arrive. But one of their number, a burglar, is left behind, at the bottom of a hole. He calls for his friends to let down the ladder, and eventually emerges to find himself surrounded by police. The camera tracks away from him as he starts saying, 'For once I'm as innocent as a new-born babe', but in the midst of his sentence there is a shot-change, so that as he finishes it he is in a new location, at a desk being interrogated by an Inspector. Time is elided, but the voice acts as a kind of bandage across the gap, ensuring realistic continuity.

Soundtrack music frequently has this function, and can be used to 'paper over the cracks' of poorly matched edits, but sound can also *draw attention to* a cut, or draw some of its own effectiveness from a cut. One thinks of the abrupt fragmentations of sound and image in some of Godard's films of the 1960s, but there are striking examples within somewhat more mainstream work. In Woody Allen's *Interiors*, (1978), there is a scene in which a middle-aged woman, who cannot cope with life since her husband left, prepares to commit suicide. It follows immediately upon a brief scene between the two of them – hardly a reconciliation: the dialogue is polite, empty and awkward, with stilted compliments and strained attempts at inconsequentiality. The published screenplay presents the transition accurately, but inadequately:

> An abrupt cut to Eve's hands putting wide black masking tape around the borders of her apartment windows, her doors. She reaches the end of the black tape roll; she breaks off the end and finishes the job with white adhesive tape. Eve's hands work methodically, exactingly; the noise of the pulling and tearing of tape is the only sound over this scene.[27]

This conveys nothing of the shock in that 'abrupt cut', which is not just 'to Eve's hands' but also, more gratingly, to 'the noise of the pulling and tearing of tape' – and it is the harsh, painful *sound*, in sequent contrast to the gently distanced words of her husband, which jolts the viewer into a poignant participation in the agony that underlies Eve's methodical sealing-off of the room (a sequence of ten close-ups of her hands at work, ten abrasive jolts) in which we finally see her arranging herself decorously to die.

In Milos Forman's *Amadeus*, (1985), Mozart's father, in tears, reads the letter in which his son mentions his marriage (the son reading the letter in voice over). As the father finishes the letter he crumples the notepaper. This sound, like the pulled tape in *Interiors*, is exaggerated, so we register its destructive finality, and it continues over the next shot. A herd of white deer scatters, apparently frightened by the noise of the crumpled paper, but then, as the transition is completed, by the intrusion of the Emperor's party on horseback, and the news of further preferment for the young musician: local sound becomes metaphor.

In each of the examples quoted so far, from *Blackmail*, *Rio Grande*, *M*, *Interiors* and *Amadeus*, the source of the sound is unambiguously present visually, but its value is intensified by several kinds of manipulation; only in *Blackmail* is the manipulated effect so striking as to be unavoidable, though in each case it is at least momentarily palpable. Such effects, in diverse forms, permeate films, contributing to the stylistic pattern of minute detail, and yet occupying a relatively minor role in the history of film criticism where it has been focused on genres, directors or individual films. I presume this is partly because creative sound recording tends to be embedded in the narrative texture without necessarily making an obvious contribution to what one might call the literary themes of the story, or the 'content' level.

Everyone notices, retrospectively anyway, the excessive orchestration in Hollywood films of the forties, or Bernard Herrmann's 'black and white' score – strings only – for Hitchcock's rigorously composed black and white *Psycho*, or the contribution made by the music in *Jaws*, (1975), or that otherwise unremarkable film, *Chariots of Fire*, but the cumulative power of the small instances I have given is really just as great. Think, for example, of all those suspense films whose effectiveness depends on guiding your anticipation through manipulation of the soundtrack until you know something is about to happen, simply because *silence* has descended. The lack of sound has no intrinsic meaning but, like a pause, or even the spaces between all the notes in music, it is charged with meaning because of its aural context.

> *Bresson*: Concerning the two automobile skids, I think that, since one has already seen the first, it is useless to see the second too. I prefer to have it imagined. If I had had it imagined the first time, at that point, there would have been something missing. ... But after that, I prefer to have it imagined with the help of a sound, for every time that I can replace an image by a sound I do so. And I do so more and more.
>
> *Godard*: And if you could replace all the images by sounds? I mean ... I am thinking of a kind of inversion of the functions of the image and of the

sound. One could have the images, of course, but it would be the sound that would be the significant element.

Bresson: As to that, it is true that the ear is much more creative than the eye. The eye is lazy; the ear, on the contrary, invents. . . . The ear is a much deeper sense, and very evocative. The whistle of a locomotive, for example, can evoke, imprint in you the vision of an entire railroad station, sometimes of a specific station that you know, sometimes of the atmosphere of a station, or of a railroad track, with a train stopped . . . The possible evocations are innumerable.[28]

One other use of sound, again frequently inseparable from movement and editing, should be mentioned as being worth students' consideration, even though it may seem trivial, and that is the substitution effect. Everyone knows that sound effects may be gathered from all sorts of unlikely sources – perhaps the best known effect of all is to make the sound of galloping horses by banging halved coconut shells together. In Penny Marshall's *Big*, (1988), there are a number of scenes in which the humour seems to arise naturally from a situation, but where it is really very precisely gauged. Tom Hanks plays with a toy, for example, holding its arms and pretending that it is boxing with him. The action is quite casual and spontaneous, but as the sequence comes to an end he makes the toy land a punch, and reacts as if hit. Immediately we are into the next sequence, without having time to wonder why the last made us smile or laugh. The crucial element, I think, is that the blow is accompanied by the *sound* of a full-size punch which, instead of being merely anomalous, gives the sequence an unexpectedly satisfying climax, which then *has* to be cut at once (cutting immediately on completion of the punch-line – literally in this case – is a technique also used very successfully in *Fawlty Towers*. It can work just as well in drama, but for contrast one might study the cutting rhythms of Ford and Renoir, both of whom will often maintain a shot *after* it has served its obvious dramatic purpose so that we attend more to the human drama than the plot around which it emerges).

Attention should also be given to atmospheric sound, implied in Taylor's account of *Juno and the Paycock*, and in the dialogue with Robert Bresson: off-screen sounds can be constructed in such a way that a very clear sense of time and place is conveyed, without necessarily being shown on screen at all. How would you suggest, for example, from a studio-built set, that the room is housed in a suburb, or in a terrace, or in the country, or by a busy street? For this kind of detail you could in fact study programmes like *EastEnders*, whose sense of location is excellent. But to consider sound as an integral aesthetic element, as important as image, it would be as well to go to Bresson. The jousting tournament in *Lancelot of the Lake*, for example, where the camera is predominantly on the legs of the horse and the collisions and crashes are heard to happen, but not shown; or the robbery in *L'Argent*, where the camera predominantly stays on the driver of the getaway car, while the sounds of shooting occur off-screen, up the street.

The only other art whose use of sound is at all comparable to that of film is radio, and perhaps it is not going too far, when noting film's affinities to verbal, visual and performance arts, to adduce the oral tradition as well. And yet, as I hope my suggestions are demonstrating, the way these borrowings are adapted and developed is distinctively filmic. By isolating and thereby unavoidably highlighting certain examples of acting, delivering dialogue and using sound, I have not meant to imply that these elements must be central to every film students make, or that they need to be studied intensively in every film watched, from beginning to end. I am simply trying to outline a few of the inexhaustible possibilities offered by film. I know that the enthusiasms of some film critics for, say, low budget films which may have banal dialogue and poor acting, are likely to strike beginning film students as inexplicable. They strike me that way too, sometimes, but there is also the possibility that the critic is reading aspects of the language that the student has not yet become familiar with. Script, acting, dialogue and sound will have differing degrees of importance from film to film; often they will be inseparably fused; at times they will be dispensed with altogether (a film can be improvised, animated, abstract, silent). They are choices, elements that may or may not be deemed essential to the particular narrative. An education in film involves the assimilation of its history: to know what is possible now we must know what has gone before; to read any work of art fully we need not only to compare like with like, but also to evaluate the smallest salient detail with a standard flexible enough to entertain at least some of its potential alternative treatments. However, in one sense the next element for consideration is not subject to choice: no film can be made without light.

Lighting

A video camera is more likely to be available in schools and colleges than a clockwork Bolex or a battery-run Super 8 silent camera. I have given some indication of what this means for synchronized sound shooting – the advantage can be a limitation, but the limitation can be turned to advantage, especially by using the dubbing facility for post-synchronization. But what does it mean visually? The concealed technology is extraordinarily sophisticated, compared to cameras and film stocks generally available in the relatively recent past. Students of mine, with no technical knowledge and only the briefest introduction to handling a camera, have brought back sequences shot at night, with only occasional street lights for illumination, which are at least as good as comparable sequences I remember making as a student in the sixties – the differences being that my students don't have to take meter readings, or use the fastest film stock available, or send it to the laboratory with instructions to push it in processing to increase its rating sufficiently for an image to form at all. The video camera, even when 'Light' is flashing in the viewfinder to plead for more of that valuable substance, will usually produce enough detail to form an image, as long as something can be seen with the unassisted eye; it can also focus automatically. To that extent, the video camera is like a much more versatile and sensitive snapshot camera – you press the button, and it does the rest. It's very easy, then, to take lighting for granted and to regard image creation as a largely mechanical operation; very impressive, certainly, but having little to do with art.

Although it is true that some television cameramen take advantage of the automatic facilities – either because they can judge that the results will be good enough for the purposes to which their shots will be put, or because they are lazy, or because the circumstances are such that it is more important to shoot quickly and obtain images than risk missing everything – this 'instamatic' approach is not representative of conventional practice. Clearly it *would* be representative if it could be relied on to procure with uniform consistency images comparable to those only achieved by greater expenditure of money, time, equipment and skill; but automatic adjustments occur in response to stimuli which often have no dramatic reason to intrude so noticeably. For example, if the camera, set on automatic focus, is tracking some characters in medium long shot when a bush comes into frame in close-up, the camera will not 'know' that the bush is extraneous and will therefore sense the reflections from the momentarily more dominant source, re-focusing as efficiently as it can while the characters blur. This can be disconcerting. Similarly, the automatic facility may find it impossible to deal with a fast-moving subject, even when it is held competently within the frame. Sensibly, then, video cameras usually have a manual override, so that the camera operator (or the focus puller) can set and adjust the correct distances. Regrettably, the same sensible option is not provided on most currently available video cameras for manual aperture setting (except on very expensive professional models).

Anyone used to operating automatic *still* cameras may feel that the advantages nevertheless outweigh the disadvantages, though I think that is unlikely. In any case, the disadvantages of automatic readings on film or video cameras are likely to become apparent after a very few shots; with every alteration in light source and intensity, the reading will be changed, or 'corrected', but the correction, which may take several awkwardly long seconds to complete, is likely to turn a nicely exposed head and shoulders shot into an unwanted silhouette. You may want to take the light for granted, but the automatic camera cannot. You can gain some control over the camera's propensity to keep on adjusting its aperture by planning and restricting its movements, and subject movement within the shot, by judicious use of supplementary lights, reflectors and diffusers, by altering the focal length of the lens (anything from wide angle to telephoto) and by careful focusing – all these variables affect the light that reaches the film or the tape. But with film you can choose sensitized emulsions of differing speeds (conventionally the slower the film the finer its capacity to resolve detail, but also, the more light it requires. Faster film enables you to shoot with less light, but with an increase in grain size and thus with less fine detail. However, such advances have now been made that fast films have many of the characteristics previously only available to slow ones), and in combination with film speed the negative may be under- or over-developed, as may the print. Video tape is considerably less flexible. And even with the variable factors you can control, the absence of a manually corrected aperture setting will limit what you can do with light.

The lens aperture is, quite simply, the hole through which light passes. Except for effects of slow or speeded-up motion, cameras run at a consistent speed, so that each frame is exposed for the same amount of time (a standard twenty-four frames per second with 35mm film, and the equivalent of twenty-five frames per second for television). If the size of the aperture is increased, then, obviously, that much more light will get through. With too much light the image will be over-exposed, so on a bright day you would stop-down (make the aperture smaller) and in poor light you would open up the aperture. Lenses are calibrated in f-stops which are inversely related to the diameter of the aperture, so that f2.8 might be the maximum aperture, while stopping-down to f22 would mean closing the diaphragm until little light could enter. A large f-stop such as f2.8 will cut down the depth of field; conversely a small f-stop such as f22 will increase it. Depth of field is the distance, starting some way in front of the camera lens, within which everything will appear to be in focus. If you only want to focus on one object at a fixed distance from the camera, then depth of field may not matter, but if the object is alive and needs to move closer or futher away, or if there are several such objects at several distances, and sharp focus is needed throughout, then the automatic aperture, in limiting your control of depth of field, may oblige you to create a different shot, or sequence of shots, from what you intended.

However, the focal length of the lens can also affect depth of field. A short focal length has a wider angle of vision than a standard lens, while a long focal length has a narrower angle of vision. Thus, a wide angle lens lets in more light than a telephoto, so the aperture is correspondingly smaller and the depth of field greater.

The other variable to be remembered when determining the appropriate depth of field is the focus, or distance setting. For example, with my 28mm wide angle lens set at f8, and the focusing ring set at seven feet, everything from about four feet to fifteen feet from the lens should appear on screen in focus. If the action within the shot moves outside that range focus will soften and soon become blurred. If I focus instead at five feet, my depth of field will range from about three and a half feet to about eleven feet; if I re-focus at ten feet, then everything from about five and a half feet almost to infinity should appear on screen in reasonably sharp focus. But the key to all this is *light*. If I can increase the light on the set enough to allow me to stop-down the aperture by three stops, to f.22, then the depth of field will extend from a little over two feet in front of the lens to infinity. Clearly this facility can influence the way in which the narrative is perceived.

The advice to bear in mind is that one should not always focus exactly on the main subject of the shot, especially if it will include movements towards or away from the camera, of if a sense of depth perspective is important. On the other hand, one may have good reason to prefer a selective focus, with foreground and background detail darkened or blurred. In that case the factors I have mentioned can be utilized more or less in reverse, that is, by reducing light levels somewhat, using a longer focus lens and opening up the aperture. Operating this way allows another refinement which can be dramatically effective if not overdone – pulling focus. For example, if there are two people in the frame, one at about six feet, the other at twelve feet, attention can be shifted from the first to the second – if the depth of field is narrow – by pulling focus, which means turning the focusing ring, from six feet to twelve feet in the course of the shot. Done subtly to pursue the natural rhythms of a conversation this can be imperceptible, but a marked and swift change of focus can be used to emphasize a shock, or a dramatic revelation.

Light does not merely facilitate some technical and stylistic features of the camera, and affect the disposition of the actors however. In combination with the set design it can characterize the tone of the film. Initially, films were shot by available light, and sets were unroofed to let the sun in; some could be revolved to continue catching the same light through the day. Later, muslin was hung to diffuse the light and eliminate strong shadows. Gradually a range of lights was added, and some of the techniques already developed for still photography were utilized, particularly for close-ups. In Germany's UFA studios in the twenties a heavily expressionistic form of lighting was used in combination with more fluid and sometimes extreme camera movements and angles – pools of light, large areas of deep shadow. This style, along with directors and camera crews, was taken over by Hollywood and absorbed. It is evident, for example, in Ford's *The Informer*, (1935) and *The Long Voyage Home*, (1940) and to varying degrees in many more of his films. It resurfaced, perhaps more highly polished, in the film noir genre in the 1940s – strong sidelights streaming through venetian blinds to cast striped diagonals across a set, or heavy table lamps with large dark shades casting wide angled beams of light below, characters moving in and out of shadow. Lighting for black and white cinematography became very elaborate, but lighting for colour gradually reduced the number of lights needed. A modelling light to separate a figure from a background of similar tone might not be needed at all once colour made the differentiation obvious, for example. And as the sensitivities of lens and film emulsions improved, the barrage of lights could be reduced even further.

After the Second World War some of the advances made by documentary cameramen encouraged a less formal look, available light for exteriors and, sometimes, portable lighting and reflectors for interiors. For film students in the sixties, Raoul Coutard's work with Godard popularized shooting wherever possible with little or not additional light sources. *A Bout de Souffle* was shot entirely on location with available light, using fast film pushed in development. Subsequently, for interiors, he used 'bounced' light to supplement the natural window light while remaining in character with it – photofloods are fixed above the windows and aimed at the ceilings, instead of giving direct modelling to the actors. Thus, the bounced light follows at least part of the route taken by the natural light, reflecting in a general, diffused way back from the ceiling and the adjacent walls. this also means that the actors and camera can move fairly freely within the interior, without the need to stop while the lighting plot is reorganized.

While more formal studio lighting is still used extensively in mainstream film and TV, it has tended to function increasingly within the realistic mode, perhaps more appropriate to colour anyway, which has less explicit modelling of features, less light and shade contrast, less implied depth, than in the classic Hollywood period. Exceptions tend to be within genres such as the horror film. The potential of lighting to create different dramatic spaces, different sets, within the frame, has been suggested in Francis Ford Coppola's technical *tour de force*, *One From The Heart*, (1982), and, less extensively, Robert Altman's film of the same year, *Come Back to the 5 and Dime Jimmy Dean, Jimmy Dean*. Moody foreground lighting will slowly fade, while lighting from another source brings up previously concealed actors on a plane further back, so that there is an effect of fading, dissolving, superimposing from one scene to the next, all done with a dreamy soft smoothness. Apparently solid walls disappear (as, more obviously, in a startling scene from Paul Schrader's *Mishima*, (1986)) and one has a sense that although the realism of narrative continuity is maintained, another realism, that drifts with the memories and hopes of the characters, is also present.

One From The Heart was an intimate film, but it cost nearly as much to make as *Apocalypse Now*, (1979), (twenty-seven as against thirty million dollars); it was a critical and commercial failure. Students are unlikely to have access to Coppola's resources, of course, but even so I do think that when they have exploited the video camera's excellent capacity to form decent images in available light, they should experiment a little with creating effects through lighting – try additional spotlights at various angles, above, below, off to one side; deflect the light, hang gauzes, bamboo blinds, coloured gels and so on in front of it. Don't accept natural light as adequate for every circumstance, but, rather, think of lighting as a major dramatic resource, as important as the shooting script – sometimes more so.

The two remaining elements I will look at in this chapter derive naturally from a consideration of lighting, but offer the possibility of a complete break from the convention I began with, of continuity editing. Multiple camera shooting attempted, while remaining firmly within the convention, to preserve the temporal integrity of performances. Deep focus, in combination with the long take, can obviate the need for master shots followed by shot/reverse shot pairs, can apparently stop the director manipulating the narrative during editing, can, in fact, emphasize the continuous dramatic narrative through the world within the shot, rather than by the association of one shot with another – can, in short, approximate to the kind of unbroken, unconstructed realism made possible (a possibility rarely exploited) by live broadcast television.

Deep Focus

The term is applied to photographic images whose evident depth of field extends from close-ups, through medium shot, to long shot; it is rarely of interest unless these three planes of action are animated compositionally and dynamically by lighting, placing of objects, and the movements of actors. Consequently, although the term refers specifically to the sharpness of three planes on the screen, it is often used rather more loosely to refer to the deliberate staging of a scene spatially across these planes, even if there is some loss of focus in the foreground or background.

Deep focus enables actors to move about freely within their environment, and to be perceived in their relationship *to* that environment and to one another. It seems to guarantee the integrity of the space in which characters move and, thus, to be fundamentally biased towards reality rather than artifice. Watching Alida Valli walking down a tree-lined avenue in *The Third Man*, (1949), approaching directly towards the camera from extreme long shot to medium shot and then off past the camera frame right we *know* the avenue is not a painted backdrop, and we know how long it takes to walk that distance because there is no editing. After an inserted concluding shot of a jeep being driven away, the final shot of the film lasts about a minute and a quarter. We may also suppose that a satisfying conclusion has not been created in editing, which is true, but we would be naïve to suppose that the director had simply chosen to absent himself from interpreting the story at this point – clearly the shot did not just happen by itself!

Edited film fragments the space and *dis*locates the actors' relations to it, but conventional narrative continuity reconstructs the fragments and relocates the actors so that, usually, no disorientation is experienced. True deep focus, however natural it appears, is essentially a photographic effect made possible by the light-sensitivity of lenses and film emulsions. If you hold up your hand and attempt to look at it, an object a few feet beyond it, and something beyond that again, you will find it impossible to keep the three planes in sharp focus; your eyes will automatically 'pull focus' as you look *from* your hand *to* the object beyond it. The two-dimensional screen image with sharp foreground, middle distance and background detail is no more truly representative of what the eyes actually see than the shot which selects a focused area and allows other planes to blur, or the sequence of shots that shift attention from actor to actor. It may convey a greater *illusion* of reality, however, because there is less opportunity for subsequent interference with the scene as it unfolds. Therefore the looser definition of deep focus, while technically incorrect, does seem to me reasonable, since it accepts the only dramatically meaningful application of deep focus, composition in depth.

Deep focus is evident in one of the first films of the Lumière brothers, *A train entering a station*, (1895). The train approaches the camera and stops, passengers alight, and there is movement towards and away from the camera. Examination of frame stills shows sharp focus on a figure moving through close-up past the camera, and on middle distance and background. The three-dimensional illusion is supposed to have been such that audiences in the 1890s screamed and ducked under their seats to avoid the oncoming train, and Godard recreates this legend of film's realism in *Les Carabiniers*, (1963). Many other more or less fortuitous examples of deep focus can be found in monochromatic or orthochromatic films until the mid-twenties, when panchromatic film was introduced. This film required incandescent lighting, which was less powerful, but also less noisy, than arc lighting; consequently the aperture had to be opened up more, and the larger the aperture the smaller the depth of field.

Jean Renoir's *La Règle du Jeu*, (1939), remains, I think, the most intelligent film structured so that deep focus is not an accident or a flashy effect but a necessary dramatic principle, A purist, however, would argue that this is not an example of true deep focus because although action takes full advantage of the places of recession, Renoir did not have the technical resources shortly to be exploited in Hollywood and, consequently, sharp focus is not maintained at all distances.

Improved arc lamps came into use in Hollywood in the mid-thirties. They were silent, and also much brighter than incandescent lights. A much faster film stock was introduced a couple of years later, with fine grain; lenses improved optically (lens coating, which allowed more light to be transmitted, began to be practised just before the end of the decade). As a result, wide angle lenses, stopped down, could be used, creating greater depth of field and stronger, sharper, more 'contrasty' images. Many directors and cameramen still favoured the softer, 'greyer' look that had become established with incandescent lighting, heavily diffused, and narrow depth of field: Gregg Toland was a notable exception. In William Wyler's *Wuthering Heights*, (1939), and more extensively in Ford's *The Grapes of Wrath* and, particularly, *The Long Voyage Home*, (both 1940), he had the opportunity to develop compositions in depth, with selective lighting on the three main planes, deep shadow between, low angle shots showing ceilings, and shots with the light source visible and shining directly into the lens. His most celebrated work is in *Citizen Kane*, (1941), (see note 29).

Precedents for the powerfully melodramatic, expressionistic compositions in depth that distinguish much of *Citizen Kane* (whose elements of surreality strongly influenced the photographer Bill Brandt, as well as informing the theories of realism advocated by André Bazin) can be found in the German cinema of the 1920s, and the Hollywood that adopted the UFA style for horror movies in the early 1930s and film noir in the 1940s.

There are, however, striking, if isolated, examples elsewhere. One shot in *A Woman of Affairs*, (1928), could almost have come directly from *Citizen Kane*, and certainly from Bill Brandt. This film, directed by Clarence Brown and photographed by William Daniels, is a plush vehicle for Greta Garbo. The pseudo-tragic heroine attempts to visit her brother, who is dying and who refuses to see her. There is a close-up of her hand on the doorknob, followed by a reverse close-up of the doorknob from inside his room. The camera tracks out rapidly from this close-up, away from the door and across the room, coming to rest just beyond the brother. He is now framed in a disturbingly large and unbalanced close shot. With an empty bottle looming large between him and the camera, and the door still visible in the background. Admittedly, the door is not as sharp as the thematically important bottle and foreground figure, but the rapid track away from it is an effective visual equivalent for the tensions on both sides of it, so its importance is not diminished by the slight loss of focus at the end of the shot. In any case, the *effect* of deep-field compositions, particularly in combination with selective planes of light and deep shadow, was never entirely lost in Hollywood in the thirties, as can be seen in several relatively minor John Ford films prior to his association with Toland (for example, *Mary of Scotland*, (1936), *The Hurricane*, (1937) and *Four Men and a Prayer*, (1938)). A curious incidental link between German expressionism, Ford and deep focus is that the two films Welles studied with most care before making *Citizen Kane* were *The Cabinet of Dr Caligari*, (1919) and *Stagecoach*, (Welles's acknowledgment of the formative influence of the 'old master', Ford, is well known).

Deep focus seems to have become little more than another transparent device, used easily and frequently without any particular dramatic emphasis. My impression is that a stronger visual characteristic of film, particularly from Europe, since the sixties has been the exploitation of the actual two-dimensionality of the screen image, rather than the illusion of perspective in depth. I daresay that a prolonged shot-by-shot analysis would prove this impression to be without foundation technically. Impressions are not dependent on mathematical accuracy however, but intermittent imagery. I think of the use of paintings and flat surfaces painted in primary colours in, for example, *Pierrot le Fou*, of the abstract shots of parts of the body in *Une Femme Mariée* and Resnais' *La Guerre est Finie*, and of the lateral tracking shot in the stock exchange in Antonioni's *L'Eclisse*. The wide screen, the lateral tracking shot and the somewhat flatter lighting suitable for contemporary colour counteract, I think, the extensive use of the zoom lens and forward and backward tracking shots (even with the added smoothness and flexibility of steadicam); but whether my impression is right or wrong is immaterial. What matters is that students should be conscious of lighting and deep focus as modes of expression, aspects of the language, along with deliberate over- or under-exposure, use of the zoom, available light shooting, and so forth.

The Long Take

The long take, usually combined with deep focus composition, tends to be spoken of less as a singular event – an extended shot or two appearing in a film where continuity editing predominates – than as a structuring practice fundamentally different from, and arguably more realistic than, the conventional practice of narrative construction through editing, or montage. The latter subordinates the shot content, elevating rather the plasticity of the material, the skill with which the elements are assembled. The long take, by contrast, subordinates editing and elevates shot content, observing spatial and temporal continuities and fixing aesthetic interest there, in the choreographies of performance and environment. The distinction is theoretically persuasive, but the most striking uses of the long take are combined with ingenious, and obviously rehearsed, camera movements which either duplicate the conventionally edited sequence of positions, or generate such an awareness of themselves that the experience is heightened by the artifice of its presentation.

The long take does tend to impart a different sense of unfolding time from classical Hollywood cutting – characteristically, time seems to be drawn out, which may either have the effect of slowing down the narrative without contributing anything, or of extending it so that a greater weight may be carried. The films of Andrei Tarkovsky fall into the latter category, and become more rewarding, more exciting, on repeated viewings. However, the summary comments of the compilers of the *Bloomsbury Foreign Film Guide* (Bergan, R. and Karney, R., 1988) on *Nostalgia* and *The Sacrifice* may be taken as typical:

> The extremely long takes, the camera moving almost imperceptibly at times, create an intense concentration on the many extraordinary images. But there are scenes of an almost perverse obscurity and the final sequence is tedious beyond belief.[30]

> The opening six-minute take of a man and child planting a tree prepares the audience to be patient. By the time the film reaches its brilliant climax – an unbroken 10-minute take of a burning house seen from a distantly-placed camera, many might have lost that patience.[31]

The final sequence of *Nostalgia* is one of the most moving and satisfying in world cinema, but I think the 'tedium' refers to the penultimate sequence which may, admittedly, seem tedious if all that has preceded it is ignored. What has immediately preceded it is the public self-immolation of a recluse who wants to warn the world of the destruction he believes it is heading for. The protagonist, Gorchakov, now lights the candle which the recluse had given him and attempts to cross from one side of the 'healing' Baths to the other, keeping the flame alight. The symbolic, ritualistic and perhaps hopeless gesture is redeemed from abstraction by what seems a concentrated force of will, and the long take is essential to its communication. The shot commences in a close-up of the candle being lit, then Gorchakov steps away to touch the side of the Baths and begins his slow journey across the puddled, uneven, debris-strewn floor, the camera tracking at his speed and parallel to him. Twice the candle gutters and, exhausted, physically and spiritually, Gorchakov moves back to the beginning, re-lights it and starts again. The third crossing succeeds and, after eight minutes, the flaming candle is set down safely, with slow care, the hands in close-up, only leaving the frame as the protagonist collapses, unseen, presumably dying.

There follow a couple of transitional shots before the conclusion, which is in tinted black and white for memories or dreams; here it may mean that the exiled Russian has, in death, found a kind of heaven that brings together his yearnings for home. The shot lasts just under three minutes and begins with him reclining on some ground, a dog quiet beside him, water before him, his country home behind him. But as the camera begins to track slowly back, and the sounds of crying from the previous sequence fade, the remembered landscape is seen to be enclosed by the vast walls of a ruined church. Snow falls, a dog's bark is heard, then sacred music. The tone is melancholic, elegaic, and certainly without any hint of ascension towards joy. Yet, though muted, it is not wholly pessimistic either. To dismiss either of these shot/sequences as 'tedious' is to fail to read them. As Mark Le Fanu remarks in a chapter on *Nostalgia*, 'An idea, in the cinema, is a camera movement, not a speech',[32] and Tarkovsky's ideas are articulated with great beauty and seriousness. (Needless to say, the opening of *The Sacrifice* does prepare the audience 'to be patient', and attentive, and its conclusion is not merely 'an unbroken 10-minute take of a burning house'.)

Tarkovsky uses the long take as an appropriate and dynamic measure for his reflective, deeply intense concerns, but even when its use seems to slow a film down the thinning effect is different from the boredom of thinness in a conventionally edited film. This is at least partially to do with narrative progression and the way one shot is joined to another. A long take has an inevitable temporal movement, chronologically forward, and if it is contained *within* a larger sequence, and is of limited duration, it may be barely detectable as a stylistic device: the take may appear fast or slow, but it has to move ahead.

Continuity editing, by contrast, can have the effect of stopping that natural narrative impetus, at least during conventional shot/reverse shot exchanges. This does not happen in the theatre, where, however static the actors, the audience must experience the passage of time along with dialogue, scene changes and any other devices that may be used to create 'drama-time' within 'real-time'; nor does it occur within the novel, whose narrative is in most respects closer to film than are any other arts. Exchanges of dialogue in the novel, for example, proceed down the page, often with only nominal reference to the individual speaker: reading, one *knows*, one is able to *follow* the exchanges without continual recapitulation. But in a shot/reverse shot exchange one is always going back again to the last speaker, who is often framed just as before. Consequently, although time passes and the dialogue proceeds, the *visual* information may appear contradictory, so that one feels one is not getting anywhere, that time present is continually being nudged by a reprise of time past.

The fluent camera, combined with a long take lasting, say upwards of a minute, maintains more easily the illusion of real-time passing in harmony with film-time. An elaborate camera movement, or an extended long take, breaks through this harmony and strengthens film-time, the experience of an art rather than the illusion of everyday reality. (And so, once one gets away from a reliance on shot/reverse shot, does the montage-based film. A static camera, moved to a new set-up for each shot, can give a powerful sense of *building*, of the narrative adding up cumulatively, and not just happening as if it were a ready-made whole. The postcard sequence of Godard's *Les Carabiniers*, (1963), with the camera fixed on the sight of postcard 'conquests', each one dropped on top of the ones below, is, among other things, a paradigm for this kind of construction. A recent and modest example is Danny Boyle's *The Hen House*, first shown on BBC2 in September 1989, with evocative and tactful camera-work by Arthur Rowell. Bresson's films express a similar clean, cool and unstoppable directedness, which doesn't destroy the realism of the enacted drama, but holds it within a defining form.)

The most famous, or notorious, use of the long take is Alfred Hitchcock's experiment in *Rope*, (1948). The duration of the original stage play was exactly the same as its drama-time; there were no act or scene divisions, but a continuous unfolding of the drama.

> I asked myself whether it was technically possible to film it in the same way. The only way to achieve that, I found, would be to handle the shooting in the same continuous action, with no break in the telling of a story that begins at seven-thirty and ends at nine-fifteen. And I got this crazy idea to do it in a single shot.[33]

The average length of a shot is rarely above fifteen seconds, and usually considerably less. Hitchcock's shots ran for approximately the maximum time possible, determined by the capacity of the film magazine – ten minutes. Walls, furniture and lights were movable, and had to be moved silently during the take, as did the camera, the sound being recorded directly. There were ten days of rehearsal for actors, cameras and lighting, followed by eighteen days of shooting. If one element went wrong at any time during the ten minute take, the whole shot would have to be re-taken. There are, unavoidably, cuts in the film, but most are not used dramatically because of Hitchcock's attempt to make it look like one full-length shot. The dramatic cuts, which tend to be on projector reel changes (every two reels, or twenty minutes), are more effective than the 'concealed' cuts, where the camera moves into the darkness of a close-up figure's back to end one magazine, and moves out again at the start of the next.

Although this experiment dispensed with editing in the aesthetic sense of cutting together discrete lengths of film to create specific patterns and effects, Hitchcock acknowledged in his interviews with Truffaut that by continually re-framing compositions he was still effectively following conventional narrative practice:

The mobility of the camera and the movement of the players closely followed my usual cutting practice. In other words, I maintained the rule of varying the size of the image in relation to its emotional importance within a given episode.[34]

It is worth noting that in this ambitious experiment with the reality of continuous time Hitchcock not only accedes to the 'rules' of continuity editing, but also acknowledges another filmic principle, the 'episode', or scene. That is, even when coming closer than anyone else in film or television to what is, potentially, television's most distinctive difference from film (the capacity for recording from a single camera a continuous live performance), both the effects of editing (establishing long shots, medium shots, close-ups) and the inherent scenic structure, even within a single scene play, are covertly maintained. Indeed, the lesson of *Rope* is drawn explicitly by Truffaut later in the interview:

Nevertheless, weighing the pros and cons – and the practices of all the great directors who have considered the question seem to bear this out – it is true that the classical cutting techniques dating back to D. W. Griffith have stood the test of time and still prevail today.[35]

It is no accident that the eight or so minutes' tracking shot of Gorchakov carrying the lighted candle in *Nostalgia* begins and ends in a close-up of his hands, or that for the rest of the shot he is shown full-figure or in medium close shot.

In its context, Truffaut's observation is an endorsement of the conventions Griffith helped to establish, and that is only likely to sound at all unusual to those who know that Truffaut's mentor was André Bazin, the critic who elevated deep focus and the long take to a position of supremacy over montage. As an informed observation within a discussion of the possibilities and limitations of the long take, Truffaut's remark goes some way towards explaining why television, too, has tended to follow Griffith. And if it can be agreed that this is indeed the case, that the aesthetic of television is essentially film, then the burden of my opening chapter, suggesting that education should prioritize *film* rather than the more nebulous *media* studies, may be seen to be logical and reasonable, albeit in opposition to current trends.

The bravura crane-shot that opens Orson Welles' *Touch of Evil*, (1958), is less than half the length of *Rope*'s ten minute takes. It looks far busier, in that it involves precisely choreographed cars, people, animals and camera, in a real town exterior shot at night, but is operated on the same principle and has the same aesthetic justification. (As does the long take already described from *Nostalgia*.) We start in a close-up of a time-bomb in someone's hands. The dial is set. The camera moves as the figure moves to place the bomb in the boot of a car. The figure exits at speed, the camera beginning to rise above the car as a man and woman get into it and begin driving. The camera rises up, tracks across roofs and descends into the street again, following the car as it negotiates this busy border town at a crawl. We know that the device in the boot is ticking away as the shot proceeds. Another couple are introduced, and the car and this second couple reach the checkpoint at the same time. Our attention is on the second couple, but we hear the woman in the car complaining of hearing a ticking sound. As the car drives on, slowly out of frame, we follow the second couple, and as they embrace the explosion occurs and the first cut is made.

All this is run under the opening credits, to music with a fast beat. A cut at any point *en route* would have allowed us to infer that another car, with dummies in, had been substituted, but by prolonging the shot and placing various fortuitous obstacles in front of the car, Welles not only describes the atmosphere and activity of this raucous night-town, and links the imminent murder to the lives of the second couple, he also encourages us to identify the nature of film with the development of narrative. Part of the tension is that we must anticipate an inevitable cut, inevitable because these real people driving this real car through this real town cannot *really* be blown up. But the shot continues and the anticipated cut is deferred. When it finally comes, the moment is suitably climactic. The passionate kiss is interrupted, we cut to the blazing car falling to the ground, then back to the interrupted protagonist, and a fast tracking shot away in front of him as he runs towards the disaster.

Rope does nothing so spectacular. As the film begins we see the two men completing their cold murder and placing the corpse in a trunk. We then remain in their apartment throughout the film, as guests arrive, eat, discuss the missing friend and, occasionally, seem about to see what is inside the trunk. The scene in *Nostalgia* is not at all spectacular. Nevertheless, in each case the avoidance of conventional cutting is intended to increase audience involvement in the physical reality of the unfolding drama. An essential part of the meaning resides in the fact of the uninterrupted long take. Hitchcock, Welles and Tarkovsky are all using close-ups, medium-shots and long-shots within the extended shot, but what connects them is not an abrupt, edited transition but a visible camera movement – what connects them is the physical integrity of the space as the camera negotiates it, ingeniously but without concealment, in time.

A somewhat different and more self-conscious purpose underlies the opening sequence/shot of Max Ophuls' *La Ronde*, (1950). It is, apparently, a foggy night. A man in a belted overcoat moves through the frame and mounts some steps. Behind him we see an impressive civic building, some of its windows lit. He addresses us urbanely, talking about his identity and the nature of reality. The camera follows him as he moves in front of a stage with footlights. He speculates as to where we are, retraces his steps and walks across the stage and past it. Behind him is a view of the city at night, but around him we see the apparatus of a film studio. He strolls on, then defines place and time: Vienna, 1900, Spring. But this period city is being created as we watch, by sets, lighting and movement. He changes costume by a coat-stand. Now it is day, a bird is singing. The shops behind him appear more substantial – more than painted backdrops, at any rate. He calls for the appropriate music and a waltz starts playing. A carousel revolves. By the end of this single shot sequence dusk has fallen again and we enter the story at the point where we would normally expect it to begin, with the illusory reality created; only this time we have been brought to it by means of this other narrative, which has laid out some of the elements before us and then swept them together into the film we enter. It is a fiction about fiction. Also a courteous and ironic way of introducing us to a story set in the past (a story, moreover, which is itself already communicated with some detachment).

Godard's use of the long take, in such films as *Vivre sa vie*, (1962) and *Weekend*, (1967), has the formal restraint one readily associates with directors like Hitchcock, Bresson and Ozu, but I think it develops rather more from this usage in *La Ronde*, at least in as much as it is one of several devices Godard deploys for a distancing effect, operating upon an already desaturated narrative. Until the alliance with the Dziga-Vertov group in 1969, most of Godard's films engaged productively with a conflict between improvisatory narrative and the forming of a style equipped to shape a fragmenting culture. The repeated lateral tracking shot across the backs of the woman and man in conversation, at the beginning of *Vivre sa vie*, have a precise beauty, and are irritating: we want to see faces, identify the voices, *get to know* the characters, but the long, authoritarian take refuses to indulge us, insists on the unknowable mysteriousness of people. Then, even when the camera seems to dwell almost lovingly on Anna Karina's features, the dispassionate, 'documentary'-style narrative (verbal, visual and edited), continually interrupts that kind of sympathetic identification. In a subsequent long take, Karina is seated facing the camera, but in front of the camera is a man with his back to us. As their conversation proceeds the camera moves laterally, until it reaches a point of stasis at one side, from which we can see the actress; then it reverses the movement, sometimes stopping on the man's back, blocking her, sometimes stopping at the far side, revealing her again. The camera movement is slow and careful, but is not matched to the dialogue. Consequently the long take is part of a separate narrative, whose other component is the subordinated accumulation of shots, the edited sequence. The long take, then, is absorbed into the director's manipulative style, instead of serving, *pace* Bazin, the staging of the drama.

Similarly, the three 360 degree pans around a courtyard in *Weekend* constitute a shot that is, on the one hand, largely empty – in that there is no narrative progression, and nothing dramatic occurs – but on the other hand, not really an interruption because the film is already being composed of apparent irrelevances, digressions and chance discoveries. Film is addressing the breakdown of civilization by asking itself what it can do, why it should not do this? Its story is self-questioning and generating, and self-destroying, for as well as asking how a story should be told, it asks what value does any story have? And the criterion of value moves outside the thing itself, beyond, say, the beauty of the compositions and structures, and tries to become affixed to ideology.

For André Bazin the strength of the long take is quite specific:

Above all, certain situations can only be said to exist cinematographically to the extent that the spatial unity is established, especially comedy situations that are based on the relations between human beings and things . . . If slapstick comedy succeeded before the days of Griffith and montage, it is because most of its gags derived from a comedy of space, from the relation of a man to things and to the surrounding world. In *The Circus*, Chaplin is truly in the lion's cage and both are enclosed within the framework of the screen.[36]

Here the 'relation of man to things and to the surrounding world' provides a realistic dynamic whose visual contrasts, counterpoints and so on could, I believe, be read as an equivalent for, rather than a term of absolute difference from, continuity editing. For the director it becomes, surely, a matter of deciding which approach is appropriate for the particular sequence or scene and not a matter of which approach is ideologically more correct.

A more problematical challenge to assumptions about what is, or is not, cinematic is made when a static long take serves a spoken monologue or duologue, for here the camera is not primarily exploring a spatial relation but recording a voice and its utterer. One might expect to find the most cinematically neutral instances in the television interview. In 1989, BBC2 resurrected the old *Face to Face* format, where the interviewer is heard but not seen, except in over-the-shoulder shots. Several set-ups are deployed to vary the positions from which we can look at the interviewee, and average shot lengths are nearer a minute than the ten or so seconds of conventional filming. But if the interviewee is saying something that promises to be unusually interesting, or that requires lengthy exposition, the camera discreetly holds to whatever position was assumed when he began. Consequently there may be a number of shots sustained for anything up to three minutes, but they may be in inappropriately extreme close-up. Even so, one watches without being distracted or bored by the monotony of the image – and monotony is traditionally held to be one of the reasons why a composition should vary fairly frequently, by camera movement and/or editing. One attends as one would attend to any interesting speaker, in fact, and the length of the shot is immaterial. But is the event filmic? I believe it is, because of lighting, framing and sound levels, because of the deliberate restriction, the concentration on *that* subject in isolation, but the expressive level is low or, rather, it is vested in the speaker.

Integration of the static long take into the fabric of a more dramatic narrative need not cause an obvious rupture, or be the site of conflicting approaches to realism. In John Ford's *Drums Along the Mohawk*, (1939), there is a scene where an exhausted Henry Fonda recounts a battle to Claudette Colbert. Apparently the battle was written into the script to be filmed, but Ford decided on the spur of the moment on this much cheaper, quicker and dramatically more risky expedient. The shot begins with a slight camera movement, but is then sustained for three minutes while Fonda describes his experience of the engagement. He is prostrate, just his head and shoulders propped up, and Colbert is dressing his wounds fussily. There is a brief cutaway to other wounded men being treated, then the same set-up is resumed for another one and a half minutes. Attention does not wander, of course, and what one experiences is not the large-scale spectacular of battle but the intimate, shocked aftermath in the dry voice of a stunned survivor. One might say that this is theatre not cinema, or the realism of performance, not the art of the director; but, knowing the circumstances in which it came to be filmed, one would have to qualify such assertions. The actor improvised brilliantly from his knowledge of character and script, to provide the feeling and meaning the director wanted.

Near the beginning of *The Grapes of Wrath*, made the following year, Ford holds a two-shot of Fonda (as Tom Joad) and John Carradine, while the former talks – not animatedly, with little physical gesture – for over two minutes. The shot is integrated into a sequence which includes several briefer shots, and others nearly as long. But in contrast to Godard's long takes in *Vivre sa vie*, the visual slowness is in part a description of character and milieu, so that we can feel we are getting to know the rhythms of Tom Joad and the almost beaten farmers. We are getting to know, without Ma Joad's assurance at the end of the film, that the migrant workers *will* endure. These steady, unhurried scenes are both bleak and strong (without the nervous energy that fast cutting could communicate, or the romantic colouring of bravura camera movements). Perhaps the best-known and most influential of these static long takes occurs in *Two Rode Together*, (1961). It is an improvised conversation by the river's edge, between Richard Widmark and James Stewart (they thought they were rehearsing), which is maintained for nearly four minutes. It has a natural spontaneity and humour that make the scene intimate and 'real'; but I suspect that its celebrity is in part due to the period when the film was released, when the next generation of young film-makers were studying contemporary American cinema closely, and discovering *auteurs* in Hitchcock, Hawks, Fuller and, belatedly, Ford.

Conclusion

As well as the areas I have introduced in this chapter, students learning the language will want to consider other expressive possibilities – various documentary styles, the uses of lightweight, handheld cameras, of the zoom lens, of grainy black and white film, tinted film; the use of natural lighting, artifical lighting, composing in colour, working with non-professional actors, improvising scripts, set design, music – the range of possibilities and combinations is enormous. What Frank Palmer says about the acquisition of verbal language is at least partially applicable to film:

There is, of course, a real sense in which we cannot teach English at all to those who already speak it. Our native language is learnt, but it is hardly taught at all. We can no more teach our own school children English than we can teach them to walk or run. They have acquired all these skills before they reach school age.[37]

Whereas children acquire verbal language by hearing and speaking it, and then by reading and writing it, film is acquired for the most part without the communicative equivalent of speaking and writing: it is seen and heard merely. (Though receptivity is not necessarily passive, and Barthes' insistence on the essentially active, associative, predictive, *writerly* ways in which we read and make meanings is applicable to our reading of film too.) Many of my generation learned to negotiate lengthy film narratives before we could read books, so against the objective historical fact of film as a new art form should be set the subjective fact that, in terms of its formative influence, film is one of the earliest, therefore oldest, arts we have experience of. By the time we possess the retentive skill, and stamina, to read novels we have already read many films – not analytically, perhaps, or with consistent attentiveness to their expressive subtleties, but then we don't read novels that way either until we learn to discover these additional pleasures through disciplined study.

To complete the process of acquisition, from seeing and hearing to communicating, enabling others to see and hear the art we make, disciplined study is, clearly, essential. I have illustrated a number of basic structural conventions and endeavoured to show how various elements of film can be used to affect the mood and meaning of a narrative, but if isolated techniques sufficed, students could learn all they might need from television adverts and promotional pop videos. These certainly have an appeal for the young, and often demonstrate quite succinctly stylistic features and even expressive possibilities, so some teachers may well want to encourage students to look carefully at them. Aside from their frequent vacuity, however, their very brevity limits their usefulness. A serious offer to educate students in film must effect a more extensive introduction. The problem is that films have been made in many countries over a period of about a century, and that every day more films are being released than can possibly be seen, and more programmes are transmitted on television than can fit into a twenty-four hour day – the problem is, where to start? how to find a principle for selecting from what must appear a ceaseless deluge of material? Should one look for a Great Tradition, with key authors rather than titles, or should one study particular *types* of films, or specific periods, specific countries, specific studios, the star system, conscious and unconscious attitudes to class, race, gender, money, humour, tragedy, school . . . ? The problem is eventually, and unavoidably, one of evaluation. Technical proficiency is one criterion of assessment, and can be scaled according to available resources and levels of experience in their use. But sometimes we feel there is a sense in which films are good despite technical shortcomings, or bad despite technical excellence. And our reason for wanting to study film, or any art, has little to do with any other factor than its capacity to move us intellectually or emotionally. How are we to approach, understand and even appropriate the ways in which it does this?

Notes and References

1 Wollen, P. (1969) *Signs and Meaning in the Cinema*, London, Secker and Warburg, p. 153.
2 Fell, J. L. (1986) *Film and the Narrative Tradition*, Berkeley, University of California Press, pp. 18–21.
3 Eisenstein, S. M. (1949) *Film Form*, London, Dennis Dobson, p. 204.
4 Berger, J. (1980) *Success and Failure of Picasso*, London, Writers and Readers, p. 70.
5 Henderson, R. M. (1971) *D. W. Griffith: The Years at Biograph*, London, Secker and Warburg, p. 14.
6 Brown, K. (1973) *Adventures with D. W. Griffith*, London, Secker and Warburg, p. 15.
   In this connection, see also Balshofer, F. J. and Miller, A. (1967) *One Reel a Week*, Berkeley, University of California Press, p. 33, for a similar description of 'putting down the lines', *circa* 1908, which suggests that the practice was not, as Brown claims, one of Griffith's innovations.
7 Brown, *ibid.*, p. 21.
8 Kuleshov, L. (1987) *Fifty Years in Films, Selected Works*, Moscow, Raduga Publishers, p. 88.
9 Quoted in Coe, B. (1981) *The History of Movie Photography*, London, Ash & Grant, p. 42.
10 MacCabe, C. (1988) 'Death of a Nation: television in the early sixties', *Critical Quarterly*, **30**, 2.
11 Bordwell, D., Staiger, J., Thompson, K. (1988) *The Classical Hollywood Cinema*, London, Routledge, p. 139. See also Happé, L. B. (1975) *Basic Motion Picture Technology*, London, Focal Press, pp. 242–44, for an ironic contrast with the above. Happé describes the introduction of some television technology into film work, to facilitate multiple camera shooting in the late sixties. It was not successful: 'Perhaps the greatest difficulty came from the operational approach required, since the shooting script had to be prepared in meticulous detail for simultaneous photography, the complete lighting plan equally closely worked out and the actors sufficiently rehearsed in advance to cover the continuous action of a complete sequence. The lighting cameraman might well feel that the uniform style of illumination necessary for multiple viewpoints sacrificed the quality which could be obtained when each set-up is composed and lit individually. Similarly some directors certainly felt that the whole system imposed unacceptable limitations on their creative abilities and that the subtle nuances of performance and editing obtainable with the repeated take of the individual shot were no longer possible.'

Acting Techniques

12 Shepard, S. (1985) *Motel Chronicles & Hawk Moon*, London Faber and Faber, p. 14.
13 Kuleshov, *op. cit.*, pp. 44–5.
14 *Ibid.*, p. 45.
15 *Ibid.*, p. 52.
16 Ford, D. (1982) *The Unquiet Man, The Life of John Ford*, London, William Kimber, pp. 85–6.

Script

17 Kuleshov, *op. cit.*, p. 51.
18 Quoted in Leyda, J. (Ed) (1988) *Eisenstein 2*, London, Methuen, p. 59.
19 Kael, P. (1974) *The Citizen Kane Book*, London, Paladin, p. 77.

20 *Ibid.*, But see also Carringer, R. L. (1985) *The Making of Citizen Kane*, London, John Murray, pp. 16–35, and Corliss, R. (1975) *Talking Pictures*, London, David & Charles, pp. 249–53.
21 Kuleshov, *op. cit.*, pp. 51–2.

Dialogue Styles

22 Abbott, C. C. (Ed) (1935) *The Letters of Gerard Manley Hopkins to Robert Bridges*, Oxford, Oxford University Press, p. 89.
23 McBride, J. (1982) *Hawks on Hawks*, Berkeley, University of California Press, pp. 80–1.
24 Quoted in Smith, D. G. (1984) *American Film Makers Today*, London, Blandford press, p. 27.
25 *Ibid.*, p. 30.

Use of Sound

26 Taylor, J. R. (1978) *Hitch, The Life and Work of Alfred Hitchcock*, London, Faber and Faber, p. 105.
27 Allen, W. (1983) *Four Films of Woody Allen*, London, Faber and Faber, p. 136. A prefatory note to this edition states, 'The italicized passages that describe the action have been provided by the publisher'. The passage quoted from is italicized yet central to the narrative; either Allen's scripts suffer serious lacunae or his English publishers are imprecise. The latter is, unfortunately, a real possibility, and published scripts are notoriously unreliable. John Ford and Dudley Nichols' *Stagecoach*, for example, was published by Lorrimer in 1971. Six years later, in *Screen Education*, Summer 1977, Mike Catto examined several screenplays, including this one, and gave detailed examples of textual inaccuracies. In 1988 Faber took over distribution of the Lorrimer list, *Stagecoach* now being a 'Revised edition 1984', but still extremely inaccurate, even in the apparatus surrounding the text. For example, a note claimed that 'significant divergences' between shooting script and release print of the film were numbered and footnoted, but no footnotes appear anywhere in the edition. I wrote to Faber in May 1988, quoting a number of errors – enough to demonstrate that the book is useless for study purposes – and the bland reply merely promised that 'if and when' a new edition was called for it would be revised. In the meantime, of course, the sloppily edited edition of 1971 is perpetuated. Such publishers evidently do not expect their publications to be taken seriously. Provision for script-based study remains patchy, as if no one has given a thought to the educational value of an accurate, clearly annotated text, based on the final shooting script, indicating earlier draft material, directional contributions and significant alterations in the cutting continuity.
28 Bresson, R., (1967) in interview with Godard and Delahaye, *Cahiers due Cinema in English*, 8, pp. 9–10.

Deep Focus

29 Toland's contribution to the development of deep focus photography is considerable and contentious. The interested reader should consult the seminal paper by Patrick Ogle, 'Technological and Aesthetic Influences upon the Development of Deep Focus Cinematography in the United States', which is reprinted in *Screen Reader 1*, Seft (1977), along with its extensive bibliography and a rejoinder by Christopher Williams. There is also an informative chapter by David Bordwell in *The Classical Hollywood Cinema*, *op. cit.*, and Carringer's *The Making of Citizen Kane*, *op. cit.*, includes a comparative analysis of *The Long Voyage Home*, with a number of frame stills.

The Long Take

30 Bergan, R. and Karney, R. (1988) *Bloomsbury Foreign Film Guide*, London, Bloomsbury, p. 410.
31 *Ibid.*, p. 484.
32 Le Fanu, M. (1987) *The Cinema of Andrei Tarkovsky*, London, BFI books, p. 121.
33 Quoted in Truffaut, F. (1969) *Hitchcock*, London, Panther, pp. 216–17.
34 *Ibid.*, p. 217.
35 *Ibid.*, p. 223.
36 Bazin, A. (1967) *What is Cinema?* Berkeley, University of California Press, p. 52.
37 Palmer, F. (1971) 'Language and the teaching of English', in Minnis, N., (Ed) (1973) *Linguistics at Large*, London, Paladin, p. 246.

Chapter 5

Language, Genres and Television

Introduction

This chapter traces the generic antecedents of some popular forms of television. The introduction suggests that the individual or collaborative work of art always emerges from the inherited and current language, and that genres are part of that pre-existing common language. The representative forms I examine (*Blind Date, News, Pop videos, Commercials* and *Situation Comedy*) generally rely on formulaic conventions rather than innovation and the articulation of a personal vision. My argument is that this tendency towards anonymity can make them peculiarly useful for the preparatory study of narrative.

We cannot say what a long take, a low angle, or an extreme close-up *mean*, except in reference to a general disposition. We refer to the usage out of which the convention has become established, a process of habituation through repetition that need not preclude *un*conventional usage and, thus, an extension of the possible range of definitions.

Conventions become a kind of articulate thought only at the level of specific implementation and deliberated interpretation, while the film is being made, while it is being studied. Meaning resides, or is invested in particular instances by the intervention of thought at the junction of style and story. The long take becomes a feature of Tarkovsky, as characteristic as his recurrence to images of fire and water. Somehow it forms part of the intense meditative fabric, the attentive silence and palpable control that urges the viewer into a collaborative effort to understand this private but not secret world. The precision and clarity of the long take may help persuade the viewer that the effort is worth making, that Tarkovsky's sometimes obscure images are not merely personal and wilfully injected into what might otherwise be revealed as a commonplace expression, but that the director is communicating, as simply as he can, a vision charged with doubts and regenerative possibilities, which could not be stated, or engaged with, without this rigour. Yet the meaning, here, may be no more amenable to translation or paraphrase into verbal language than the meaning of a musical phrase in its context, or the brushwork or colour of a painting (which isn't to say that we should abandon the attempt to think through a work, only that that process might be helped if we don't altogether dismiss the non-academic, affective experience of first giving ourselves up to it). Tarkovsky's long take cannot be abstracted as a meaningful figure in its own right: it means something different in Hitchcock's *Rope*, Ophuls' *La Ronde*, (1950) and Andy Warhol's *Beauty no. 2*, (1965).

Of these, the easiest to imitate would be Warhol's, where the camera is immobile, with the pan and tilt head of the tripod evidently locked off. All one need do is estimate camera height and the angle of its tilt towards, in this case, the bed, then switch on and leave the camera running. Theoretically it would be possible to abstract and duplicate the set ups for complete films. As far as I know no-one has ever done so, though re-makes of successful films do sometimes attempt a slavish imitation of the camera plots and cutting rhythms of key sequences (as they sometimes incorporate some original footage). Unsurprisingly, the result is never a reproduction of the style or evocative power of the originals. The most intricate choreography for camera is meaningless without its filmed content: that relation is a unique bond. The elaborate camera movements of many pop videos mean so little because instead of relating the content they are substituted for it; conversely, many films with intrinsic dramatic and narrative interest lose potential impact because no exchange with the camera has been initiated.

But the unique bond implies that, however derivative or uninspired, every film ever made must promise some redefinition of the language; it certainly seems to be the case that *some* interest, however momentary and fortuitous, can be found in the least promising of vehicles. As in all narrative arts the possibility of a transcendent moment exists because the possible combinations of words, sounds and images are never exhausted. To admit the essential uniqueness of every sustained utterance is not the same thing as to confer value, is not to say, for example, that one current British sitcom, chosen at random, is as good or bad as another, or that either would be as rewarding to experience repeatedly as, say, a Buster Keaton two-reeler or a Howard Hawks comedy from the 1930s or 1940s. They might be, of course, but where do we look for the criteria that enable us to judge?

The conventions we have looked at should be of some help, if it is understood that, as Lindsay Anderson says, 'Poetry is created when the way of saying *becomes* the thing said',[1] but we need to balance our awareness of the uniqueness of every work with the coeval truth that that uniqueness is embedded in familiarity: every artwork is derivative; to use a more Leavisian formulation, we do not invent the language we use.

Without the English language waiting quick and ready for him, Lawrence couldn't have communicated his thought: that is obvious enough. But it is also the case that he couldn't have thought it. English as he found it was a product of an immemorial *sui generis* collaboration on the part of its speakers and writers. It is alive with promptings and potentialities, and the great creative writer shows his genius in the way he responds. Any writer of the language must depend on what his readers know already (though they may not know that they know) – must evoke it with the required degree of sharpness or latency.[2]

Because of its hybrid form, its conscious and unconscious drawing together of narrative practices from other arts, its ceaseless cultural promiscuity, the language of film cannot be the product of '*sui generis* collaboration' – and I'm not sure that English is that, either – but the burden of the passage may be appropriated, legitimately, I think. Amongst the 'promptings and potentialities' of the living language of film I would include those established formal structures which provide the framework for an artist's thought and, while doing so, contribute more than may be acknowledged to its shape, texture and kind. The artist, concerned with 'the current language heightened', contributes to the continuous collaborative production of a language which, beyond its lexis, includes idiom and even cliché; and again, beyond the familiar and almost transparent locutions that stud its discourse with helpfully easy connections, includes archetypal themes and these vital generic forms. It seems to me that we need to be able to recognize these, their extensiveness, their inherent anonymous creativity, their usefulness and their limitations, before we can set up judgmental criteria that aren't merely expressions of relatively uninformed personal preference.

The modes of realism which have, despite alternative movements in the arts, dominated modern narrative, may appear too diverse to be susceptible to an inclusive definition, since they inhabit different genres and, indeed, different arts. But if for the moment we accept Northrop Frye's classification (albeit simplified and contrived to fit a theory) of fiction into five modes – myth, romance, high mimetic, low mimetic and ironic – and if we generally concur with his historical declension,[3] we may accept that realism, for all it has opened up, has nonetheless operated within a restricted field – low mimetic and ironic – with the consequence that the potentialities of the three great earlier modes have been all but closed off. (That they still service some kind of human need may be evinced by their perpetuation in comic-based films with indestructible super-heroes.)

If certain modes become too outmoded for current use, then certain kinds of thought become literally unthinkable. For example, the particular turns of thought made possible by the Petrarchan sonnet structure are subtly changed by the structural shift to the English sonnet; again, *vers libre* coaxes thought in a new direction, which cannot be reckoned a *progression* from preceding forms. What it constitutes is thought of a different kind. Now, the poet may be free, up to a point, to choose his form, but the form will also, up to a point, co-write his poem. And this relation, which Leavis characterizes elsewhere as 'the interplay between the living language and the creativity of individual genius',[4] does suggest a way of putting our grasp of film language to use on confronting the intimidating torrent of filmic matter that flows unstoppably through cinema, television and video.

With film more than with the novel or play, and with television more than with film, we are likely to be more aware of the generic forms of the language than the unique responses which might perhaps modify those forms – the author is harder to find, the qualities of authorship seem too diffuse. All art is collaborative in the sense adverted to by T. S. Eliot in 'Tradition and the Individual Talent':

> Someone said: 'The dead writers are remote from us because we *know* so much more than they did'. Precisely, and they are that which we know.[5]

That sort of collaboration rarely stops us ascribing works to particular authors (we won't demote Donne for not having invented the sonnet, or Turner for not having created landscape painting single-handed), or organizing courses around the study of authored works. We may shape our courses around historical movements or periods, but it is not *only* institutionalized practice that returns us to the same groups of major and minor names: we may give some attention to other ways of documenting and revealing the set period, may question the legitimacy of some of the recurring authors, but there is something inevitable about their perpetuation, as long as the balance of our interest favours aesthetic and moral responsiveness rather than the socio-economic history of the time in which the art was created. The death of the Author-God and the instability of those notions of absolute value that were ultimately derived from a no-longer-tenable concept of a stable, fixed identity do not really make authorship, in this sense, a problem. The work ascribed to various artists remains their work: we simply learn what we should always have known, that the ascription does not confer God-like status. Consciously and unconsciously, artists borrow plots, characters, symbols, themes, interests, generic forms, ways of seeing, feeling and thinking, much as the rest of us do so long as we are alive in and to a particular time, experiencing its art and the art that has preceded and contributed to it. But, again like the rest of us, artists aren't *merely* borrowers, and the art they make is not merely an imitation or a reflection.

There is art, however, in which variation, the signature of the individual, may be less important than repetition, the restatement of the key pattern, the monolithic form. Think of the collaborative history of certain architectural periods, styles and motifs, of folk literature, folk music, folk art: forms that embrace the singularity as well as the diversity of peoples, values, beliefs, forms of communality that don't require the cultivation of artistic temperament, the artist-type, or the cult of the artist as hero or scapegoat/martyr. And the mass media, or popular arts, seem to straddle somewhat uneasily the boundary between art of this kind and the art of the individual creator.

Quite apart from considerations of ideological bias, it seems to me understandable that advocates of film and television studies should, in the last quarter of a century, have attempted to dispose of 'art' and replace it with 'media'. Popular film and television are manifestly not the aspiring utterance of the people, and it is a curious collaborative art that is rooted in commercial enterprises on such a vast scale; on the other hand, its individual creators aren't really individual *enough*. To insist on 'art' is almost to invite the accompanying adjective, 'bad':

> Consider, for instance, the incidence of bad art, by which we are surrounded, and its potential for deleterious behaviour. One only has to turn a knob, and bad art is at one's command most hours of the day and night through radio and television – and this is the art that most people absorb from their environment. The whole question and role of bad art in our society needs very careful consideration.[6]

This voice, so closely echoing I. A. Richards in the 1920s, F. R. Leavis and Denys Thompson in the 1930s, and R. G. Collingwood, also in the 1930s, happens to belong to G. H. Bantock in the 1980s. It is a voice from a fine, humane tradition; a decent and authoritative voice, in many respects. I don't think it will cease to be heard by pretending that the aesthetic is not part of the discourse. What needs to be scrutinized is the confident relegation of an art form to an arena where it may only be perceived in terms of 'its potential for deleterious behaviour'; what needs 'very careful consideration' is the routine presumption of guilt. On what is it based? – I mean the ascription of badness, rather than the association with behaviour. The voice concedes that this is an art, but, perhaps uniquely, an art that is bad. Should we assume that this familiar, sometimes avuncular voice has a clear understanding of the language of this art, or is it possible that the language has been ignored, treated as a transparency through which every impartial eye can observe at once that the emperor has no clothes?

More often than we care to admit in intelligent discourse I am afraid we do delimit our fields of study in the latter, more cavalier way. On television we are presented with an immediately replaceable product, offered and usually accepted as a momentary distraction, like popular drama in the sixteenth century, or the novel in the nineteenth century. Both passive enjoyment and passive scorn of the medium are to be expected. Only by deliberate intervention with as few preconceptions as possible, by breaking the continuum and subjecting selected programmes to a more sustained gaze than their scheduling encourages, is it reasonable to hope for a more discriminating response, one which should, if it affirms the connection with film, and so with 'art-speech', help to extend rather than foreclose the potential disciplines of thought available in our age.

What I hope to establish is that art pervades the medium of television. It would be easy enough to point to numerous documentaries, television plays and television films. However one might 'place' them critically, it is clear that works like Tarkovsky's *Nostalghia*, Wenders' *Paris, Texas*, Fassbinder's *Berlin Alexanderplatz*, Reitz's *Heimat*, Bergman's *Fanny och Alexander*, and other European and Latin American soaps, are conceived, executed and read as films, whether or not they also have a cinematic release. But to substantiate the claim that art pervades the medium I want to avoid the prestigious or exceptional and go instead to the most popular and least filmic forms, initially. It may well be the case that the art they produce is bad, but I would invite the reader to defer that judgment, at least until we have looked more closely at the characteristic use and potential of the languages of a few generic types.

Blind Date

With my emphasis predominantly on film as the art of telling stories, it may seem odd to turn to quizzes and gameshows (where, no doubt loosely, I locate *Blind Date*), yet part of their enduring appeal lies in the fact that their narrative basis is at least as ancient as Homer and Virgil, and that it extends beyond oral and written literatures into rituals of celebration and competitive prowess, combat, exertion, defeat and victory.

The adventures of Ulysses, Aeneas, Jason and Perseus are delivered from another age, as are those of Arthur and Gawain, and the Ancient Mariner, Jane Eyre, Captain Ahab and Huck Finn. Their matter is travel and travail, quest and test. *Blind Date* deals facetiously with the matching and mismatching of couples. But if we ask 'What is it about?' doggedly enough, most classical narratives will give up a kind of generative essence which does link them to *Blind Date* and its ilk.

A protagonist has a goal but may not reach it directly. The goal is a prize which may be won only after certain tasks have been performed successfully (or ordeals endured, or obstacles dealt with). The prize may be the love of a lady, laurels of victory, the securing of peace in the realm, social hegemony, finding the Holy Grail or Golden Fleece, spiritual or material wealth. (Jane Eyre gains moral quietus, spiritual growth, identity, a lost family, a fortune and a respectable marriage.) The obstacles may be monsters, distracting and destructive temptations, threats, or riddles. The protagonist may need physical strength, grace and beauty, or mental agility, or spiritual resources. The narrative may be epic, tragic, romantic or comic, its formula being adjusted as appropriate as the conclusion is neared. The romantic or comic protagonist will attain the goal, as, probably, will the epic; the tragic will likely fail and die; the low mimetic, realistic or ironic will sometimes win, sometimes lose.

Aristotle sees the plot as the refining away from story of all inessential matter, until the salient features remain. Unities of time, space and action are observed and the plot has a beginning, middle and end. (Godard claimed that his films did too, 'but not necessarily in that order', which is one way of expressing modernism's legacy from Chekhov.) Such a schema is, obviously, extra-literary and applicable not only to quizzes and chess, but most games and sports. Aristotle also links story with the historically real, and plot therefore with the effective heightening of essential or universal reality. Bakhtin, writing of the Greek prose romances that emerged five hundred and more years after Aristotle, locates what I think it's fair to call reality in the individual rather than the plot, the individual who does not so much perform set tasks satisfactorily as put up with the vagaries of Fate:

> ... things occur simultaneously by chance and also *fail* to occur simultaneously by chance, ... events have no consequences, ... the initiative belongs everywhere exclusively to chance ... In essence, all the character's actions in Greek romance are reduced to *enforced movement through space* (escape, persecution, quests) ...
> ... While it is true that his life may be completely passive – 'Fate' runs the game – he nevertheless *endures* the game fate plays. And he not only endures – *he keeps on being the same person* and emerges from this game, from all these turns of fate and chance, with his *identity* absolutely unchanged.
> ... In this way Greek romance reveals its strong ties with a *folklore that predates class distinctions*, assimilating one of the essential elements in the folkloric concept of a man ... No matter how impoverished, how denuded a human identity may become in a Greek romance, there is always preserved in it some precious kernel of folk humanity; one always senses a faith in the indestructible power of man in his struggle with nature and with all inhuman forces.[7]

Contestants in gameshows tend to emerge from their trials unchanged: they are ordinary at the outset, and ordinary they remain. The paradigm is not used to effect transformation, simply to entertain, as it has been entertaining people for thousands of years. Programmes such as *Blind Date* are not so much a debasement of the formula as an under-elaborated repetition. So, too, sporting contests and tournaments repeat the ancient formula effectively and simply, and give witness to human skill or ingenuity within a controlled narrative framework. Perhaps it even becomes understandable that commentators should cry out during these events that a minor mishap has been a tragedy, a disaster. (The interchangeability of the terms expresses confusion as to whether the event is art or nature, while their use at all suggests merely a mistaking of the event's place in narrative development.)

We could jump from the observation that gameshows enact a simple, archetypal human drama of passage through test to reward, to the judgment that they remain, nonetheless, a species of junk, but we should still be failing to give credit to other elements in their production. Because in one way or another they are always there we are inclined to take these elements for granted, yet some of these shows have a structural efficacy which deserves recognition. The comparison I want to evoke here is with our responsiveness to simplicity in art.

Paradoxically education, by whose means we grow aware of the ambiguities, complexities and profound uncertainties of the world and our relations with it, increases our capacity to appreciate – often as something transcendently beautiful – true simple rightness. In music and painting simplicity often seems synonymous with balance, perfect harmony, and even if the work is ostensibly secular the aesthetic response is hard to dissociate from an occasion of spiritual uplift. Something of this is present too in verbal and filmic narrative – is, for example, part of the experience of fatalistic bleakness in Robert Bresson's *L'Argent*, (1983), a narrative as logical as a mathematical formula which, though formally detached, evokes pity at the human condition when we follow the helpless lives of those ordinary people caught within such a pitiless trap. In fact, the rigour and clarity of outline in this film make it a more convincing and terrible work than the melodramatic treatment of a similar theme in, say, Hardy's novels. Related to this experience of a spiritual element in art that may be nihilistic there is, after all, the familiar observation that in great works of doubt or despair – *Job*, *King Lear*, some of Eliot, Tarkovsky and Ford – we sense too the positive creativity that brings them into being and gives them permanent shape and authority.

Simplicity of this order is in part valued because it is a summation of an aesthetic and moral response to life. The extent to which we are capable of giving ourselves up to the experience may indicate our relative sophistication, but also a refinement of our creativity. The act of appreciative reading is itself an opening which both receives and gives, so that the accompanying sense of released potentiality, of perhaps renewed faith or commitment, new power emerging, is in no sense passive or secondary – certainly not illusory or irrelevant. It is the sense that gives and makes meaning and value – the aesthetic sense which leads to developments in science as well as in art.

Is the simplicity of a great theorem or a great motet of a wholly different order from the simplicity of, say, a folk tale, an anonymous ballad, a nursery rhyme, or a gameshow? Since we cannot readily ascertain and quantify the quality or depth of anyone's response, the answer must surely remain relative. That a children's rhyme, or a picture-book illustration, or the vibrant blue of a day-for-night shot may now strike me as trite and sentimental, or inept, need not make me embarrassed to recall that it once was marvellous enough to awaken a desire to write, or colour, to dream of other places, other ways of being. I am not suggesting that *Blind Date* feeds thus the imaginations of millions, but I suspect that there is a level of unconscious aesthetic satisfaction there, received along with the pleasures of watching people make contact. And I suspect that this level, always operating across the medium, may well counteract the surface reading that enables critics to articulate their concerns about the deleterious behaviour that may be encouraged in others (never themselves). The aesthetic level is present in organizational clarity, order, simplicity and control, in the plot and the visual design. The set is arranged in three main areas, designed to suit the stages of the narrative.

In the first area three high chairs are fixed in a line against a neutral backdrop. (In the current series the backdrop has windows, but nothing lies beyond them.) On these chairs sit the three suitors, who will compete to be selected for a blind date. They wear their own choice of clothes, but because they are so completely isolated from their usual environments they resemble the sitters in Irving Penn's photographic studies: clothing, hair style, gesture, intonation, etc., are accentuated by this initial removal of the individual from any habitual context.

In the second area another uncomfortably high chair is set, and the date has to perch on it, unable to see or be seen by the suitors. The date will ask three questions, each question being put in turn to each of the three suitors.

Between areas one and two, and central to the game, is a retractable wall, a familiar enough symbol of division, familiar, too, as a challenge to separated lovers. We, the hostess and the studio audience, have privileged access to what is occurring on both sides of the wall, but date and suitors are in this sense blind. Almost everything depends on the date's evaluation of the answers, but this may be complicated by the hostess', and the studio audience's, reactions. We know more than the date knows. The date knows that and must assess laughter and applause which come in excess of the verbal question and answer. The suitors compete to sound wittier, more vain, or more fetching than one another, while the date is also being tested, watched, always liable to make the 'wrong' choice.

Once a choice has been made the two losers are introduced for momentary dismay, embarrassment or relief, and then the wall retracts to reveal the winner. This is the first climax. Now an envelope is opened, and the couple discover where they will go for their date, at the show's expense, and accompanied by a film crew. (In a previous series there was only a stills photographer, but success increases budgets.) The couple promise to return next week to tell us how they got on.

The third studio area, then, is where the resolution and recapitulation of the narrative takes place. Now, instead of dauntingly stark office furniture, the couple will be encouraged to relax, their ordeal over, in a more domestic setting (which is still isolated from any realized domestic interior). The hostess sits on one sofa, the couple on another. They tell us what they thought of each other. Sometimes they plan to meet again, sometimes not.

> . . . to be learning something is the greatest of pleasures not only to the philosopher but also to the rest of mankind, however small their capacity for it; the reason of the delight in seeing the picture is that one is at the same time learning – gathering the meaning of things, e.g., that the man there is so-and-so . . . [8]

It is not the smallness of mankind's capacity for learning but, rather, the smallness of what is there to be learned that makes gameshows easy targets for derision. I have not enumerated all of the devices employed in *Blind Date* (the suitors are 'summed-up' in a fatuous male voice-over, while the date struggles to decide which of the three vacuous egotists will prove the most complimentary companion; the bizarre dress-sense of the hostess – a different costume each week – must exert its own fascination for some viewers; the resolution scene is interrupted by previously shot interviews, and these separate sequences of candid reminiscence are intercut for ironic counterpoint, while on the inset screen the couple react 'now' with predictable pouts and embarrassment at the revelation of their 'private' ruminations), but I have tried to make it clear that the structure does have a compelling simplicity whose wide appeal is less a sign of the collapse of civilization than of the timidity and conservatism of popular taste.

The pattern is repeated in the course of the programme, with only the nominally individualized dates and suitors changing. Commercial breaks work rather like intermissions, occurring at suitably conclusive moments, but of course the narratives cannot develop any significant dramatic complexity. (At times one is aware that the couple found so few moments of interest together that they are unable to spin our the minutes of discussion – the hostess is obliged then to apply desperate variations on the questions she's already asked, as if pushing them to have a last minute insight before the break comes and allows them to resume their private lives, far from this brief concocted fame.) Each narrative has its own closure, deferred to the following week to provide a series of little enticements to the viewer: we see the resolution of last week's stories, and anticipate next week's resolutions of this week's stories. Each completed narrative repeats the ancient plot of the protagonist (date) or the contestants (suitors) seeking a goal (election as the chosen couple) and undergoing a form of trial (making up or answering the three questions, which often take a low-key riddling form and attempt humour). Each narrative is enacted within the three stylized settings whose minimalism could perhaps inspire Sister Wendy Beckett[9] to speak of their spiritual value. *Blind Date* could almost be a post-modernist masterpiece.

But it isn't. And the reason it isn't is that generic continuity with a universally understood narrative formula is not enough. However, it does clearly satisfy an aesthetic need, and its minute variations on endlessly repeated exchanges within the structural confines of the sets may also satisfy a need – the pleasure of learning, as Aristotle says, 'that the man there is so-and-so', but more than that the pleasure which, for Kierkegaard, inheres in repetition itself:

> The dialectic of repetition is easy; for what is repeated has been, otherwise it could not be repeated, but precisely the fact that it has been gives to repetition the character of novelty. When the Greeks said that all knowledge is recollection they affirmed that all that is has been; when one says that life is a repetition one affirms that existence which has been now becomes. When one does not possess the categories of recollection or of repetition the whole of life is resolved into a void and empty noise. Recollection is the pagan life-view, repetition is the modern life-view.[10]

I want to give what deserves to be given to what is, on the face of it, a disturbingly bland type of popular distraction. Kierkegaard's lively reflections may, I think, be applied without condescension to the phenomenon of the widespread appeal of trivia:

> ...it is only of the new one grows tired. Of the old one never tires...It requires youth to hope, and youth to recollect, but it requires courage to will repetition...But he who does not comprehend that life is a repetition, and that this is the beauty of life, has condemned himself and deserves nothing better than that which is sure to befall him, namely, to perish.[11]

Repetition gives the reassurance of familiarity to the otherwise chaotic new, and we all, at differing levels, respond to its stabilizing power. But even if this helps to explain (and justify, if that is necessary) why undemanding entertainments collect mass audiences, it still leaves us with the problem of evaluation unresolved; indeed, if we acknowledge the technological sophistication, the narrative antecedents and the structural and aesthetic simplicity of the form, the problem of evaluation has become more complicated. I doubt it can be resolved by appeals to seriousness, maturity, meaning and absolute values – not, anyway, these alone; I think we must address our appeal to Time.

Shows like *Blind Date* are formulaic and adaptable. You or I could reproduce the format in a school or a village hall, at a party, almost anywhere, with or without video cameras, changing the goal and the types of questions, without really plagiarizing – since the formula is common property – and without becoming 'authors' – without doing anything very original or specifically filmic. We could call it *Mastermind*, *The Krypton Factor*, *Pot Black*, or whatever, and we might well have an entertaining time. But if we happen to know that this narrative game is also capable of giving us *The Odyssey*, *Sir Gawain and the Green Knight*, *Pilgrim's Progress*, *A Portrait of the Artist as a Young Man*, and so on, we shall perhaps feel that our time has only been passed, not used economically and for lasting enrichment. I suppose any art can function as a soothing break between one activity and the next, but to use television solely for its soporific effect is to limit its potential unnecessarily, and in the context of education we must deal in economies of time.

One reason why we all need stories is that our own lives are finite – we simply do not have sufficient time to develop the possible selves within us; we make choices, and in making, live by them and not by others. Stories are the accretions of possibility that extend sensibility and understanding, expand the selves we are becoming. But stories also exist in time, *our* time while we attend to them. We may wish to 'fleet the time carelessly as they did in the golden world', but once we hear 'Time's wingéd chariot hurrying near' we'll welcome the plot which removes irrelevant, time-consuming details from the story. Narrative, with its root meaning in *gnarus*, knowing, is art's great response to the frustrations of mortality, and education resembles narrative in that it doesn't seek to embrace everything (story) but is perforce highly selective, as well as competitive with other disciplines, other plots. *Blind Date* may already be heavily plotted, but that does not mean it offers as rich an experience as may be got from any similar narrative of the same duration. If we are concerned with the selection of texts (and necessarily the exclusion of many more) as formative of an education, we have a duty to be concerned with their comparative weight.

The antecedents of *Blind Date* are worth alerting students to, as are its visual styles and its particular ways of fictionalizing real people into brief iconic celebrity, and real issues (how to initiate relationships) into trite, if impersonally memorable, vignettes. These things can be brought out usefully, enjoyably, and relatively easily. But then what? Perhaps there are further layers of intentional and rewarding meaning in the text, but soon one has to impose external meaning by applying the methodologies of other discourses (a sociological reading, a feminist reading, a psychoanalytical reading, etc.). The text and its medium cease to have intrinsic interest; substituted texts from different media could serve as well. In that case, *Blind Date* has no value of its own, but is the occasion for something else, and learning resides in that something else, the theoretical discourse and its own perspectival limitations. That's fine, but so long as our educational purpose is to make available a major aesthetic form it is premature; too easily, and mistakenly, it returns the medium to unproblematical transparency.

The limitation of *Blind Date* is the limitation of genre study: it lets us discover its parameters and conventions, but once these are grasped offers little more, unless we shift our attention to the strategies of another discourse, or look within the genre for significant modifications of its language. To some extent these will evolve anonymously with the language, but dramatic differences, which begin to take a particular work out of the genre we ascribed it to, are more likely to occur through the intervention of intelligently creative individuals, through, in other words, attributable authorship.

Beyond the properties already mentioned, what do shows like *Blind Date say* as film? The studio lighting is even and constant, with little or no variation for shifts in mood or creation of particular atmosphere. (After a long absence, I watched a recent episode and saw the candid reminiscences done in surprisingly low light, but this turned out to be the accidental effect of an attempt to introduce an interesting background – filming through a window, correctly exposing for the exterior, the interior figure wasn't given sufficient supplementary or reflected light.) Colour tends towards that familiar, somewhat garish blend of theatricality which *is* a style, but which is so pervasive and lacking in subtlety one wants to call it styleless. Lighting and colour merely announce the brash occasion, without nuanced attention to how they might add further dimensions to the narrative. The same goes for the camerawork. We see master shots of the studio spaces, and mechanical, predictable series of two-shots, medium close-ups and reaction shots – nothing that could be termed imaginative, inventive or adventurous.

As film language, *Blind Date* operates at the level of an early Ladybird book, not inappropriate for the level of verbal exchanges it records. And yet I remember reading somewhere that in a poll of MPs' favourite television shows *Blind Date* came first. From what I can gather, it's also popular with academics. Such groups might be less willing to admit that their preferred relaxation-reading consisted of Ladybird books, since these are accepted as being designed for children whose experience and vocabulary are limited. Light entertainment is for anyone with nothing better to do, and it doesn't have to do much to 'work'.

Insofar as we are sitting still, not conversing, and moderately attentive, *whatever* we see on television will be interesting. However narrow the margin, the shifting colours, movements and sounds, the verbal and dramatic flavour, will provide us with something more dynamic than a blank wall. We easily become a captive audience. We easily become involved, albeit mildly, curious to discover what will happen next, even if we can guess. We smile at these people, laugh or grimace at their jokes. But the emotional content is neither autonomous nor fully directed. That is, none of these people who entertain us for a few minutes is allowed to be much more than a cipher, a minor contributor to the narrative, and none is exactly a character either. Each has a defined role, but none may reveal an aspect that warrants and gets more extended treatment. We can't turn to the author/director and demand that so-and-so's part be built-up, because the show *has* no author in that sense. The framework is fixed, self-writing and self-perpetuating, and the contributors are fixed within its fixed pattern, yet not quite as embodied as fictions.

If we decide now to make the judgment that *Blind Date* is bad art it is not because we really suspect it has *no* art. We have made some attempt to recognize the art it possesses, and we have probably gained a sense of its unrealized potential; we have evaluated and decided that it will not do, because it will not do *enough*. I see some point in introducing genre through shows of this type, and some of the basic conventions outlined in Chapter Three – the educational point is to start where the children or the MPs are. Would other types of show serve our purpose better?

I should say here that the existence of programme types is not always as evident as that of genres in other arts. Always coming from the same part of the room, always moving from one show into bridging material that fills the gap before the next show begins, and always susceptible to the viewer's channel-changing, television could be read as a kind of bumper-size narrative whose origins are already forgotten and whose end is nowhere in sight. Actors, newsreaders, hostesses, resemble, in their representation on television and as subjects of newspaper gossip, minor characters, and in this particularly baggy monster, the ongoing, all-inclusive media-novel, the shows are little more than oddly fixtured paragraphs whose ultimate coherence will never be realized and is not wanted.

Such a fragmentation of unity, such apparent loss of the need for any more serious meanings than can be got in brief narratives and the random collisions of narrative information, makes within our culture a pseudo-meaning of its own, which Michael Ignatieff (in a disappointing television series of his own) called 'the three-minute culture'. Taking television seriously does imply a determination to recover its potential to be more than that, and classifying genres helps us to isolate that potential from the flow.[12]

News

Interviews, documentaries and news broadcasts bring us about as close as we can get, without really being there, to unmediated reality, life's raw material, as yet unimagined, simply and fully happening. They are, we might suppose artless – story, not plot – and that is their peculiar value. We want impartial news. If it is too clearly authored we shall discern bias rather than creativity. If it has to be structured, the structure should appear inevitable and unquestionable, like something agreed to long ago, something communal, traditional, anonymous and right. But the medium cannot give us both the totality of an actual event and a structure. News is already plot, not story. Sometimes an interim report of what *is* happening, sometimes a prediction of what *should soon* happen, news depends most often on the past tense: it is a reconstruction of what *has* happened. News is as formulaic as *Blind Date*. The games it plays with reality may be more serious, depending on how seriously we take its 'players' and the events that have made them newsworthy. We certainly obtain a stronger sense of the world 'out there', if only because that seems to be where news is collected from, but the broadcasts are still constructed as a series of discrete narratives. And neither the method of construction nor the themes it serves are essentially filmic in origin, so, given that television news is a type of film show, we can work towards the question – What does the film dimension add?

First, the method of construction, which is that of an agenda rather than a menu. The items on the agenda need have no relationship, but tend to be sequenced in descending order of gravity and immediacy, so that the lead item will be the most calamitous – a natural disaster, a large-scale accident, a financial crisis, a political crisis, an act of terrorism, a war – and the concluding items will be about sports or some other lightweight, if possible humorous, occurrence. Thus, even within the mundane structure of an agenda, a separable *emotional* plot is formed whose analogy is not with artless life but, surprisingly, Shakespearian comedy. The rule of order is initially threatened by destructive forces (in the perception of the rulers, of course: the converse is that the young, good and true are threatened by a repressive order). After the potentially tragic opening there follows a transitional section where some licence is allowed and where some values are challenged, explored or modified. (How seriously are we to take yet another squabble between prominent ministers whose narrative role is rarely to do anything other than provide, without verse or much verve, regular flyting matches?) This leads to a conclusion where a more merciful order is established, harmony restored, and happiness allowed, at least for the moment, to rule the day. Interestingly, the transitional items on the agenda, that so frequently deal in personalities (clashes between, or scandals involving well-known politicians, for example), have a precedent not only in medieval flytings and some of the classical eclogues of Theocritus and Virgil, but also in the Old Comedy of Aristophanes, with its social and political satire and belittling portraits of named contemporary figures.

The agenda is constructed to inform, occasionally to investigate, and to entertain. In principle the order of items could be reversed, so that every news broadcast would describe an emotional arc closer to tragedy, or to something even more despairing, because unresolved, continuing. The agenda of comedy is preferred, but not because it is necessarily more true to life; it enables us to maintain a sane distance from perpetual turmoil; it is reassuring, a fiction we can bear to see repeated nightly.

The television news agenda tends to follow the standard pattern of newspapers, which headline main items, then have sections of home, international, general and leisure news. But we don't need the multiple sections of the weekend press to be reminded that with newspapers we can turn to the parts we wish to read first. With television and radio news we are obliged to follow the set agenda through, from gravity towards levity.

The determination of the raw stories that will be selected for the evening's plots again owes little to a specifically filmic mode of representation. What surprises is not the degree of unanimity about newsworthy items across the media, but those occasions where one of these organs either misses a story, or scoops one missed by the others – the implication being that the news items have already detached themselves from the world and are merely waiting to be found. There must be lacunae in the agenda, but the typology is decided *prior to* the specific events about which news appears to be composed. I have listed some of the categories above, and because they are inevitable and perennial, the news we receive has something of the unfortunate quality of an agreed, fundamentally familiar and congenial, fiction. As with *Blind Date*, the participants change while the narratives remain the same.

That we do not altogether lose our capacity for pity and terror is due less to the honesty of the medium than our sympathy for human suffering, which can transcend the contrived agenda and even, I think, manipulated appeals to feeling, and attach itself to that level of reality which the filmed report merely glimpses. Even so, the agenda, repeated several times daily with only minor variations, must inevitably dull our responsiveness to the particularity of many items. This level of structural repetition generalizes, rather than universalizes, feelings which should probably be individualized anyway. But news conventions rule out a fuller, more imaginative use of the medium than can be obtained by editing and commentary.

The discovery, definition and construction of news *could* be one of the greatest challenges facing anyone interested in narrative. The story, which may be unfolding anywhere, is not yet isolated from the numerous stories that intersect it; the point at which it will be said to begin has not been fixed; its location may be known, but not the manner in which that is to be presented. The story is immensely complicated while it remains embedded in the world. Closest to the story are its participants and witnesses, next, advisers, experts, and none of these tells the whole story; everyone carries a facet, maybe a crucial element, but still only a point of view. To construct news is to observe, intervene, assess, select and rebuild according to one's own more or less informed perspective. It is to perform an operation on the world and the story, removing the latter in such a way that it will seem complete rather than torn away. A delicate business. But the precision, the ethical and aesthetic tact that should accompany this operation, have been redundancies of formulaic convention and repetition. Only students of film coming freshly to the language and questioning these monolithic assumptions are likely to see the extent of the challenge and endeavour to meet it.

I should add that in England extended programmes like Channel 4's news and BBC2's *Newsnight* have proved capable of more detailed examinations of individual items, have broadened the scope of what is newsworthy, and been able to avoid the emotional structure of comedy, though usually by moving from one solemnly-treated topic to another. There is no opportunity, apparently, for a news seriously conceived as absurd, surreal or anarchic.

News, more aware than any other mode of communication of its imminent obsolescence, stakes everything on realism, immediacy and impact, and on the intrinsic value of its contents to constitute those recurring aspects of heightened reality that are humanly interesting. Heightened reality here, of course, resides in the event depicted, and not in the depiction of the event. Form serves content, but content is not the unshaped story: it is the plot, and so it is the form too. A passage by John Berger, in a piece on Barbara Hepworth, may be useful here:

> ... there is a fundamental confusion about the relationship between form and content. (Here I should emphasize that content is not the same thing as subject matter: it is what the artist discovers *in* his subject.) It is its content that makes any work of art dynamic. It is the content that the artist distils from life and which, through its influence on the spectator as he comprehends it, flows back into life. The function of the form of the work is to concentrate, to hold the pressure of both the artist's and spectator's experience of the content.[13]

News is an aesthetic form whose agenda has no author and whose regular manifestations are authored collaboratively. How much subject is 'discovered' by these perhaps unwitting artists? How well does the news form 'hold the pressure of (our) experience of the content'? That the answers may be disappointing should not persuade us that the questions are inappropriate. The medium is *not* transparent, even here where we seem most inclined to conspire to believe it is, and within its terms a reading of artistic quality is the means by which we can reach the subject.

News catches our attention with a musical theme and graphics. The tone could be characterized, not unreasonably, as urgent (*Newsnight*'s graphics even include, as well as fast tracking shots, high-speed shots of night traffic, as if the world is going by too fast to be reported at normal speed), though there are times when the agenda is thus made to seem anticlimactic, simply because its pace differs. Because the announcing theme is the programme signature it cannot be changed to accommodate the actual items, which are themselves bereft of musical accompaniment (presumably because music was not part of the story, but neither were the camera operator, sound recordist, editor, etc.) and so must either risk resting a mite dully on their own merits (the operations of part of the available form and content on subject) or be pumped up by editing and narration to match and sustain the mood.

Newsreaders do, of course, read news, but they also function as hosts. They are 'anchors' – they anchor the free-floating items together by working in between them, talking over some of them, generally sustaining the illusion of a flow rather than a series of broken spurts, and they anchor the viewer by imparting a sense of stability and concomitant authority. Their function in the narrative bears comparison with that of Theseus in *A Midsummer Night's Dream*, but also, more disturbingly, with Duke Vincention in *Measure for Measure* – the newsreader appears an impartial arbiter, but at times we may be unsure that this really is the case – whose version of this item are we getting? We may also sense, of course, that the newsreader is only a performer, the mouthpiece of an *unseen* author or authors (producer, editor, corporation).

What television offers above other news media is that excess referred to in Chapter Two: filmed reality, seen to be true. The visible record and proof of an event urges us to accept its plain veracity, where a verbal account is obliged to describe and gather potentially interpretative colour and ambiguity. But we know that each filmed shot is calculated anyway, and even if we see on screen a reporter/author whose impartiality we trust, we know that the report will probably have been edited by someone else before transmission. The event may be strong enough for these qualifications to be merely quibbles, but very often the advantage of visual proof turns out to be a lame contrivance – we listen to a commentary which is less full than a newspaper account, while we look at a library still of a public building, or shots of people entering or leaving cars. These shots have only the most trivial link to the story. Most authors would cut them from the plot. (I suppose an exception would be Chantal Akerman who, in *Toute Une Nuit*, (1982), made an entire feature out of nocturnal comings and goings, and deliberately eschewed the conventionally more important passages of contact in between.) In short, the visual advantage is not much use if the camera operator is excluded from most of the dramatic centre of the story, and since most stories have begun before the news team's arrival that will often be the case. Which is one reason for a heavy reliance on anchors and, indeed, for blue screens and inset shots, back projections, and as many technological aids as may be brought in without turning the news too obviously into a stylistic simulacrum of pop videos.

As a model for practical work in film, however, news has greater potential than quizzes and gameshows: the latter happen to use film language, but could use the languages of other arts without significant losses – their usage is prosaic. We may contend that news too lacks real 'aesthetic universality' and answers only to the needs of 'objective validity'. (I am using Ernst Cassirer's terms for Kant's *Gemeingültigkeit* and *Allgemeingültigkeit*[14].) But objective validity, when compared with treatments of the same story in other media, reveals differences which *are* significant and have to do with creativity and convention in the form used.

Thus, because the same agenda tends to be used in other media, and because each of these media has a number of reasonably distinct organs, the opportunities for analysis by comparison and contrast – of one medium against another, then of one organ in a given medium against another in that medium – are extensive. It would be a false economy to limit such analyses to the revelations of ideological bias that will emerge. How and why do the newspaper items differ from the television items? Answering should help students to prepare cogent aims before filming stories for their own news programmes. These may well be local in matter, but the artistic and sometimes ethical issues raised are fundamental: the students are intervening in reality, perhaps at first to extract a 'typical' item, but, if a questioning spirit has been encouraged, they may well create news out of material that does not 'look' like news at first sight – does not, that is, fit the conventional categories that effectively delimit and fictionalize the world.

To follow the news model through, the filmed material should be edited by other students. The several items filmed should be coolly compared, their eventual duration decided partly on the intrinsic interest of the edited sequence, partly on a scale of relative importance in the agenda – the whole to be coordinated by a presenter with a commentary, and with the use of whatever graphics the available equipment is capable of producing. (Even without expensive editing suites, for example, one of the current generation of home video recorders could be connected to an older model to introduce into the editing procedure mosaic and solarization effects, picture-in-picture, freeze-frame and slow motion – none of which requires technical skill to achieve.)

Such an exercise should certainly develop narrative awareness and stress the importance of disciplined pre- and post-production planning. It contains areas where collaborative activity is important, as well as areas where creative control shifts from one group to another, and so should provoke animated discussion about involvement and impartiality, the possessiveness or rights of authorship in a situation where work is valued for subject rather than treatment. To what extent does the overall news editor become the author/coordinator of items which each film crew will have put considerable effort into making? *Feeling* the issue raised by this question seems to me more valuable than merely approaching it theoretically. (Why is the director the *auteur*, rather than the scriptwriter, camera operator, editor, actor or producer?)

The agenda structure is appealing because it lends itself readily to organizing full classes into small, well-defined groups. But the main drawback to learning film through news is also implied by that structure, and beyond that by documentary, for both can appear, at the level of handling the camera, too easy; both can perpetuate a kind of visual illiteracy by ignoring – and sometimes managing extremely well without – the conventions outlined in Chapters Three and Four. Reliance on the intrinsic interest of the basic subject matter can appear to legitimate imaginative laziness. One is not responsible for sets, lighting, actors, and may not have the opportunity to 're-draft', to re-take a scene. If there are several shots one will seek elements of continuity, but it may not be possible to construct the sequence conventionally. This does not mean that in shooting a documentary one works to different aesthetic norms; rather, one seeks equivalents or relies on the general acceptance that because this is 'real' and not wholly controlled, a certain narrative jerkiness is permissible. Some logical connections or continuations may be missing, some footage may even be imperfectly shot, the composition not ideal, the image over- or under-exposed. For the shot one really wanted, a dramatic moment central to the event, one may have had to make-do with a somewhat flat substitute. Up to a point, all these things can be overlooked as unavoidable eventualities, and the sympathetic viewer might value all the more highly the film-maker's ingenuity in handling material in difficult circumstances. But one has been recording, not thinking freely about the best camera placement, angle or movement; one hasn't been developing the relationship between self, subject and audience that the language is capable of forging.

The results of working with various constraints may, seen often enough, begin to resemble deliberate style. Despite improvements in lenses and the resolving power of high speed colour film, for example, the word 'documentary' can still evoke a memory of grainy, black and white images, very obviously shot from a hand-held 16mm camera. I remember shooting footage like this myself in the 1960s, when it was already fairly well established as a desirable stylistic approach to 'actuality' (because of the impact of films by Allan King, the Maysles brothers, and Don Pennebaker); but then it was also necessary. To obtain any kind of useable image while shooting inside a lift in a dimly-lit food-packing plant late at night, for instance, I had to use a lightweight 16mm camera, hand-held obviously, and the fastest available film, which was black and white. That was then sent to the laboratory with instructions to push-process it, thereby increasing its speed several times. The returned footage was very grainy but images could at least be seen. As far as I was aware they couldn't have been made by any other means, unless we'd had the facilities and permission to set up banks of lights. Given the circumstances, then, the results were acceptable. Given other circumstances they might not have been. But what was the expedient has become part of the grammar – 'Let's go for a sixties style!' Fine, if it happens to be appropriate, but otherwise it is simply a reference without a meaning to amplify.

I am not suggesting that one shouldn't take particular conditions into account when responding to a work, only that the conditions under which a documentary or a news item may have to be filmed will not always be the most propitious for students of the art. The discipline of making a news item, to last perhaps a minute on screen, is valuable, but the danger is that it could lead away from the creative possibilities of the shot-by-shot involvement of camerawork and editing with subject – away from Berger's committed definition of context.

The structure of the news broadcast as a whole conspires in this. It is intentionally easy to read, but not exciting or involving. People speak directly to camera, then there may be a two-shot for a scrap of conversation. A long shot may involve a pan, followed immediately by another talking head, or another long shot, or a back-projected still. A location film may consist of extreme long shots or distant helicopters firing missiles, or of distant detonations. We accept the circumstances and accept the shots accordingly, admire the bravery and skill of those who made them, but within the larger structure these shots do nothing to add coherence to the visual hotch-potch.

The agenda is merely linear. The arrangement of items does have its characteristic emotional arc, but taken shot-by-shot visual continuity is bound to be sporadic and, therefore, of little use in training students to use film as a fully articulate medium. At worst it could stifle imaginative development by demonstrating that mis-matched shots and sequences that don't build up or lead into one another can still be understood. What might then be questioned is the level of this understanding, and what might be remembered is that news accepts its ephemerality: what it is trying to say is of interest for and adequate to the moment, but it rarely makes more substantial claims on our attention (until we become historians) than that implies.

A New Art?

A quarter of a century ago Susan Sontag made a plea for a criticism that would move away from its interpretative function in order to recover 'the sensory experience of the work of art':

> The aim of all commentary on art now should be to make works of art –
> and, by analogy, our own experience – more, rather than less, real to us.
> The function of criticism should be to show *how it is what it is*, even *that it is
> what it is*, rather than to show *what it means*.[15]

This bracing project was receptive to the theoretical encroachment of semiotics and structuralism, then deconstruction and post-structuralism, but the *critical* function began to seem redundant since, despite the assumption that it could simply adjust its focus, its lens effectively dropped off when it could no longer 'show *what it means*'.

A decade after Sontag's *Against Interpretation*, Robert Alter, in *Partial Magic*, made a similar observation, not based on the changing requirements of the reader/audience/critic, but on what was happening inside the contemporary novel:

> Film, because it is a collaborative artistic enterprise involving a complicated chain of technical procedures, almost invites attention to its constitutive processes; and there is a clear logic in the involvement in film-making of several of the French New Novelists, or in the repeated recourse to cinematic composition by *montage* in a writer like Robert Coover. The close parallels between what is happening now in the two media suggest that the self-consciousness of both may reflect a heightened new stage of modern culture's general commitment to knowing all that can be known about its own components and dynamics. [16]

A culture in which both critics and artists have adjusted their attention to the fictive nature of fiction and reality must have limited life-expectancy, but it has been a significant factor in the intellectual climate of the last twenty-five years, and the doubt it has raised about the authority of the author and the possibility of locating meaning does make it difficult to argue against the kinds of genre study that centre on works conventionally regarded (by a critical concern with intentional meaning and interpretation, by an aesthetic concern with how and why these meanings are articulated) as mediocre. Leavis's famous 'Yes, but...', which should initiate a scrupulously sensitive qualification to his 'This is so, isn't it?', gets blocked off before it can be completed by 'No, that isn't even part of the discourse any longer'.

There is a problem here which has implications outside an academic debate about criticism, theory, theoreticism, and what now constitutes a subject, and which can only be exacerbated by rigid adherence to one position. Practically, however, the developments and conflicts can be useful, especially if one modifies the ambitious claims that tend to accompany every new or revived theory. Attention to archetypes, genres, narrative forms and patterns – to the inherited communal structures of languages in the arts – provides a necessary introduction. But the educational model should be progressive rather than static, and what it should progress towards, it seems to me, is what it used to take too much for granted – the meaning that the artist saturates and enchants the given form with. We should continually return, as Kuleshov said, with a difference, the difference being our assimilation and adaptation of the currents of contemporary thought.

Anyway, I want to apply again for deferred judgment – my own, as much as anyone's – while I examine the educational potential of two related forms whose value I am ambivalent about: pop videos and commercials.

Promotional pop music videos and commercials are sometimes referred to as a new art form. What is meant, presumably, is a new category or genre. Many young people have no difficulty with this notion and if they wanted the claim taken seriously might point out that well-known film directors (Ken Russell, Ingmar Bergman,

Derek Jarman, David Lynch, Lindsay Anderson, Martin Scorsese, Penny Marshall, Chris Menges, Adrian Lyne, Francis Ford Coppola, Claude Chabrol, Michael Apted) and 'top' cinematographers (Nestor Almendros, Billy Williams, Gordon Willis, Vilmos Zsigmond, Sven Nykvist) have made them. This is not a decisive argument, even if one allows that not all these film-makers make films that look like commercials. The film-makers themselves point out that these short forms can provide employment and training on the job, and even allow for experimentation. The form has its uses, displays a greater range of technical and stylistic devices than *Blind Date* or the news, and in many ways seems ideally suited for training students, from primary school to university, in the 'how' of film-making.

Promotional films, whether advertising goods or pop songs, usually express something more than information about a product, but selling the product remains their purpose. The narrative art of film, like the narrative art of the novel, interests me because of the ways in which it creates new realms of human experience. The means by which it does this are important *as* means, and are not ends in themselves. The human experience reflected in or created by a commercial or a pop video tends to be slick, stereotyped, sentimental and, however vivid and even evocative, shallow. The means may appear innovative but they, too, are usually derivative. These are popular forms, but are they suitable models for emulation? Aesthetically they foster an interest in style as effect; ideologically they validate consumerism, and indeed locate their art inside a system of materialistic values as, precisely, the commercial arm of those values. The aesthetic is reductive, moving towards self-referential closure – art for art's sake, to the extent one takes the salesmanship as art – lacking the substance of contact with real life. Would an education in any other language or art confine itself to such parameters?

As the preceding paragraph implies, I very rarely enjoy pop videos; but, inconsistently, I *do* frequently find commercials amusing, exciting, touching, even thought-provoking (though I have difficulty remembering the products associated with the advertisements that strike me as good).

Pop Videos

Commercially, pop videos are made to promote the sales of songs in the short term, and to promote their singers in the somewhat longer term. Aesthetically, these two aims may conflict: the desired 'image' of the singer or group may not be related to the verbal sense of the lyric or the mood of the piece of music; the film-maker's efforts to illustrate or interpret the latter may be sabotaged by the requirement to interpolate shots of the former. There is an analogy with the oral tradition, in which one may return periodically to sense the shaping presence of the storyteller, but it is rarely evoked with any inner necessity; on the other hand, the form is not free enough of pretensions to narrative coherence to rely wholly on rhythmic editing and visual resonance. It is characterized, rather, by a kind of scrappy randomness, a compilation of sometimes beautiful fragments which almost communicate a story, almost generate a mood and almost portray the band.

The pop video differs from the commercial not only by being longer but also by including *as an integral element* that which is being sold: you actually hear the song which you are being asked to purchase – a peculiarly generous, guileless form of advertising. One assumes that in most cases the song is still conceived, performed and recorded prior to the making of the video, and that a sense is retained that multiply-duplicated aural recordings represent the desirably authentic version, sans images. Consequently, the video must both enhance the specificity of the song it contains and be somehow *less* than that song – the apparent contradiction has traditionally been resolved by reference to the superior quality of sound on record players, compact disc and tape. Increasingly, however, one also has the opportunity to buy the video, and some include, as an added incentive, additional material that may not have been shown on television.

In some ways this is the easiest form of brief, shaped narrative for students to undertake. The song itself sets the length of the piece, while the continuous flow and evocative power of the music will help to retrieve the visuals from potential incoherence and inept construction. The professional model is characterized by attention to composition and movement rather than a firm conception of narrative, so although the shots may accumulate and be repeated (repetition of shots being more easily and quickly accomplished by tape-to-tape video editing than when editing film) this is hardly ever done with an informed sense of what might add substance to the emotional changes of pitch being aimed at. The shots can just end when the song ends, not because they have reached a satisfying resolution. The pop video offers a sort of art college conception of film art; strong on a range of filmic visual styles, animation techniques from McLaren to Duning, and contemporary graphic design, but weak in continuity, development and purpose. The form is easy to emulate because it sidesteps the challenges of working intelligently with a set duration; its disadvantages as a new animated visual art are its lack of textural surface and its movement, which seems to devalue the striking graphic qualities that may be found in the still image.

If students are to work from professional, pre-recorded music, then shots of the performers can be dispensed with at once. The task is clarified to a visual response to sound, which may be a matter of making abstract or semi-representational patterns (unusual angles, extreme close-ups based on the natural environment, for example, or a collage of images found in magazines), or of using actors to play, without dialogue, a story. There is some scope for suggesting mood by camera placement and movement, by effects of lighting, and by editing. There is no need to restrict the choice of music to an amenable pop song. Derek Jarman could be said to have extended the scope of the pop video by making a feature-length 'promo' (or do duration and subject make it too serious to be called that?) of Britten's *War Requiem*. Earlier, Vaughan Williams' settings of *Ten Blake Songs* were written for a documentary, and several could provide ample, if unusual, material for illustration or interpretation. Whether a folk, classical or pop repertoire should provide the source would itself be worth discussing with students of course.

Two student efforts seen recently, and demanding little technical proficiency to be quite effective, were an autobiographical piece using repetition and gradual narrative development until the point of the repeated shots was revealed, and a non-narrative piece in which several dead fish and fish-heads were animated into a bizarre dance. (For animation some students prefer to work on Super 8 first, editing and sometimes adding scratch rhythms on the emulsion, before videoing the projected images.) The films that seem to me to work least well are those that students are often most keen to make initially, starring themselves as moody surrogate pop-singers, striking poses while a wobbly hand-held camera moves around them and zooms in and out rather desperately seeking a frenetic style. Older students also seem inclined towards making portentous statements about inhumanity, the death of the planet, and so forth. These are usually very sincere, but facile, and morally dubious when documentary footage or newspaper stills are incorporated into the statement and are expected to carry the argument on their own emotional impact. That point where the aesthetic collides with the unwittingly exploitative raises issues which young film-makers might deal with more articulately after having acquired greater experience with the language they are using.

Anyway, the characteristic features of the model are its imposed duration and the subordination of the visuals to an illustrative or interpretative accompaniment. If the students move on to composing the sound as well, then the potential of the form is, naturally, extended.

Commercials

Statistical analysis based on market research has little connection with the aesthetic use of language, yet its results may form the basis of sophisticated short narratives which do not work by direct, prosaic displays of information, but by allusion. The power of commercials is associative: the product need not be sold as itself, but in terms of its location in people's lives, and its supposed transformative effect when introduced into those lives. The product, then, becomes the occasion for a realistic or idealized vision of how some of us live, or might wish to live. If the vision is attractive or memorable enough, the product – the advertisers hope – will be seen as the means of realizing it. Over the years the visions have become deeply conventionalized and difficult to affix to specific brands. A competitive market ensures that advertisers keep trying to overcome this, and one of their methods has been to make the vision ever more seductive, the 'sell' softer and subtler, so that the product again tends to become elusive, while the narrative becomes more memorable.

The emphasis on desirability leads to the construction of fictions which are positive, enthusiastic, light-hearted, comic, sentimental, dynamic and so on – a world of happy families, friendship groups, successful romantics, cute pets and children, thriving loners, a world of romance and comedy where consumption is conspicuous without seeming to be greedy. Darkness and gloom enter this world in public health and safety films, where the product is a habit or attitude to be avoided, and in commercials about personal finance, security and investment; though in these, the gloom can be dispelled once the characters involved join the right bank or insurance company.

Like the pop video, the commercial can make extensive use of computer-aided animation techniques, graphics, and borrowings from printed and other sources. It may use original music – a 'jingle' which becomes the brand signature and will be used for consistency when the visual elements are changed – but is at least as likely to borrow from existing sources. The range is reasonably eclectic: Vivaldi is now associated with cool modernity, the exhilarating freedom of driving far from cluttered urban centres; pop songs of the fifties – Sam Cooke, Fats Domino, etc. – seem to resonate easily with adolescent nostalgia for an imagined community of the self-aware and autonomous young, and will be used to promote jeans or batteries for personal stereos; opera has begun to be used in the late eighties to popularize almost anything Italian or sophisticated, from cars to sherries and sauces. These borrowings, sometimes as effective as pop videos in re-selling songs, are made in quick response to, rather than in advance of, taste. Arguably, the original music is tarnished by this new association, but it is also disseminated widely and may nurture an interest in kinds of music the viewer had not previously responded to.

Commercials endeavour to appeal to the *current* values and interests of those groups whose taste will shortly spread to much larger groups. There is an element of prediction, but not of real innovation. An example of this is the speed with which set designs and special effects from feature films are borrowed: *Indiana Jones, Blade Runner, 1984, Brazil and The Abyss* have all spawned imitative commercials, and in some cases these have been shown even before the films have been on general release. For the moment, however, I am less concerned with the ethics of plagiarism than with the stylistic conventions of the form which, however accelerated, can be related to the customary practices of the narrative film and film genres (and to the inevitable borrowings that situate any art in its language and its time).

The structural conventions are simple: the product or its brand name should be displayed prominently in the final shot (the pack-shot). Where possible it should be shown in use within the narrative and, because it competes with a range of similar products, the structure may be simply comparative, but designed to show the superlative nature of the advertised brand. This device is so clearly a fictive convention that there can be few viewers left who would assume that any objective demonstration had been enacted. The product is merely a character in the fiction. It just happens that more than other narrative arts, film has the capacity to make 'things' dramatically important. (Think, for example, of how suspense can be sustained by repeated cutaways to the second hand on a clock face, or to a gun which someone will soon pick up. On a richer level, look at the sequence in *Notorious*, (1946), where Ingrid Bergman has to steal the key from her husband's key ring and pass it to Cary Grant without being detected.)

Unlike pop videos, which address a predominantly youthful audience and are tailored to slight perceived differences within it, commercials could potentially address the *whole* community, so a market analysis of the targeted audience for any given product is required. Here a sense of audience will call for more than minor adjustments in the tone of the narrative: it may very well prompt the type of narrative selected, and suggest much of its shape. Instead of merely being asked to make a short film that satisfies their own tastes, students will be expected to become more exploratory, more conscious of stereotyping, perhaps more impersonal, and to compose their stories for audiences of, say, small children, middle-aged couples, nuclear happy families, young businessmen and women, or distant lonely relatives. The disciplined brevity of the form clearly imposes limitations on the complexity and depth of utterance, but it also develops specifically filmic narrative skills in ways that longer, less precise forms may not.

How many shots, on average, are used to make a commercial lasting less than a minute? And to obtain that finished effect, what would the shooting ratio have been? It should never be assumed that effects just happen. Does the editing follow conventional visual sequencing, is it timed to a musical beat rather than the narrative exposition, or is the rhythm built on cutting to movement within the compositions?

Often these three methods are combined. Coca Cola ads, for instance, employ a distinctive musical theme, varied slightly over the years, and a narrative based on the brotherhood of man, the linking of peoples of different nations, and the linking of children, adolescents and the elderly into one enormous, happy, soft-drink imbibing family – a vision of how American business interests would wish to be interpreted around the world. The shots are cut to music, but their disparate nature requires a further integrating element, which could have been provided by showing whoever is in shot swigging Coca Cola. The solution is actually subtler than that: everyone is linked because they are having fun, and this is manifested in irrepressible physical movement (supposed to look spontaneous), the cuts on movement then cementing as rhythm the narrative of active people everywhere heeding the call to drink Coca Cola. And the drink, supposedly, sustains and even gives this joyous energy. The current ads have become as awkwardly self-parodic as late Hemingway. In place of spontaneous natural movement, waited for and captured by editing from much more extensive footage – the illusion of the real and the transient – the sequences are composed of very contrived little gestures and jigs, set in a 'real' location, but made, therefore, to look even more absurd. These, one feels, are not ordinary, fun-loving people, caught on the off-chance as tempers fray or exuberance gets out of hand; they are posers or hysterics, and if Coca Cola makes this sort of thing happen to you it is a drink to be avoided at all costs.

As well as possessing a number of thematic similarities (as Tolstoy observed in *Anna Karenina*, 'All happy families resemble one another'), sequences of commercials display, even to the untrained eye, surprising diversity. Lighting, choice of film stock, filtration and tinting are used with a care one rarely encounters elsewhere on television, a care proceeding, no doubt, from the commercial challenge to make *this* short narrative distinct from the next. The Coca Cola ads just mentioned tend to use rich browns, contre-jour shots that flood the image with orange-browns, reds on hoardings etc., to link the visuals to the colour of the soft drink and its packaging. The beautifully polite child who has difficulty tying her shoelaces in a corn flakes ad is bathed in appropriately golden light. Scintillating sharp blues and whites are used for yoghurt, toothpaste, washing powder and anything connected with health and cleanliness.

The only recent use of filtration or tinting in television drama that seems comparably apt was in a mini-series about international drug-dealing, *Traffik*. It was employed because the shifts across continents from sequence to sequence might otherwise have been confusing. So, Germany was cold, with a blue cast, Pakistan hot, with a yellowish cast. Simple and effective, this device goes back to D. W. Griffith and before. (There are a couple of dramatically effective tinted sequences in Derek Jarman's version of *The Tempest*, too, where the world of nature beyond Prospero's domain is cold and blue – it could be argued, though, that this was a means of integrating black and white stock footage into the opening sequence, and of attempting day-for-night later.) The point I would wish to make is simply that commercials are helping to keep the language open, both by incorporating current devices and by reviving conventions that the mainstream has forgotten.

Even so, I think the commercial is a less easy form for students to master than the others we have looked at. With the video equipment currently available in schools and colleges, which make rapid and precise editing extremely difficult, it is perhaps hardly worth embarking on. One really needs film, even a small gauge like Super 8, which can be handled, *seen*, measured, and cut to the frame. Commercials are worth studying, though, and it would be useful if compilation tapes, with credit lists, were available. Precisely because of their emphasis on current taste, their reflection of contemporary mores, commercials can offer a curious sidelight on the social history of our times; but there is also an aesthetic interest, which may be suggested by looking at one type of commercial.

I am thinking of the type that conflates temporal sequence, for various purposes. In the past few years a number of narratives have been structured around the idea of time passing, either to suggest continuity (fashions change, but the product remains popular), or the ageing process (before you know it you'll be old, but a good skin cream will retard the inevitable), or loss (children will grow up and leave home, but you can always bring them back if you've captured them on your video camera). The products are varied but the technique is similar, a variation on time-lapse photography where, by exposing single frames at intervals, a speeded-up life-cycle will result.

One 'continuity' version has a couple facing the camera, and being allowed to make only slight movements while their costumes, hair styles, etc., are changed, along with the background music, to give a rapid chronology of twentieth-century fashions. The message is that the product, a drink, remains fashionable despite all these changes, but as the couple remain the same there is another message about human continuity. It may amount to no more than the truism that we were all young once, but it adds to that a self-deprecating humour that implies toleration of the more outlandish fashions our children might otherwise alienate us with.

The 'ageing' versions, which prey on vanity and fear, tend to be less boisterous than this, and are usually gentle, rather delicate affairs. One of the most effective begins with a close-up of a fair-haired child, which is replaced by close-ups of adolescent and then adult women, all of whose features are similar enough for us to accept that this could be the same face. Instead of a straight cut or a dissolve, the transitions are affected by a technological special effect that is surprisingly poetic: the whole screen image breaks into hundreds of small squares, which peel and drift away across the screen, the later image appearing below. There is an association with the traditional metaphor for time passing – the turning of leaves – and also a sense of the fragility of surfaces, the peeling away of layers. Whether or not we rush off after watching this commercial to buy a skin cream to keep our faces in good repair, seems to me less interesting than the beautiful and yet rather melancholy presentation of beauty and transience which the narrative so economically creates. 'Loss' is communicated in one commercial by the simple device of showing people leaving – first a child leaving a room, then someone a little older, shots from a hallway of the front door, eventually the daughter as bride, leaving the home and driving away. A poignance is captured here, not merely a sentimentality, that does express something about families and love, and does so through the art of film.

The ulterior motive – all commercials are selling products – may leave one's moral and ethical reservations intact; but when the aesthetic experience has little to do with the product any inclination to dismiss the form wholesale as 'bad art' seems facile. It might be more productive to accord the short form the sort of status enjoyed by the epigram in relation to a poet's oeuvre and, remembering that commercials are approximately the same length as the Lumière films of 1895, to study the form as a history of narrative techniques and conventions, rather than assume that, tainted by commerce, it can provide nothing but exercises in style devoid of meaning.

Situation Comedy

The last programme type I want to consider is one of the most characteristic forms of television and, I think, one of the least likely to be defended as film art. Sitcoms and gameshows often originate on radio, and translate successfully to television, but no further: cinema versions of popular sitcoms generally work less well than their originals, and the originals would not work at all on a cinema screen. (Though it should be noted that the development of the form can be traced back not only through radio but also popular series of low budget, 'B' pictures. The Andy Hardy films, for example, with their emphasis on small-town virtues and family security, their narratives of domesticity and courtship, derived initially from Clarence Brown's film of Eugene O'Neill's *Ah, Wilderness*, (1935), taking over most of the original cast for the first in the series. Such ventures did not cease with the spread of television, they moved into its domain.)

If sitcoms transfer with relative ease from radio, the implication is that television copes with predominantly verbal humour, adding, presumably, little more than a visual frame of reference. The pedestrian visual articulation of the bulk of programmes tends to bear this out. But verbal humour is not the only component of the sitcom. It can handle sight-gags, and develop farcical situations which rely as much on visual as on verbal plotting. The 'situations' tend to be domestic, or at any rate confined to a small group seen week after week in the same sets, with location shooting, limited to the occasional exterior scene, as an exception rather than a convention. The sets are evenly and too-well lit, and have the quality of stage sets. Because a studio audience is usually present during filming the theatrical sense is probably stronger than the filmic. Yet the actors' freedom to move and be followed through several connecting sets is greater than would be feasible on stage.

The experience of a sitcom, then, though analagous to that of a stage play (even down to the slight hollowness within which dialogue operates, the lack of convincing ambient sound associated with a studio production), differs sufficiently for us to think of it as televisual. Sets, lighting and sound quality lack the textured realism of film, and the scripts seem both verbose and too unambitious – and often, of course, if not always related to their modest aims, trivial.

I think all these points have a general validity, though production values are obviously higher in some cases than others, but I don't think they touch the argument that the form of these shows is filmic – that they would be weakened by projection onto a cinema screen is irrelevant. They are conceived to work on a small domestic screen, only conceived *filmically*. I'll use a sequence from *Fawlty Towers* as an example; it is the concluding sequence of an episode titled, on the video compilation, *Basil the Rat*.

The main strands of this particular script involve the Spanish waiter's pet hamster and the visit of a health inspector. Manuel's hamster is a rat, which eventually escapes. The imperative is to recapture it without alerting the inspector to its existence. The closing sequence, lasting approximately one and three quarter minutes, is confined entirely to the dining room set. This, like all the main connecting sets on the ground floor of *Fawlty Towers*, seems to have one wall missing, in that none of the camera positions includes it. The absent wall heightens the theatrical impression. If the show was being staged the audience would be there, looking in. A simplified plan of the sets would look something like *Figure 5.1:*

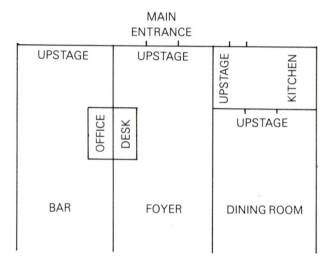

Figure 5.1 A simplified plan of the *Fawlty Towers'* stage set.

The kitchen area, glimpsed through swing doors but not included in this sequence, situates the audience at 90 degrees from the implied proscenium of the other three areas. Upstage is a door leading into the foyer; stage left are the swing doors into the dining area, and stage right, oddly, is a door leading outside – oddly because the exteriors of the hotel show no such door. It would have to be somewhere near the main entrance. This peculiarity is appropriate enough, given the name of the place.

Although one always has a general impression of the proscenium effect and can therefore easily judge the disposition of actors moving from room to room, it *is* only an impression, for the camera set ups are surprisingly varied. They rarely cross the upstage line, and in that broad sense observe the 180 degree rule, but they do admit of numerous local directional changes in the line, for close-up, shot/reverse shot pairs and so on; consequently there is a far greater narrative flexibility in the camera plot than would be possible if the director was merely making a record of a stage production.

In the sequence there are three general camera loci. I won't give an exhaustive analysis of its composition – anyone may buy or rent the video and check the details.

For my present purpose it is enough to take up the implication of the fact that to 'tell' this part of *Basil the Rat*, in less than two minutes, more than thirty shots are needed.

A simple plan of the dining room set is given in *Figure 5.2*, including the six visible tables (we don't have a clear idea of the extent of the downstage area) and the basic camera positions:

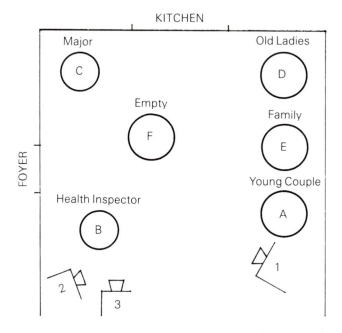

Figure 5.2 A simplified plan of the *Fawlty Towers'* dining room set.

Prior to this sequence the rat concealed itself in a young lady's bag at table A. Only the staff are aware of it, and their efforts to retrieve the rat without alarming the guests – especially the inspector seated at table B – offend the young couple, who exit to settle their bill in the foyer. Basil Fawlty pursues them and eventually gains access to the bag. The rat escapes and runs across the floor, back towards the dining room. At this point the final sequence begins.

The first shot, from position 1, is a transitional long shot across the dining room and through the open door to the foyer, showing the rat racing in towards the camera. The second shot, along the approximate axis of position 2, is a medium close-up of the waiter's backside as he plunges under table A, where the rat has gone to ground. The third shot is the reverse of this, taking the approximate axis of position 1 for a close-up of the health inspector at table B. He has chosen this awkward moment to call the waiter. This exchange of camera positions alternates again through shots four and five, by which time Manuel is clutching the unseen rat, and in the sixth shot we see the situation from position 3. This gives us the health inspector at table B, Manuel beyond him anxious to dispose of the rat, and in the background the Major at table C. Shot seven appears to be from position 1 again, a medium shot which pans with Manuel and then zooms or tracks in slightly as he places the rat in a biscuit tin at the Major's table. By now the visual parameters of the sequence are clear, and the audience will probably be attempting to anticipate the impending disaster.

Basil Fawlty re-enters the dining room in shot eleven, and immediately fawns on the inspector, who wants cheese and biscuits. Shot thirteen is a long shot from position 3, foregrounding the inspector, while in the background we see the Major giving the biscuit tin to Polly. In the next-but-one shot Manuel is panicking, panting, looking for the biscuit tin which Polly is by now holding out for the health inspector. In shot eighteen he looks at the rat, which is sitting up and turning its head.

In shot twenty-five Basil covers the tin, which is taken away. There is a state of general shock – the worst thing that could have happened has happened, and Basil appears to have internalized his anguish. The health inspector is so stunned that he may be persuaded it was an hallucination. Sybil Fawlty continues talking blandly to him. It is only six shots later that we can deduce what has happened to Basil Fawlty, for in the background of shot thirty-one, which concludes the episode, we see the waiter dragging him out by the feet.

This deferment of the resolution depends neither on dialogue nor the theatrical staging of the sequence, which unfolds in 'real' time. It is, specifically, a narrative event created by camera positions (too close to reveal what is going on elsewhere on the set), editing and timing. Basil Fawlty's fainting on camera (on stage, as it were) would be, for the audience, satisfying and in character – something, given our understanding of his inability to cope with the crises he so often precipitates, we half-expect to see. But our attention is directed to the unconcerned others until the last shot reveals what *has* happened (making their coolness even more desperate, since it is no longer only an attempt to cover the rat's appearance). This economy, this additional layer of inventiveness, is a characteristic of the series and is also consonant with the intelligence of the script and the acting, which is a play on formally controlled excess.

At its worst the sitcom takes little advantage of its aesthetic, merely batting back and forth from speech to reaction, from long shots to include significant movement within the set, to close-ups to emphasize points that are probably being made plainly enough by other means. At its best, as in this sequence, the aesthetic is imaginatively integrated. Either way, what we are watching is not radio with pictures or a stage play with close-ups: it is television, and therefore it is film. Where it differs from a cinema film is in the proportionate weight and distribution of elements. The staginess of the sets and lighting would become obtrusive on a much larger screen because we have accepted greater solidity and naturalness as a norm. (The sets in turn-of-the century films could still be quite primitive, just flats and, sometimes, obviously painted doors and windows.) Audience laughter, similarly, would seem an unnecessary amplification of the intention, rather than an occasionally irritating nudge to responses. On television these elements may contribute to an effective spontaneity which the scale and manifest physical reality of the location shown on a cinema screen should supply anyway.

Spontaneity, so useful for the accelerating chain of events in a series such as *Fawlty Towers*, is also an effect of the shooting procedure, which appears to use multiple cameras running simultaneously. It's difficult, and perhaps unnecessary, to determine exactly how many cameras are actually used. Shots eleven and twelve in this sequence are from camera positions so close as to make the reason for the almost invisible cut perplexing: it involves a slight change of angle, to include Sybil in the frame, and the camera seems slightly higher than before, but these developments could have been allowed for by adjusting the position in shot eleven. I think it is likely that a director planning the same sequence for a cinema film would have used fewer than thirty-one shots – there is a quick roughness to some of the framings that makes them no more than adequate, unless, that is, one reads them as rapid responses to the images coming up on a bank of monitors. And that, which seems in isolation a minor technical quibble, may have wider implications when we are considering how best to place film on the curriculum.

Conclusions

By the end of the 1980s there were colour television sets in over 90 per cent of British households, with at least two sets in over 50 per cent and with video recorders also in over 50 per cent (figures from the Government's *General Household Survey*, to 1988). Such information gives weight to a passage I quoted and took issue with in my paper on Film in *Living Powers*:

> . . . if a film is to be analysed as mass culture and ideological effect, then in the seventies and eighties, television, journalism and soon video have a greater claim to centrality; if film and society or cultural analysis are the issue, then the disciplines for the study of society have equal claim with the specificity of particular media . . .[17]

If the hypotheses are accepted then the consequences are reasonable. Television and video do in some ways 'have a greater claim to centrality' than films made for the cinema. But what if the film is *not* merely 'to be analysed as mass culture and ideological effect'? What if 'film and society or cultural analysis' are *not* the only issue? What if we want our students to be able to respond intelligently and creatively to art, and to sense that there is a difference between good art and bad art? It is then, I think, that my quibble about the multiple camera shooting of a sitcom and my comment about the necessary compromises involved in actuality filming for documentaries and news items, become more significant, for there is no constraint to teach film art with examples whose conventions have already introduced expressive limitations, especially when we remember that this art is a century old, is not confined to popular television, and is international.

I do believe that the diverse forms of television constitute a sufficiently important part of the language that children should be conversant with them, and I have tried to suggest hints for several approaches in the selection of generic types above – plainly, my observations are not prescriptive or exhaustive. The sitcom, for example, would be worth comparative study, relating the English to the American product. The latter sometimes has the acerbity and the comic sense of domestic nightmare of *Fawlty Towers*, but whereas the characters in *Fawlty Towers* are consistent and sometimes poignant in their role-entrapped states, those in American sitcoms are more self-consciously role-playing actors, whose scripts are sweetened with whimsicality and a deadening dependence on the delivery of homilies. Rather like Coca Cola ads, American sitcoms need to reassure their audiences that families are warm and cuddly, and that unpleasant individuals can also be vulnerable and cute. Aside from rare exceptions like *Fawlty Towers*, however, English sitcoms re-use stereotyped family groupings without wit or purpose. (The single parent's adventures with growing children, a friend, a relative and a potential romance, or the separated/divorced couple's thwarted inclinations to reunite are two combinations which seem to crop up with dire regularity.) But this sort of comparative study, though it examines narrative types, soon becomes essentially sociological and inattentive to what *specifically* is being said and why – inattentive to 'art-speech'.

Another useful but limited approach is to note the differences between series and serials. The episodes in a *series* may be self-contained, though in practice there is often some chronological development to take advantage of the recurrence of the same set of characters. The *serial*, however, is obliged to remain an open form. Nevertheless, in practice it is composed of numerous sub-plots, each of which *will* have its closure; these are staggered so that enough will carry over. The serial, then, is perpetually reaching climaxes, yet at the same time deferring the major resolution which would bring the full cast to a sense of an ending at that same time. The serial, clearly, has affinities with the serial publication of the Victorian novel, also with radio serials, comic book serials, B movie serials, and picaresque and quest forms back to *The Odyssey*. It is neither new nor particularly challenging on television. It *could* be, though, and that is the value of the formulaic message in each of the types I've looked at: they could be modified, subverted, inverted, extended, improved, but only by the involvement of a creative intelligence disciplined in the aesthetic of film.

Sitcoms and soaps, because of their duration, have a potential for narrative depth, but usually lack the relevant aesthetic intelligence to exploit it; pop videos and commercials employ a sophisticated, highly literate film aesthetic to create stylish little narratives, usually of negligible substance. It's often remarked that the commercials are more pleasurable than the programmes, and it's often true, precisely because they use the dynamics of film with so much more assurance, but they do also illuminate the observation that skill and style are not enough. As in any art, technical skill, fluency with past styles and competence to work within a genre are admirable, but may leave unanswered such questions as 'Why are you saying this? To what end?'

I have not dealt with 'serious' drama on television, simply because it is less contentious – that is, it is nearly always unequivocally film, though, in England at least, film with an emphasis on dialogue, and dialogue too often with a theatrical ring. The author is usually the scriptwriter, whose collaborators tend to serve the script instead of letting the script serve amongst the other elements of the film.

Approaches based on generic types can reveal unexpected antecedents for their narrative forms. They can provide stimulus for creativity and the acquisition of a vocabulary and a set of styles, but they evade life, or touch it with the glance of cliché. They fail to engage the intellect or the emotions artistically, and in some cases set up slickness and fatuity as time-filling alternatives to such an engagement. This strikes me as a false economy, since we could be encouraging our students to encounter films which can teach the language equally well, while also managing to be about something – films whose art communicates more than a recording of an un-entered reality, and more than a glossy surface.

The argument for starting with what's on television is that that's where the children, and most of the adults, are. The argument for starting with genre study is that it occupies part of the domain of the common language, and part of the domain of the language heightened into art. The argument for moving on from the starting point is that the meaning we want to understand, the meaning we may aspire to make, the understanding we seek from the past to live in the present, are not all located on television programmes or in the recurring genres of the arts. The argument for moving on to consider authorship is not about retracing a theoretical debate, but about recovering what is most significant, most necessary, about film: its 'instinct for life'. I am appropriating the phrase from D. H. Lawrence, who used it, not of films, which he disliked, but of the novel, which could help you 'to develop an instinct for life . . . instead of a theory of right and wrong, good and bad'.[18]

We need to learn the language of film – techniques, skills, styles, conventions, devices, how this is done, as well as how it might have been done – so that we can fully experience its art, and much of its most interesting art is to be found in films made for the cinema. Video has given us extraordinary access to many of these films, enabling us to study them as closely as we would a novel or a poem – what is there to stop us? The lack of a film culture.

Notes and References

1   Anderson, L. (1981) *About John Ford*, London, Plexus, p. 85.
2   Leavis, F. R. (1976) *Thought, Words and Creativity*, London, Chatto and Windus, pp. 26–7.
3   Frye, N. (1973) *Anatomy of Criticism*, Guilford, Princeton University Press, pp. 33–5.
4   Leavis, F. R. (1975) *The Living Principle*, London, Chatto and Windus, p. 49.
5   Eliot, T. S. (1946) *Selected Essays*, London, Faber and Faber, p. 16.
6   Bantock, G. H. (1981) 'The Arts in Education', in Abbs, P. (Ed.) (1989) *The Symbolic Order*, Lewes, Falmer Press, p. 16.
7   Bakhtin, M. M. (1985) *The Dialogic Imagination*, Arlington, University of Texas Press, p. 105.
8   Aristotle, translated by Bywater, I. (1967) *On the Art of Poetry*, Oxford, Oxford University Press, p. 29.
9   See Sister Wendy Beckett (1989) 'Less is More', in *Modern Painters*, **2**, 3, pp. 118–19.
10 Kierkegaard, S. (1964) *Repetition*, London, Harper Torchbooks, pp. 52–3.
11 *Ibid.*, p. 34.
12 See Williams, R. (1974) *Television: Technology and Cultural Form*, London, Fontana, especially pp. 78–118.
13 Berger, J. (1969) *Permanent Red*, London, Methuen, p. 75.
14 Cassirer, E. (1972) *An Essay on Man*, Yale, Yale University Press, p. 145.
15 Sontag, S. (1967) *Against Interpretation*, London, Eyre and Spottiswoode, p. 14.
16 Alter, R. (1975) *Partial Magic*, Berkeley, University of California Press, p. 219–20.
17 Gledhill, C. (1981) 'Introduction' in Gledhill, C. (Ed) (1970) *Film and Media Studies in Higher Education*, London, BFI Education, quoted in Watson, R. (1987) 'Film is Dead: The Case for Resurrection', in Abbs, P. (Ed) (1987) *Living Powers*, Lewes, Falmer Press, p. 124.
18 Lawrence, D. H. 'Why the Novel Matters', *Phoenix*, London, Heinemann, p. 538.

Chapter 6

Film and the Narrative Arts

Introduction

Where is there a place for film, a major contemporary narrative art, on the curriculum? 'Narrative' suggests its affinities with literature, but 'contemporary' adverts us to the difficulty of locating film in a traditional syllabus, whose emphasis is on perceived continuities within established disciplines. My argument necessitates a digressive reflection on 'English': the difficulty of assimilating film, it seems to me, co-exists with the difficulty of assimilating the best of international contemporary literature. Therefore I propose a policy of greater openness, of inclusion rather than exclusion, focused on the concept of Narrative Arts, rather than the national tradition. In conclusion I offer outline readings of two commercial American films of the 1980s; these readings suggest that various kinds of background knowledge can be as necessary to an understanding of popular contemporary films as to established 'great' works in any of the arts, and that a prerequisite for an educated response to film art is an education in its traditions – significant periods, movements, conventions, styles, directors – its continuity with other narrative arts, and its presence in and impact on contemporary culture.

Medium, Language, Art

The reader of the foregoing chapters will probably be aware of a certain looseness in usage, or implied usage, as if medium, language and art could almost be synonyms. Language is a medium in which art may be made, but there are media whose languages do not make art (morse code, shorthand) and media which do not produce languages (telephone). In all cases the medium has an effect on the message it transmits, but in some the effect is an accepted limitation, in others a creative opportunity. Semiotics, by encouraging us to discern systems of signs and symbols permeating our cultures at all levels, has blurred distinctions between medium and language, while either recognizing that art is too problematical to be brought within a comprehensive system or attempting an inclusion that is necessarily reductive. The formulaic and structural conventions I have been describing could be construed as constituents of the medium or language, and only elements of an aesthetic in so far as my summary illustrations and comments justify that application. The major difficulty in writing about the art of film is that one has no adequate and direct means of quotation. Any argument therefore relies far too heavily on assumptions already shared with the reader. I may claim, for instance, that film is a major art without expecting much in the way of rigorous opposition, but is that because we all know, having experienced, major film works, or because we can see that the medium is ubiquitous and may therefore deserve to be studied?

To insist on making *art*, and not merely *language*, central to the case for film is to admit a necessary complication, because it depends on concrete evidence, which can be alluded to but not produced. Traces of some ancient languages exist, unread because scholarship has not yet successfully conjectured or deduced the pattern of relationships that would make deciphering possible. We have to translate in terms of concepts we can understand. And yet these traces *are* recognized as fragments from another language, even if we cannot make sense of it, because they include enough external features common to languages. (Series of pictograms, say, arranged vertically or horizontally.) The medium for the ideas, feelings, information or whatever, may be words or images; in another sense the medium may include ink, brush and paper, or incising tool and stone. Our aesthetic response to the finish or sophistication of the marks, and our awareness of the ease or difficulty with which those marks could have been made, may provide insight into the sophistication of the producing culture and the relative importance of the actual fragment. (A message incised in wet clay could perhaps be a shopping list; one chiselled from granite would probably be more significant.) But that is about as far as we can get without some fluency in the language. Where there is a language the *possibility* of an art exists, but not the proof. If we can speak of film as a language rather than merely a medium through which other languages pass, then we can admit its aesthetic potential, be we can only speak of its art when we have acquired enough fluency to refer to achieved and experienced works. Film cannot be claimed as an art, great or otherwise, simply because of its pervasive presence; there must be individual works, pointed to and subjected to the kind of attention that great art can sustain and give a purpose to.

Critically and theoretically film has had such attention. Its status as an art is not in doubt, but its presence in schools, colleges and universities is still minimal. This is not because film art can be dismissed, as G.H. Bantock dismisses television, as 'bad art', but it may well be due to certain ingrained educational habits.

Literacy, Culture and the Contemporary

When I think of the art film I do not think of England, and that is both typical and somewhat unfair. Through the pioneering efforts of Louis Le Prince and, later, the contributions of R. W. Paul, Birt Acres, Cecil Hepworth and others, England has as good a claim as France and America to a position of some importance in the birth and early history of the medium. The English work of such directors as Alfred Hitchcock, Carol Reed, Michael Powell, David Lean and Lindsay Anderson should suggest a distinctive, if diverse, national cinema. (Films by Lean and Powell, in particular, have been seminal influences on contemporary American directors like Martin Scorsese and Stephen Spielberg.) There have been important movements and genres – the documentaries nurtured by John Grierson in the thirties, the wartime documentaries of Humphrey Jennings, those of the Free Cinema movement in the fifties; the output associated with Korda and London Films, or with the Ealing Studios under Michael Balcon; the Hammer cycles; even, I suppose, the *Carry On* films. But while one may still occasionally hear that England produces the best television in the world – a sentiment that is often disputed, but not regarded as ludicrous – I don't think it has ever been said that England produces the best *films* in the world. The fact that many successful American films, especially those requiring advanced special effects, may turn out to be *made* largely in England, employing English craftsmen and artists, or the fact that, say, Stanley Kubrick has lived and worked in England for decades, is not sufficient for one to think of film as a central 'component of the national culture', to use Perry Anderson's phrase. The presence of the late Joseph Losey, Kubrick or Skolimowski isn't quite the same as Henry James, T. S. Eliot or Joseph Conrad.

When I think of the art film I think of Russian cinema and German Expressionist cinema in the 1920s, of Bunuel's first surrealist films, of Gance's ambitious undertakings, of Italian neo-realism in the forties, the Japanese cinema of Ozu, Mizoguchi and Kurosawa, of the French New Wave in the late 1950s and early sixties. I could go on to recite the standard 'key' names that would stand for the art and its importance, and the names and nations would not be English. This readiness to approve the art but see it as essentially foreign is, I think, a commonplace. Despite its massive influence on world cinema, despite the *politique des auteurs* and the English critics associated with *Sequence* and *Movie*, the American film is still generally perceived as popular entertainment, or an art tainted by mass production. The English film is the American film writ small. What this suggests to me is that the language of film art has continued to be curiously opaque – assumed to be transparent, even non-existent, when its verbal language is that of the audience, assumed to be legibly present when its verbal language is incomprehensible or interpreted through subtitles. As a consequence, even where film is recognized as an important art it has been easy to regard it as of marginal significance to our culture.

Because of its strength as a narrative art, film's closest affinity is with literary forms, especially the short story, the novel, the narrative poem and the play, but no decisive national continuity has emerged, so there has been no marriage, no general sense of a *need* to educate children and students in this art. It is not exactly philistinism or inertia that have to be overcome, though these elements are always with us, but a limiting institutionalized concept of education. Somehow we need to shape a discipline flexible enough to embrace and not be consumed by the insularity of our conventional approaches to the arts, to literature in particular.

Anyone who has attempted to broaden the syllabus in response to multi-culturalism, or in an attempt to introduce some of the classics of world literature in translation, or in response to some of the most interesting contemporary writing – anyone, that is, concerned with socially relevant reading and response, or with the best that's been known and thought *anywhere*, or with the challenges of late-twentieth century literature, anyone whose abiding interest is the vital art of literature rather than the national product – will be aware of the problem. There is a measure of freedom in the primary and secondary sectors, but as one moves towards final examinations, further and higher education, specialization becomes more apparent. Language courses enable students to experience some foreign literature, but English begins to shed the flavour of the contemporary in favour of the tradition. The national literature is part of our shared heritage, our identity; it happens also to be one of the great world literatures. There is no adequate argument for denying our children the means of access to it. On the other hand, there *is* a rational argument against the teaching of contemporary literature – because it is around us, addressing us now, we shouldn't actually *need* to be taught how to read it. (If we do, then presumably there's something wrong with us, or with it, that education isn't likely to fix.) The contemporary and 'third world' token selections I have seen on various syllabuses seem to be based on fairly traditional notions of excellence in the predominantly realist mode, rather than a perceived need to comprehend what modernism signified in relation to what preceded it, and what postmodernism has signified in relation to modernism. If Alan Wilde was correct in arguing that postmodernist literature has been a largely American phenomenon[1] then our slowness to relate to it has its usual excuse – simply refer back to the centrality of the national literature.

It would be convenient if I could share the dislike of some theorists for the notion of a great tradition, but the writers who constitute it, from Chaucer to Lawrence, have obviously given us something far more substantial than a prop for the dominant ideology. I am not English and feel no patriotic prompting to sustain a national literature, but I need, and think we all need this common heritage. Film, rather like contemporary literature from other cultures, and literature in translation, doesn't seem to flow naturally on from this model, and yet has had depressingly little impact as a discrete discipline.

Without being sanguine about its chances, I want to propose an alternative model:

English + Film = Narrative Arts

A literature with the longevity and richness of English literature could obviously be approached in a number of ways, from the chronological survey, which maps the historical territory without filling in much local detail and colour, to the specialized study of a single period, author or form of writing. Many syllabuses seem to be composed on a 'pick n' mix' principle, selecting half a dozen or a dozen exemplary highlights from the glorious heritage of some six hundred years, and offering them up by turns for close study. Even allowing for attention to the cultural climate within which each work was made, this approach has a curiously dislocating effect. Most people will end up having 'done' Shakespeare (but not necessarily Chaucer, Spenser, Wyatt) and Marlowe (but not necessarily Webster, Ford, Jonson) and Donne (but not necessarily Herbert and Marvell) and Milton (but not necessarily Swift, Pope, Johnson), Wordsworth (not necessarily Coleridge, Byron, Crabbe), Jane Austen (not necessarily Scott), the Brontës and George Eliot (but not necessarily Disraeli, Mrs Gaskell, Carlyle) . . . and so on. Enormous gaps, sometimes trivial, often not, are inevitable; higher education will fill in some of them, and self-education is more likely to supply one's real needs. Shakespeare, of course, just *has* to be there, but the other names, in and out of parentheses (and others not listed) seem to be regarded as more or less interchangeable, because all are approved and established facets of the great cultural jewel, the common heritage. So, you may never have 'done' Milton, but you've 'done' the Metaphysicals, so you know your way around; you have a blind spot for Dickens but you love Jane Austen; you've never read the Augustans but you have passages from *The Prelude* by heart, so, by and large, we speak the same language.

But there are other, perhaps more crucial gaps. I used to expect, when I taught 'A' level students, that we'd experience difficulties with some of T. S. Eliot's literary references and their contribution to the qualities of the poems. I used to expect that we'd have to struggle together with some of Sylvia Plath's obscurely personal images. I didn't expect, when teaching *Paradise Lost*, to find that some students had never previously encountered the story of Adam and Eve, the serpent, the forbidden fruit, had never heard of the Garden of Eden. Perhaps the example is extreme, but others could be found easily enough. Hellenic, Judaic, Arabic, Celtic – the myths and legends, the deep symbolic layers of our common culture are, simply, missing for many of us. The aspect of this disturbing gap that interests me here, however, it not how best to fill it (some of these things, I suspect, have died a natural death, and it would be both unnatural and unrewarding to attempt mouth-to-mouth at this late date), but its implication for how we might approach literature more openly.

The gap is exacerbated by an accidental insularity. I don't feel any need to justify the pleasures I get from reading Chaucer, or the desire to enable others to share those pleasures. *The Knight's Tale* seems to me superior to what I've read of Boccaccio's *Il Teseida*, but I don't think it's necessary to go to that source before one can understand the tragic vision underlying Chaucer's chivalric romance. (Though it helps to deepen one's appreciation of Chaucer to go on to read *The Miller's Tale*.) Similarly, one doesn't *have* to read Holinshed, Greene's romances, Whetstone and Cinthio, or Plutarch's *Lives* in order to read Shakespeare, because the sources are transformed and improved. What *is* worth registering, though, is that these quintessentially English writers did draw, openly and extensively, of whatever happened to appeal to them, and what appealed – what was, obviously, available – was often from Europe, or the rediscovered classical past, sometimes in the original language, sometimes in translation. And that pattern of borrowing extends throughout the literature and is one of its great strengths (how much smaller Blake and Wordsworth would be if they had deliberately deafened themselves to the sounds and potentialities of revolutions beyond England's shores).

In English we look at the work produced by English writers, but these English writers were not themselves so insular: they looked outward at the contemporary world and drew in what they could use. Their particular sources may or may not still matter to us; their openness certainly should, for they, as T. S. Eliot said, 'are that which we know'. And, surely, we know them and find them *worth* knowing because they are the truly educated men and women of their respective ages. We need an education that can enable us to know their work as that which lives in and converses with our present; so we need an education that admits a balanced interest in the contemporary. The parochial triviality and adolescent realism of much contemporary English literature does not present a particularly stimulating context, but if we are going to respond to the contemporary then 'English' is already too narrow an invitation; even 'literature' may not be sufficiently open.

The only real context – perhaps I mean arena - in which we can meet the art of the past is the one where we find ourselves alive. I don't mean to imply that we should attempt to translate everything that might constitute 'the present' into the controlling matter of education, but I do mean that any introduction to the great art of the past is necessarily impoverished if it has not been made vivid by a lively commitment to the art of our own time. And the art that addresses us most significantly in our own time will not necessarily have been made in England. In short, it seems to me likely that we will bring more to and gain more from our meeting with Chaucer, Shakespeare, Donne, Wordsworth, George Eliot, Dickens and Lawrence if, instead of supposing our contemporaries are only, let's say, Margaret Drabble, William Golding, Dennis Potter and Martin Amis, we also admit Nadine Gordimer, R. K. Narayan, Donald Barthelme, John Barth, John Gardner, Milan Kundera, Gabriel Garcia Marquez and, for the sake of economy to curtail the list here, Italo Calvino.

'English' is too limiting a term if what we are concerned with is a living tradition of literature. But 'literature', too, is limiting where what we really want to effect is a stimulating introduction to the extraordinarily fecund art of storytelling, which joins literary arts but continues making connections with *other* arts – most promisingly, with film.

I am not interested in distinctions between high and low culture, but I think that those who dismiss manifestations of popular entertainment *tout court* are as misguided as those who embrace them. Some art is more difficult to recognize because it is in a popular mode. Some is more difficult because its matter is original or complex. Education is about helping as many people as can be helped – as many as discover they want to be helped – to overcome the obstacles that the *lack* of education puts in their way. Its process is never completed, but is marked rather by the satisfaction of achievements that nourish further aspirations, whose goal is not, cannot be, social superiority but, I think, a kind of communality of understanding. As I have probably indicated, for me the films of John Ford and Andrei Tarkovsky are summits of film art. If, after years of primary and secondary education, after further years of higher education, our English graduates are still not equipped to 'read' these films seriously enough to agree or disagree intelligently, then the system has failed to educate them in what art is, what moral poetry is, what narrative is.

Film, as much as the traditional forms of literature, is the great contemporary narrative art whose presence should be part of the context within which Chaucer's narrative art continues to live. But within the scope of this book 'great' and 'art' remain, stubbornly, little more than assertions. All I can attempt, in the few remaining pages, are some specific readings that touch on genre and authorship and may suggest one or two ways of proceeding further.

Genre and the Auteur

I once made some sarcastic comments to my grandmother about a film we were watching and she, to my dismay, was deeply offended by them. My grandmother, a benign, tolerant and good-humoured woman, was a Baptist. The film was one of the Hollywood biblical epics popular in the fifties. I think I was responding to the rigid camerawork, stilted acting and wooden dialogue, though I do remember remarking, with callow assurance, that the film was actually irreligious to the point of blasphemy, that *it*, and not my criticism, was what was offensive. My grandmother was not persuaded. As far as she was concerned the film treated an important subject, and that was enough to validate it. In belittling the film I was belittling the Bible and her faith. She rarely went to the cinema and had no interest in whether or not the film was an art, but she knew when it could be taken seriously. So did the nuns at the convent where my wife was educated: they told all their pupils not to see *The Robe*. I remember, too, my naïve surprise when, in the sixties, I went to see the latest Pasolini and noticed among the usual student audience an unprecedented row of nuns. But the film was *The Gospel According to St Matthew*.

The supposed seriousness of films with a religious subject can be extended to historical reconstructions, biographies of notable politicians, scientists and artists, adaptations of classic novels and, of course, Shakespeare, and it will always be the case that the seriousness of the subject does not guarantee the seriousness of the film (with the possible exception of news footage). Equally, the triviality of the subject does not guarantee the triviality of the film. The subject is not likely to be altogether irrelevant, but as a criterion of value it may well be misleading. Depending on its treatment, an apparently trivial subject may be a consummate work of art while an apparently serious subject may be risibly inept. However obvious this is, the history of the arts is littered with the débris of works that were applauded in their day. Retrospectively we think we have learned to see more clearly, and yet many of us would still dismiss television as bad art, and assume that the popularity and accessibility of many American films removes them from serious consideration. On occasion I have heard children grumbling, before a film starts, 'It's not *silent*, is it?' Or, not *foreign*, not with *subtitles*, not *black and white*! These prejudices are no more silly than Professor Bantock's animadversions against the mass media. Nor are they sillier than those – as likely to be articulated by academics as children or the general public – that complacently, even proudly, dismiss entire genres ('I never watch crime/horror/science fictions films'; 'I can't stand musicals'; 'Isn't there something disturbing about anyone who likes Westerns?').

The *politique des auteurs*, initiated by the critics associated with *Cahiers du Cinema* in the fifties, was an attempt to retrieve from the anonymity of the Hollywood studio system the director, as author of a distinctive *oeuvre*. The director was usually under contractual obligation to a studio, and was therefore less likely than some European directors to be involved with a film from its conception to its completion. He might periodically work on cherished personal projects, but would also be assigned to direct pictures which were already scripted, cast and budgeted. These assignments could be congenial, well suited to the interests and talents of the director. They could also be uncongenial, but if a director was deemed an *auteur*, then *all* his films were worthy of study. A positive effect of *auteurism*, then, was convincingly to relocate 'seriousness' well away from those prestigious productions with worthy subjects, in an aesthetics of treatment – characteristic stylistic motifs, recurring themes and emphases – which might cut across different genres and different studio house-styles to reveal layers of interest residing in previously ignored B pictures as well as commercially successful but critically underrated A features.

A handful of directors had always received a measure of critical recognition – and, more importantly, had influenced the great Russian, Japanese and European directors – among them Griffith, Vidor, Hitchcock, Lubitsch and Ford. But the *Cahiers* critics, and those associated with *Sequence* and *Movie* in England, and Andrew Sarris in America, helped to awaken interest in much less celebrated figures, such as Edgar Ulmer, Samuel Fuller, Nicholas Ray, William Wellman, Raoul Walsh, Frank Tashlin, and so on. What, in their enthusiasm, they tended to underestimate was the contribution of the language, in its network of conventions, established practices, generic structures – their *auteurs* emerged *despite* rather than in collaboration with the studio system. Raoul Walsh, for example, was already a prolific and established director when he made his first film for Warners, *The Roaring Twenties*, in 1939. Hal Wallis was an executive producer. The following extracts are from Wallis's memos to Walsh during the shooting of this film:

> . . . I don't like your [camera] setups; those straight-on two-shots, and individual close-ups are going to get monotonous and make for choppy cutting . . . Get a little composition into the thing and a little grouping so that we don't have to cut from one big close-up to another and just have a series of portraits on the screen with the people speaking the lines . . .
>
> . . . When Cagney comes into the church steps, instead of that close shot on the stairs where he runs into it and then runs up a few steps and then falls down, pick Cagney up down the street and pan with him as he staggers into the shot of the church steps, let him stagger up against a pillar on the left of the church, where we will distinctly see that it is a church, then let Cagney go up two or three steps and stagger half way across the stairs and fall down. Then cut to Gladys George, picking her up down the street where you picked Cagney up, and pan her into the shot on the church steps and let her go in and kneel down beside Cagney as she did in the other stuff . . .
>
> . . . At the end of the scene from her close-up, after she reads the line 'He used to be a big shot,' pull back and up into a long shot, so that we leave the three small figures on the church steps, the girl holding Cagney in her lap, the cop standing alongside, and we can use that for our fadeout shot . . . [2]

The *effective* director here is Wallis rather than Walsh, and his directions cover actors, compositions, camera movements, editing, narrative pace and tone. (Paradoxically, this example may help to show how the extraordinary Turkish film, *Yol*, could be accepted as a work by Yilmaz Güney despite the fact that he was serving a nineteen-year prison sentence while it was being shot – he was able to escape to edit it.)

The word *auteur* applied to a film maker has misleading connotations; 'director' is more accurate; nevertheless, although the *auteurists* were sometimes incorrect in seeing as directorial felicities touches that had been contributed by others, or which were inherent in the language or the iconography of the genre, their policy did help to make Hollywood films approachable. By the late sixties, however, the gaps and inadequacies in this approach led to a new interest in genre study, which seemed to be capable of filling in the gaps by studying many of the films that *auteur* study had left out of account. By the eighties the gaps and inadequacies of genre study were also becoming apparent, and it was realized that the *auteur* could still be a useful 'site of meaning'. Another area, which had been progressing rather quietly through the sixties and seventies, began at last to flourish more openly as critics and theorists noticed that scholarly historical research could modify and enrich their understanding.

In the light of these developments, I want to look at a couple of popular Hollywood films of the eighties, assuming that you have seen them or can easily obtain them on video. The first, *Down and Out in Beverly Hills*, (1986), could be called a social comedy, the second, *Witness*, (1985), a crime thriller. These designations would be implied by trailers, posters and the machinery of publicity – it's very difficult to attend a film about which one has *no* preconceptions – and would therefore prepare the audience for a particular kind of experience, which the titles would reinforce or even focus more clearly. The single word 'witness' in the context of a crime story suggests quite specifically what kind of thriller this will be: the 'witness' will witness a crime and become the criminal's potential victim. The residual legal and theological meanings are not necessarily implied by the genre, and may add density to the film if taken up. But I will return to *Witness* shortly.

Down and Out in Beverly Hills

'Down and out' could be associated with boxing, but that's unlikely because boxing films are made infrequently and this genre more or less excludes them anyway; nevertheless, the metaphor is apt enough, since a down and out is, conventionally, a loser, a tramp, an outsider. There may be an intentional reference to Orwell, in which case the predicate 'Beverly Hills', rather than 'Paris and London' gains a parochial irony. Beverly Hills is hardly a great capital city, and has none of the complex cultural accretions we can associate with a metropolis. For most of us it probably means America, modernity, conspicuous wealth and superficiality. A film about being down and out *there* will inevitably use the rags and riches contrast to assess materialistic values, but the examination will almost certainly be comic because Beverly Hills does not signify what is representative or typical about America. It is American success caricatured by excess (one might usefully contrast the documentation of Paris, as experienced by the impecunious musician in Eric Rohmer's first feature film, *Le Signe du Lion*, 1959), and the values that one might wish to criticize are already so manifest that a serious dramatic exposure would be redundant and bathetic.

Without knowing anything of the author(s), without having seen any of the film, one knows what to expect – skilful repetition, confirmation of one's anticipations and, perhaps, a freshness in the treatment of local detail that will be enough to provide novel thematic variation – the unexpected – in place of anything original or disturbing. The film will attempt to entertain and flatter, reinforce standard attitudes by offering a mild critique of materialism while at the same time indulging the escapist desire to wallow visually in luxurious surroundings.

Colour is muted in the opening shots of an anonymous but evidently depressed downtown area on a Christmas morning. A dishevelled tramp, immediately recognizable as the physically imposing star, Nick Nolte, is discovered pushing his meagre trolley of belongings. There are a couple of shots of 'real' down and outs, one of whom also pushes his belongings, and the purpose for their inclusion seems to be merely to add veracity to Nolte's wardrobe and props. The name Beverly Hills first appears, no doubt significantly, on the side of a waste skip, inside which Nolte is foraging for scraps for his dog. Having registered the shock that there is dispossession in Beverly Hills, we are quickly moved on – before the credits have finished – to the mansions, swimming pools, fine lawns and palm-lined, sunny avenues we expected.

Nolte's dog deserts him. He weights his pockets with ornamental stones and, aware that he is being observed, jumps into a private swimming pool. The observer, Richard Dreyfuss, rescues him from drowning and makes him a household guest. The ensuing narrative simply uses the figure of the tramp as catalyst. He is flexible enough to provide whatever is missing in the lives of the wealthy family members (and their maid), and can even help the family dog, which had been seeing a psychiatrist. He reminds the father, whose wealth is in the manufacture of coat hangers, of his hippy ideals of the sixties, offers therapy and sex to the mother, confidence to the confused son, sex to the flighty daughter, sex and political awakening to the maid, and he shares meals with the dog. Eventually he is revealed as something of a charlatan, though his 'cures' work, and he leaves, but in the closing sequence he returns, to everyone's satisfaction, and in the last shot, when everyone has gone back towards the house, we see the father looking thoughtful. After all, in some ways the tramp has been disruptive; it is also the case, however, that he has been absorbed into the bourgeois world of the father. Though there was never much of a contest, the Dreyfuss character has really won, the family's neurotic problems having turned out to need only minor adjustment, their wealth built on coat hangers remaining intact, their general decency and tolerance having re-emerged as sustaining forces.

It's a genial entertainment, very smoothly shot and edited, full of bright clean surfaces, as bland as a family sitcom, with perhaps a slightly more convincing theme of fundamental human frailty and goodness. It could be read as a gentle apologia for affluence, a typical, rather impersonal commerical product of the eighties, when a number of adult movies explored middle-class domestic mores in a television style, with attention to dialogue and star performances rather than camera, lighting, editing, etc.

But if *Down and Out in Beverly Hills* is read as a director's film does it become more interesting aesthetically? It might, if only in the sense Robin Wood adverts to in his 'Reflections on the Auteur Theory':

> A great artist's failures are often interesting, certainly, but the interest lies
> in the light they throw on and the context they provide for the successes:
> that is to say, it is a passing interest. My interest in *Sergeant York*, for

example, ceased when I felt I had understood its relation to Hawks's successful works – which is another way of saying, when I had accounted for its failure. I have seen *Rio Bravo* something like twenty times, and would see it again tomorrow; I have seen *Sergeant York* thrice, and have no particular desire to repeat the experience. One can blame Hawks or not for the failure of *Sergeant York*: either, 'the material was uncongenial, Hawks was ill-at-ease', or 'the failure of the film indicates clearly Hawks's limitations'. Both seem to me true; it is the latter that gives the film its passing interest.[3]

Paul Mazursky's films do exhibit some consistencies: they are personal projects, films that he wants to make, and personal too in that they usually explore, or parade, contemporary themes which can be related to his own experience. He deals with the emotional problems of well-to-do Americans who are fond of articulating their anguish with a candour that is sometimes facile rather than painful. This peculiarly personal cinema should make him an *auteur*, but doesn't, because he has no sense of film, only a sensitivity to actors. Several of his films have flopped, but several have been enormous commercial successes. One could say he has maintained his artistic integrity, and some critics esteem his work for its idiosyncratic performances (these are 'characters', rather than stock characters) and serious subject matter: coping with permissiveness, creative blocks, old age, divorce, and so on. But these qualities encourage one to read the films sociologically, for their reflections of little aspects of society at a given time. And documentary value, in an artwork, implies that the artist is both sufficiently representative and self-effacing to be an *accurate* mirror. For greater insight one requires somewhat more of the artist. What is unusual about Mazursky is his infatuation with European cinema. Unlike Woody Allen, Mazursky has not been able to absorb and transform the influence.

In the early sixties, before his four-year stint as a writer on 'The Danny Kaye Show', he wrote a short film parody of *Last Year at Marienbad*, called *Last Year at Malibu*. His second film as a director, *Alex in Wonderland*, (1970), was about a successful film director (Mazursky had become successful after *Bob and Carol and Ted and Alice* the previous year) who can't decide what to make next, and who fantasizes. Fellini popped up in the film, which was clearly indebted to *8½*. A decade later, in *Willie and Phil*, Mazursky transposed the *ménage à trois* of Truffaut's *Jules et Jim* to Greenwich Village in the seventies. Both films had perceptive and sensitive moments, but both seemed narcissistic, self-indulgent and pretentious, their director locked in a dream of sixties European art-films.

Down and Out in Beverly Hills, then, invites a third kind of comparative reading, one that takes into account its apparent genre and its director's interests, a reading of historical sources and influences. The credits acknowledge that the film is based on *Boudu sauvé des eaux*, the play by Rénè Fauchois. Jean Renoir's *Boudu sauvé des eaux*, (1932), was of course based on the same play:

As usual, I had made great changes in the original story. Fauchois, the author, took this in very bad part and threatened to have his name removed from the credits. Thirty years later, upon seeing the film again, he was astonished by its enthusiastic reception. He was brought onto the stage, and the ovation he received caused him to forget my unfaithfulness to his story.[4]

Renoir's 'changes' were radical, as Alexander Sesonske suggests:

The play chronicles the successful attempt of a left-bank bookseller, M. Lestingois, to make a contented bourgeois of the uncouth tramp, Boudu, he has rescued from drowning. The author, Fauchois, had played Lestingois in the Paris production of the play. But Renoir's adaptation, with Michel Simon turned loose in the role of Boudu, transforms the film into an anarchic romp with Boudu as its center, a work very far in spirit from the triumph of middle-class culture presented on the stage.[5]

The film was unpopular initially, and was not released in England until 1965, when I saw it for the first time and was enthralled by its rough freshness and the appalling/appealing contemporaneity of Boudu, 'the perfect hippy', as Renoir later called him. *Boudu* was released in America in 1967, and at last discovered an enthusiastic audience. It was part of the sixties cinema that Mazursky is so fond of, yet in *Down and Out in Beverly Hills* he reverts to Fauchois' original intention: middle-class values are vindicated, Boudu is made a bourgeois. It is not that Renoir's Lestingois is unsympathetic, but that Renoir's tolerance is far more complex. He can make Lestingois humane, cultivated, enlightened, and still reveal the emptiness of his life. He can make Boudu a simpleton with disgusting habits, who nevertheless embodies – and finally retains – a natural and enviable freedom and innocence. Renoir's film has a liberating, subversive power quite alien to Mazursky's. Mazursky has to make his tramp acceptably literate, sophisticated, and a drop-out by choice, so that he can be a catalyst who merely adjusts lives a little, so that he can be essentially the same, only free from neurotic traits.

Another, unacknowledged influence on *Down and Out in Beverly Hills* is suggested by Mazursky's fascination with sixties cinema, by the attractive colour and smoothness of his film, and by certain internal changes, such as making Dreyfuss a businessman rather than a cultured bookseller, and extending the family to include two children. In 1966 Pier Paulo Pasolini visited America and was profoundly affected by the experience. Two years later he wrote the novel and at the same time made the film, *Teorema*, the latter intended to have been shot in New York. The catalyst in *Teorema* is supposed to be God, rather than a tramp, but he functions in the same way. In the form of a sixties icon of potentially depraved innocence, Terence Stamp, God enters the household of an industralist and seduces the father, mother, both children, and the servant. Perhaps Pasolini borrowed inadvertently from Renoir. It would seem to me an extraordinary coincidence if Mazursky had not borrowed from Pasolini.

Is *Down and Out in Beverly Hills* a different film now? I don't think my suggested readings can have made it a *better* film; for me they have made it more irritating and cowardly, a film that makes deliberate compromises to be palatable, a film that is knowing in a very negative way. But this is neither an argument against commercial cinema nor against the *auteur*. This particular commercial, and very successful, product, has a clear relationship to more distinguished works, and an awareness of their precedence can sharpen our response from a condescending acceptance of *Down and Out* as an effective enough film on its own, fairly anonymous level, to a precise dissatisfaction with its specific form and tone, which are the responsibility, not of the studios or any inevitable inferiority in American films, but of the limited sensibility of the director, a Beverly Hills resident.

(It is worth noting that remakes of important films, even those as individual as Renoir's, can be done intelligently enough to stand on their own, or to make comparative study reveal the particular strengths, as well as weaknesses, of the directors. Renoir's *La Chienne*, (1932) and *Le Bête Humaine*, (1938), were remade in Fritz Lang's American period as *Scarlet Street*, (1946) and *Human Desire*, (1954); *The Diary of a Chambermaid*, (1946), in Renoir's American period, was remade in 1964 as *Le Journal d'une Femme de Chambre*, by Luis Bunuel; *Les Bas-Fonds*, (1936), based on Gorky's *The Lower Depths*, was filmed by Kurosawa in 1957.)

One scene in *Down and Out in Beverly Hills* nicely reveals Mazursky's debt to Renoir and his unwillingness to assimilate it adequately. Dreyfuss, having cleaned up Nolte, proudly takes him out to dine. Nolte recognizes another tramp, passing by on the sidewalk, and invites him to join them. Dreyfuss, after a moment's hesitation, seconds the invitation. Other diners may be shocked, but Dreyfuss has demonstrated his liberality. The tramp, however, declines to eat with them and, after a brief conversation with Nolte, gets up to leave. As he passes other tables he steals rolls, blatantly and, as he had been offered food, unnecessarily. The action is perverse and unsettling. In *Boudu sauvé des eaux* by Renoir, that is how Boudu behaves, repeatedly. But here the inspired moment is effectively sanitized by being given to a tramp whom we don't have to accommodate for long – he is about all that remains of the spirit of Boudu in this film. Personal projects are no guarantee of the seriousness of a film.

Witness

Witness was not conceived by its director. According to the reviewer in *Sight and Sound* 'it reached him third hand, via producer Edward Feldman and star Harrison Ford, the latter exercising his by now well established prerogative to choose his own director'.[6] In outline it is a conventional thriller with pleasantly old-fashioned aesthetic and moral values. It is the kind of film that dozens of contract directors working for the studios in the forties could have turned out efficiently – a model of the system at its best, with capable star performers, a proficient crew, a solidly plotted story and a humane message. Does it become anything more by being a Peter Weir film? Or, to put it another way, would it have provided more or less the same experience had it been assigned to Paul Mazursky?

Plot and characterization are familiar and cross several genre boundaries. The tough, dedicated, honest cop, capable of using force where necessary, but also capable of courtesy and sensitivity, is at least as old as Chaucer's 'verray, parfit gentil knight'. He is wedded to 'Trouthe and honour, fredom and curteisie', so although he might find a suitably ideal love, she will quite possibly die violently, thus precipitating his violent retributive mission (*The Big Heat*, (1953)), or be left because his journey is unfinished (*Shane*, (1953), *My Darling Clementine*, (1946)). The hero may discover that organized crime is not restricted to the 'underworld' but has corrupted politicians, judges, journalists and the police (*Scarface*, (1932), *His Girl Friday*, (1940), *The Big Heat*, (1953), *Point Blank*, (1967), *The Ipcress File*, (1965), *Serpico*, (1973), *Defence of the Realm*, (1985)). If the hero is wounded or hunted he will often take refuge with ordinary, innocent people, who may be put at risk as a result: he will be willing to sacrifice himself if necessary, to protect them (some Westerns and thrillers, any number of war films, especially if dealing with resistance movements).

The witness as potential victim is again a popular theme that provides the narrative basis for many plots. The witness is usually either unaware of the threat, or vulnerable, (or both). Often a woman, whom the hero will save at the climatic moment (he is too late in De Palma's *Blow Out*), the witness is more rarely a child (*The Window*, a B feature made in 1949, is probably the best known example), or an incapacitated adult (*Rear Window*). *Witness* had not only the child, but also the woman (his widowed mother) and the wounded man (the honest cop/knight who hides out with the family, falls in love with the woman, but leaves at the end).

The poignant plausibility of that departure is at the heart of the film's success, for the thriller elements are carefully structured to force a confrontation between two cultures that cannot be fused together without destruction. *Witness* begins in fields, a line of people emerging through the crops, then more, with horses and buggies, all on their way to a meeting, women in bonnets, men in broadrimmed hats, simple contrasts of black and white. A title informs us that this is Pennsylvania in 1984, so we are not actually in the past but amongst a community which has renounced some of the manifestations of the present, maintaining traditions of simplicity, piety and hard rural work. These are the Amish, a pacific people, who do not wish to be contaminated by the technologies and violence of the urban world with which we are more familiar. The honest detective, played by Harrison Ford, is committed to the struggle for law and order in the urban world – without it he would lose his identity as a knight. The woman, Kelly McGillis, could not leave the Amish community without questioning its values and losing her own identity. People here function and are defined socially, and love does not prove stronger than rootedness.

However selective and idealized it might be, the view of the Amish presented in *Witness* is attractive. Functional simplicity in tools, furniture and fittings had been fashionable since the sixties; the film led to a fashion for Amish-style clothes. But despite the nostalgia and novelty, the representation of this community was not something new. Stern, patriarchal figures whose authority can be benign are familiar icons. The Amish were represented as non-violent and vulnerable to gangsters in Richard Fleischer's 1955 film, *Violent Saturday*, whose climax hinged on whether or not the family would have to resort to violence; but Quakers have much the same role and dilemma in William Wyler's *Friendly Persuasion*, in 1956, and so do the Mormons in John Ford's *Wagonmaster*, (1950). The Amish are simply the latest representatives of pastness, otherness and spiritual integrity. As in *Wagonmaster*, they are treated with dignity and respect, but allowed moments of irreverence and humour so that they will be sympathetically human.

The Amish in *Witness* do not resort to violence themselves, though violence occurs. Harrison Ford tricks one of the rogue-cops into a grain elevator and releases the shoot, so that the man is suffocated and drowned in good honest Amish grain. This device has been used elsewhere a couple of times, and derives ultimately from the drowning in white flour in Carl Dreyer's 1931 *Vampyr*. In a nice touch the Amish themselves become witnesses, surrounding the man who has the power to kill the boy who was the initial witness to a killing. One witness is vulnerable; a community of witnesses overwhelms violence.

What, then, might be the director's contribution to a film which, in many respects, we have already seen? Given the plot, the themes and conventions, what can particularize this film? What most people seem to have responded to is the sincerity and warmth of the performances, an atmosphere of menace that *is* menacing because of the delicacy with which moods and relationships are evoked.

I don't know how much of this can be ascribed to the director. Some, but not all of it, is conveyed in the dialogue, some in costume and sets and locations, some in Jarre's music score, some in John Seale's beautiful photography, and some in the leading performances. But similar costumes, sets and locations have been used elsewhere without being so effective, and the same could be said of Maurice Jarre's film scores. There is equally brilliant cinematography, by Nestor Almendros, in Terence Malick's rather phony *Days of Heaven*, (1978). Prior to this film, Harrison Ford had not revealed such wit and sensitivity, even if his charismatic presence suggested the capacity. Almost by a process of elimination, then, we reach the director, but none of Peter Weir's previous films has the expositional clarity of *Witness*; they are strikingly evocative, have delicate moods and a sense of unseen menace, but the narrative meanders or seems muddled. Not exactly empty, the earlier films are more than stylistic exercises – *The Last Wave*, (1977), at least, has a dramatic power lacking in *Gallipoli*, (1981) and *The Year of Living Dangerously*, (1982) – but frustratingly less than cohesive works. Harrison Ford's decision to employ Weir seems apposite, however, because as well as an ability to communicate dramatic intensity Weir has retained a way of perceiving the delicate mysteriousness of the ordinary, and this, although it drifts into vagueness in *Picnic at Hanging Rock*, (1975), adds a subtle warmth and innocence to the solidly worked-out scheme of *Witness*.

I'll try to illustrate this from a sequence of a little over three minutes, where the Amish boy has been brought into the police station to attempt an identification of the murderer. An affectionate rapport with the Ford character has already been established. We know the boy likes to wander around curiously, and we have been acclimatized to point-of-view shots and camera set-ups at his height. The scene is an important one, because the identity of the killer is discovered, but it is treated without sensationalism and, on first viewings, appears low-key and naturalistic. There is no significant dialogue in the sequence.

We open close on the man and boy, leafing through mugshots at a desk. They seem tired, as if they have been at it for some time already. Ford has his arm around the back of the boy's chair in a relaxed protective gesture. He take a phone call and this distraction is enough for the boy, hesitantly, to get up and begin to wander.

American police stations are often presented as dark and cluttered, rather chaotic, and filled with eccentrics being noisily booked. (The television series *Hill Street Blues* mimics the stereotyped presentation effectively.) This environment is busy, but seems a bright and reasonably efficient office, clean and well-lit. A woman beckons to the boy and offers him a biscuit, commenting that he is pleasant; then a man who looks a little like Ford beckons him, and there's a quick cutaway to the handcuffs that secure him to his chair as he tugs at them and grunts.

The boy wanders on, camera at his level so we see adult torsos passing by, occasionally a friendly hand patting his head. Throughout this the ambient noise of the office is naturalistic, if slightly muted. The boy bends to study the contents of a trophy cabinet. His attention is drawn to a cutting in the cabinet, a newspaper report about a narcotics officer's recent success. From the boy's point-of-view we begin a slow zoom in on the photograph. It is the killer. We see the boy's wide eyes, then the continuing zoom, and a sustained, eerie note comes on to the soundtrack. Gradually the ambient noise is faded out completely. There's a medium shot of the boy, still bending towards the cabinet, but looking back over his shoulder. The reverse shot shows Ford still on the phone. The rhythmically binding exchange of shots – the photograph, the boy and Ford – continues under the sustained high note of sound. When Ford notices the boy his reactions are slowed down almost imperceptibly. In the surrounding silence he moves in continued slow motion towards the cabinet, and crouches beside the boy, who stands straight and becomes taller in the frame than Ford. Slight physical movements become, in close-up, a rhythmic ballet that works closely with the editing to involve us emotionally in this unspoken realization of danger. The boy points his finger, and Ford nods and gently covers his hand. No-one else must know, of course. The safe, pleasant atmosphere of the office was deceptive. Anyone around them could be involved with the corrupt narcotics officer. The strongest feeling communicated in the scene is the tenderness evoked by facial expressions, eye contact and the protective physical gestures. Yet the naturalness has been created in part by quite unnatural manipulations of film speed and soundtrack. Release from this intimate tension is provided by the abrupt cut at the end of the sequence, to a rush of movement back at the apartment.

I am conscious of the inadequacy of this description, which obviously cannot substitute for a close viewing of the sequence. But stills would not help either, since the effectiveness depends on attentiveness to rhythms of movement and sound, on the continuous flow of narrative. It can't be conveyed by the script, couldn't be acted on a stage, or communicated by the camera alone, or the sound alone, or the sets or the editing alone. It is the narrative art of cinema that coordinates *all* these elements to communicate economical descriptions of place and character, subtle nuances of mood, dramatic tension and the complexity or directness of the developing story. The sequence is a modest enough example, but could nevertheless serve as a model of how carefully the elements of a film are brought together, how conscious and deliberate an art it is. It may also stand for *why* anyone should bother to learn the techniques and conventions, for here the form is not obtrusive, it *in*forms the content and touches life.

We might stand back from the film as a whole and say that a greater film maker, like John Ford, would have been able to differentiate the individual members of the Amish community, show a wider range of their activities and thus give a deeper sense of lived reality to their world, but if students can read sequences like the above they should be able to respond to work of greater density.

Almost any film can be watched and, in a sense, understood with no training at all, but, as all literary students know, the understanding that comes from a first reading is rarely complete. And, just as when reading a novel no-one would suppose its essence lay in the conversations, and that the descriptions, comments, reports and so on could be ignored, so, when reading a film one needs to learn to read the *whole* film, to see how the lighting on a face might ironize what is being said, how a camera movement might suggest a subtler mood than the positioning of the actors or their exchange of dialogue might be indicating.

Bunuel says this: 'To be a good director in the cinema is the same as being a good writer — to have clear ideas, to know what you want to say and to say it as directly as possible'.[7]

Renoir says this: 'I got nearer and nearer to the ideal method of directing, which consists in shooting a film as one writes a novel'.[8] And this: 'In my view cinema is nothing but a new form of printing – another form of the total transformation of the world through knowledge'.[9] And this: 'Everything that moves on the screen is cinema'.[10]

Film is a collaborative narrative art which we can only read in terms of specific works. What we bring to our reading is our experience (including our own film-making) and our capacity to read, both of which are educable in terms of history, tradition, convention, technology, technique, style, genre and authorship, which may then be aligned with whichever discourses we find congenial or unavoidable.

This book is intended merely, and without condescension, as a primer in some of these areas; necessarily it leaves much still to be said, but the general drift has, I hope, been clear enough: it is not enough to incorporate film with other media as a somewhat elderly and soon disposable relative. Film, which includes television and video, is a contemporary narrative art whose place on the curriculum is amongst all the arts, and whose most valuable place would be in a newly constituted field of narrative studies.

Conclusion

Whether or not our children will learn to use the language of film for reflection, expression and the considered discourse of art depends entirely on the recognition by teachers of its importance. Exercises in storyboarding, scripting, planning the shot and the sequence extend narrative skills, develop creative awareness and a critical faculty. The abilities to make films on video and to read films sensitively do not threaten verbal skills, or the child's capacity to draw, act, dance or make music. Each discipline is enabling in its own right, but by itself is unnaturally fragmented from the culture it both springs from and exists in. Together, their affinities and differences forming part of the emerging understanding, the arts are mutually enriching, and offer our children an education of formidable integrity and power. But it is up to teachers, not government ministries, to recognize the need, take the action and, by their example, prove the case for the arts. In the current climate acquiescence is an invitation to Thomas Gradgrind:

> You can only form the minds of reasoning animals upon Facts: nothing else will ever be of any service to them.[11]

Dickens opposed Fancy to Fact, and Fancy triumphed. But hard times are here again, and again the arts need a vigorous and sustained defence. Those arts whose place is less than assured, such as film, need the passionate advocacy of men and women who *know* that the creative intelligence, nourished from infancy, is of the essence of human life. In the short term one has to look for 'slots' where film can be introduced, across the curriculum, in General Studies, Integrated Arts courses, where they exist, in Media Education, obviously, and in English; but these are the compromises of expediency, and the goal is more ambitious. The language and art of film have expressed the twentieth century more widely, and perhaps more fully, than any other language or art. It really is time that all our schools, colleges and universities notice this and discover that it *is* possible to respond.

Notes and References

1   Wilde, A. (1981) *Horizons of Assent, Modernism, Postmodernism and the Ironic Imagination*, London, John Hopkins, p. 12.
2   Behlmer, R. (1987) *Inside Warner Bros. (1935–1951)*, London, Weidenfeld, pp. 93–4.
3   Wood, R. (1976) *Personal Views, Explorations in Film*, London, Gordon Fraser, p. 174.
4   Renoir, J. (1974) *My Life and My Films*, London, Collins, pp. 116–17.
5   Sesonske, A. (1980) *Jean Renoir, the French Films*, 1924–1939, Harvard, Harvard University Press, p. 112.
6   Roddick, N. (1985) review in *Sight and Sound*, **54**, 3, p. 221.
7   Aranda, F. (1975) *Luis Bunuel: A Critical Biography*, London, Secker and Warburg, p. 34.
8   Renoir, J. (1974) *op. cit.*, p. 265.
9   Renoir, J. (1974) *op. cit.*, p. 11.
10 Renoir, J. (1974) *op. cit.*, p. 11.
11 Dickens, C. (1854) *Hard Times*, Harmondsworth, Penguin, (1975 edn.), p. 47.

Bibliography

Periodicals

For reasons of economy and practicality I have not attempted to collate useful articles and essays, though many of those that have been influential are reprinted in the anthologies which *are* listed. Retrospectively, the journals of the last twenty-five years that retain more than an historical interest would include *American Cinematographer*, *Cahiers du Cinéma*, *Film Comment*, *Film Culture*, *Film History*, *Film Quarterly*, *Jump Cut*, *Movie*, *Screen*, *Screen Education*, and *Sight and Sound*. Currently *Premiere* provides, as well as ephemeral gossip, some insight and background information on American film production, while the Canadian journal *CineAction!* contains some of the best contemporary criticism.

Pamphlets and Teachers' Packs for implementing film (usually in the context of media education) in Primary and Secondary schools are available from the British Film Institute Education Service, from whom film and video extracts, slides, various 'dossiers' and so on may also be hired.

'Film Education' (37–39 Oxford Street, London W1R 1RE at the time of writing) offers to schools, and for no charge, a range of study guides to current releases and information packs on the film industry and on various approaches to teaching. The films dealt will often seem negligible, and the guides little more than banal comprehension exercises; the simulation exercises mimic professional practice, and I admit I do not see the necessity, beyond the usefulness such exercises have, particularly for developing interactive skills, oracy, mutual responsibility, etc. (But why film, rather than any other industry?) Video, surely, should give children opportunities to get *away* from the large-scale studio model and explore themselves and their environments with more independent freedom?

Teaching Film and the Media

BENNETT, T. *et al.* (Ed) (1981) *Popular Television and Film*, London, BFI.
This is an Open University reader which includes, *inter alia*, several essays on the Documentary Drama (textually centred on *Days of Hope*), Colin MacCabe's controversial 'Realism and the Cinema: Notes on some Brechtian Theses' and Thomas Elsaesser's 'Narrative Cinema and Audience-Oriented Aesthetics'.

BOBKER, L. R. (1969) *Elements of Film*, London, Harcourt, Brace and World.

DAVIES, H. and WALTON, P. (Eds) (1983) *Language, Image, Media*, Oxford, Blackwell.
Opens with a usefully thorough, if naive, chapter by the editors, 'Death of a premier: consensus and closure in international news', an analysis of how the same news story is treated by different television networks.

DRUMMON, P. and PATERSON, R. (Eds) (1988) *Television and its Audience, International Research Perspectives*, London, BFI.
In the section on Subcultures there is a paper by Eric Michaels, 'Hollywood Iconography: A Warlpiri Reading', which, in suggesting why 'electronic media have proved remarkably attractive and accessible to such people where often, print and literacy have not', effectively warns us against extending preconceptions based on our own readings into the minds of those whom we wish to educate.

DUNKLEY, C. (1985) *Television Today and Tomorrow, Wall-to-Wall Dallas?* Harmondsworth Penguin.

FERGUSON, R. (1969), *Group Film Making*, London, Studio Vista.

GLEDHILL, C. (Ed) (1981) *Film and Media Studies in Higher Education*, London, BFI.

HALL, S. *et al.* (1964) *Film Teaching*, London, BFI.

HARCOURT, P. and THEOBALD, P. (Eds) (1966) *Film Making in Schools and Colleges*, London, BFI.

HARTLEY, J. *et al.* (1985) *Making Sense of the Media*, London, Comedia.
Comprising ten booklets, this huge work seems to me a product of *Screen's* ideology; it's particularly interesting, therefore, to consult Cary Bazalgette's distancing review in *Screen*, **27**, 5, September–October 1986.

HIGGINS, A. P. (1966) *Talking about Television*, London, BFI.

HUSS, R. and SILVERSTEIN, N. (1968) *The Film Experience, Elements of Motion Picture Art*, London, Harper and Row.
Less traditional, more perceptive American approach than Bobker, *op. cit.*

KENNEDY, K. (1972) *Film in Teaching*, London, Batsford.

KITSES, J. and MERCER, A. (1966) *Talking About the Cinema*, London, BFI.

LOWNDES, D. (1968) *Film Making in Schools*, London, Batsford.
This is unpretentious and full of practical ideas, which have not dated even if some of the equipment shown has. It is much better than Ferguson, Kennedy and

Rilla, *op. cit.*, and has an engaging directness which the knotty ideological partisanships of *Screen* would shortly render untenable.

LUSTED, D. and DRUMMOND, P. (Eds) (1985) *Television and Schooling*, London, BFI.

McMAHON, B. and QUIN, R. (1986) *Real Images, Film and Television*, South Melbourne, Macmillan Australia.

This contains numerous exercises on the various 'codes' of film and television; similar in approach to much BFI material, it nevertheless seems to me to retain a somewhat stronger sense that film matters as an art.

MASTERMAN, L. (1979) *Teaching about Television*, Basingstoke, Macmillan.

MASTERMAN, L. (1985) *Teaching the Media*, London, Comedia.

MORLEY, D. (1986) *Family Television, Cultural Power and Domestic Leisure*, London, Comedia.

Sociological approach, with lengthy interviews to discover how and what people watch.

PIKE, F. (Ed) (1982) *Ah! Mischief, The Writer and Television*, London, Faber and Faber.

POSTMAN, N. (1986) *Amusing Ourselves to Death*, London, Heinemann.

RILLA, W. (1970) *A–Z of Movie Making*, London, Studio Vista.

WILLIAMS, R. (1974) *Television, Technology and Cultural Form*, London, Fontana.

WINSTON, B. and KEYDEL, J. (1987) *Working with Video*, London, Pelham Books.

There are a number of books available for the amateur video enthusiast, and this seems to me one of the best. It is not specifically designed for school use, but nonetheless provides simple guidance through the technologies of video, rehearses the conventions thoroughly and draws where applicable on the aesthetics of film.

Technology and Style

BORDWELL, D. *et al.* (1988) *The Classical Hollywood Cinema, Film Style and Mode of Production to 1960*, London, Routledge.

Much of the information in this massive book does seem to me useful, though the methodology is entirely suspect – see the important and devastating essay by Andrew Britton in *CineAction! Winter 1988–89*, 'The Philosophy of The Pigeonhole: Wisconsin Formalism and "The Classical Style"'. Not for the first time, I find myself in accord with the scrupulously detailed critique yet unwilling to dispense with the slaughtered text.

COE, B. (1981) *The History of Movie Photography*, London, Ash and Grant.

FIELDING, R. (Ed) (1983) *A Technological History of Motion Pictures and Television*, Berkeley, University of California Press.

An anthology from the pages of The Journal of the Society of Motion Picture and Television Engineers – and much more fascinating than that might sound.

HAPPÉ, L. B. (1975) *Basic Motion Picture Technology*, London, Focal Press.

NEALE, S. (1985) *Cinema and Technology: Image, Sound, Colour*, London, Macmillan BFI.

SALT, B. (1983) *Film Style and Technology: History and Analysis*, London, Starword.
This is both idiosyncratic and authoritative, the most rewarding and lively of the books in this section.

Conditions of Filming

ANDERSON, L. (1952) *Making a Film, The Story of 'Secret People'*, London, George Allen and Unwin.
A chronicle, in diary form, which also includes the shooting script and an account of the sorts of changes that occur as a script is transformed into film.

BACH, S. (1986) *Final Cut, Dreams and Disaster in the Making of 'Heaven's Gate'*, London, Faber and Faber.

BOORMAN, J. (1985) *Money Into Light, 'The Emerald Forest', A Diary*, London, Faber and Faber.

DE NAVACELLE, T. (1987) *Woody Allen on Location*, New York, William Morrow and Co.
A day-to-day account of the making of 'Radio Days'.

GOODE, J. (1986) *The Making of 'The Misfits'*, London, Limelight Editions.

LITWAK, M. (1987) *Reel Power, The Struggle for Influence and Success in the New Hollywood*, New York, Sidgwick and Jackson.

PIRIE, D. (Ed) (1981) *Anatomy of the Movies*, London, Windward.
Includes contributions from Martin Scorsese on directing, and Robert Towne on screenwriting.

ROSENTHAL, A. (1971) *The New Documentary in Action: A Casebook in Film Making*, Berkeley, University of California Press.
Extensive interviews with the makers of many of the most influential non-fiction films of the last thirty years or so, for example, Wiseman on 'High School', Watkins on 'The War Game', Sandford on 'Cathy Come Home', and Pennebaker on 'Don't Look Back' and 'Monterey Pop'.

ROSS, L. (1952) *Picture*, London, Gollancz.
Famous account of the making of 'The Red Badge of Courage', with less insight into the creative and practical processes involved than Anderson and Boorman, *op cit*.

ROSTEN, L. C. (1970) *Hollywood: The Movie Colony, The Movie Makers*, Arno.
Reprint of a 1941 sociological account of the industry.

Directors Talking

In this section directors' names are listed alphabetically, with the names of interviewers or editors appearing after the titles, except in the case of group anthologies.

BERGMAN, INGMAR (1973) *Bergman on Bergman* (interviewed by Stig Björkman, Torsten Manns, Jonas Sima; translated by Paul Britten Austin), London, Secker, and Warburg.

BERGMAN, INGMAR (1988) *The Magic Lantern*, London, Hamish Hamilton.

BUNUEL, LUIS, (1984) *My Last Breath*, London, Jonathan Cape.

CAPRA, FRANK (1972) *The Name Above The Title*, London, W. H. Allen.
Capra's densely emotional, populist films sometimes leave a taste similar to the compacted sweets in George Herbert's great poem, 'Vertue'; this large autobiography explains the stickiness and makes Capra a smaller and less agreeable man than one might have supposed.

CHAPLIN, CHARLES (1964) *My Autobiography*, London, Bodley Head.
Interesting but, as history, sometimes misleading due to omissions, distortions and various inaccuracies.

DZIGA VERTOV (1984) *Kino-Eye* (Edited by Annette Michelson; translated by Kevin O'Brien), London, Pluto Press.
A valuable compilation from the articles, diaries and film projects of this most radically innovative Soviet film maker whose pseudonym, Michelson explains, stands for movement and the sound of a hand-cranked camera ('dziga, dziga, dziga'). An incidental, unexpected link with American cinema – Vertov's brother, Boris Kaufman, was the cinematographer of several Elia Kazan films, including *On the Waterfront*.

EISENSTEIN, SERGEI (1943) *The Film Sense* (translated by Jan Leyda) London, Faber and Faber.

EISENSTEIN, SERGEI (1949) *Film Form* (translated by Jan Leyda) London, Dennis Dobson.

EISENSTEIN, SERGEI (1968) *Film Essays* (edited by Jan Leyda) London, Dennis Dobson.

EISENSTEIN, SERGEI (1985) *Immoral Memories, An autobiography* (translated by Herbert Marshall), London, Peter Owen.

EISENSTEIN, SERGEI (1988) A series edited by Jan Leyda, consisting of four shorter works:
On the Composition of the Short Fiction Scenario, London, Methuen.
A Premature Celebration of Eisenstein's Centenary, London, Methuen.
Eisenstein on Disney, London, Methuen.
The Psychology of Composition, London, Methuen.
At the time of writing there is no complete collected edition of Eisenstein's

writings and sketches in Russian, though I understand an edition is under way. English translations, including previously unpublished material, are appearing from several publishers. Each of Eisenstein's films is flawed in one way or another, and although the *oeuvre* will retain more than an historial importance it seems to me at least conceivable that their value ultimately may reside in the practical basis they provided for the development of one of the most important bodies of theoretical work in aesthetics of the twentieth century. Unfortunately, that work, like Coleridge's, may always be irritatingly diffuse, digressive and lacking in systematic cohesiveness, but it also has the virtue of engagement with the moment, with the process of capturing an emergent art.

FORD, JOHN (1978) *John Ford* (interviewed by Peter Bogdanovitch, and first published in 1967, this edition includes supplementary material by Bogdanovitch), Berkeley, University of California Press.

GEDULD, H. M. (Ed) (1967) *Film Makers on Film Making*, Harmondsworth, Penguin. Interviews and articles by directors from Lumière to Kenneth Anger, taking in many American, British, Japanese, Russian and European directors along the way.

GODARD, JEAN-LUC (1972) *Godard on Godard* (Edited by Jean Narboni and Tom Milne, with translation and commentary by Milne, and an introduction by Richard Roud), London, Secker and Warburg. Includes Godard's criticism and film reviews, plus interviews.

GRIERSON, JOHN (1946) *Grierson on Documentary* (edited by Forsyth Hardy), London, Collins.

HAWKS, HOWARD (1982) *Hawks on Hawks* (interviewed by Joseph McBride), Berkeley, University of California Press.

HEPWORTH, CECIL (1951) *Came the Dawn*, London, Phoenix House. An unassuming, thoroughly charming memoir about the early years of film making in England, manifestly the work of a gentleman and an enthusiast.

HITCHCOCK, ALFRED (1968) *Hitchcock* (interviewed by Francois Truffaut), London, Secker and Warburg.

HUSTON, JOHN (1981) *An Open Book*, Basingstoke, Macmillan. Several of Huston's films remain popular entertainments, but he seems to me an uninteresting director. The opening sequence of *Prizzi's Honour*, for example, looked ineptly edited because the close-ups wouldn't cut with the magisterial crane shot; and the uncertainty of intention in this sequence permeated the film. The challenge of making a romantic comedy about mafia murderers was largely evaded by a tactfulness inappropriate in the 1980s – the killings were 'clean', or took place off-camera. In some circumstances one might be critical of explicit violence, but here its absence seemed aesthetically and morally dishonest. Directors' autobiographies, with a few exceptions, contribute little to our understanding of films, so I have not included many in this section.

KAZAN, ELIA (1988) *Elia Kazan, An American Odyssey* (Edited by Michel Ciment), London, Bloomsbury.

> Lectures, articles, notes and so on, by another 'actors'' director (nevertheless, a more complex film maker and a more rewarding writer about film than Capra and Huston).

KOSZARSKI, R. (Ed) (1976) *Hollywood Directors, 1914–1940*, Oxford, Oxford University Press.

> This, together with its sequel, is a valuable anthology of short and otherwise obscure articles by famous and neglected directors.

KOZINTSEV, GRIGORI (1967) *Shakespeare: Time and Conscience* (translated by Joyce Vining), London, Dennis Dobson.

> Much of the book is concerned with *Lear* and *Hamlet*, and the director's lifelong involvement with Shakespeare, but there is a sixty page Appendix, which comprises his diary entries on *Hamlet*. Kozintsev's film of this play is certainly the best interpretation I have seen (I was less satisfied with his *King Lear*).

KULESHOV, LEV (1987) *Selected Works, Fifty Years in Films* (compiled and annotated by Ekaterina Khokhlova; translated by D. Agrachev and N. Belenkaya), Moscow, Raduga Publishers.

LOSEY, JOSEPH (1985) *Conversations with Losey* (interviewed by Michel Ciment), London, Methuen.

POWELL, MICHAEL (1986) *A Life in Movies*, London, Heinemann.

PUDOVKIN, V. L. (1949) *Film Technique and Film Acting* (two seminal works translated by Ivor Montagu), London, Lear Publishers.

RENOIR, JEAN (1974) *My Life and My Films* (translated by Norman Denny), London, Collins.

> In this case the life and the films are warmly related, and despite a relaxed manner Renoir has many perceptive remarks about the art of film.

SARRIS, A. (Ed) (1981) *Hollywood Voices: Interviews with Film Directors*, London, Secker and Warburg.

SCHICKEL, R. (Ed) (1977) *The Men Who Made The Movies*, London, Elm Tree Books.

> These eight interviews were culled from a television series which Schickel wrote, produced and directed (Walsh, Capra, Hawks, Vidor, Cukor, Wellman, Minnelli and Hitchcock).

TARKOVSKY, ANDREI (1986) *Sculpting in Time* (translated by Kitty Hunter-Blair), London, Bodley Head.

TRUFFAUT, FRANCOIS (1980) *The Films in my Life* (translated by Leonard Mayhew), London, Allen Lane.

> A collection of Truffaut's film criticism, rather than an account of his own films, but more recently (1989), and unusually for a film director, the *Letters* have been translated and published by Faber.

VIDOR, R. (1973) *King Vidor on Film Making*, London, W. H. Allen.

Many directors have not written critical or theoretical work, nor been interviewed at book length, nor written their memoirs. Robert Bresson's *Notes on Cinematography* struck me as disappointingly pretentious when I first saw it, so I didn't buy it and haven't been able to find a copy to reconsider that response; a book of interviews with Martin Scorsese is due as I write. Any other important omissions are due to ignorance, forgetfulness or obscurity rather than bias.

Cinematographers Talking

ALMENDROS, N. (1985) *A Man With A Camera* (translated by Rachel Phillips Belash), London, Faber and Faber.

> Almendros describes his work on American films, such as Robert Benton's *Kramer vs Kramer* and Terence Malick's *Days of Heaven*, and this can be compared and contrasted with his accounts of working in Europe, particularly with Eric Rohmer and Francois Truffaut.

BALSHOFER, F. J. and MILLER, A. (1967) *One Reel A Week*, Berkeley, University of California Press.

> As well as reminiscences about the very early days of American cinema, and the invention of devices now taken for granted, such as the apparatus for moving the camera, there are insights from Arthur Miller into John Ford's working methods (as other cameramen have testified, Ford never looked through the camera; he could judge the framing accurately from the focal length of the lens being used).

BROWN, K. (1973) *Adventures with D. W. Griffith* (Edited and with an introduction by Kevin Brownlow), London, Secker and Warburg.

CAMPBELL, R. (Ed) (1970) *Practical Motion Picture Photography*, London, Zwemmer.

> Campbell, a contemporary of mine from the, then, London School of Film Technique, writes for the apprentice professional, so the book deals with light meters, filters, and a range of shooting situations; it also quotes extensively from eighteen professionals in feature, documentary and television.

HIGHAM, C. (1970) *Hollywood Cameramen: Sources of Light*, London, Thames and Hudson.

> Interviews with seven major cameramen, including checklists of their films which reveal that even a top cameraman cannot save a poor film.

LASSALLY, W. (1987) *Itinerant Cameraman*, London, John Murray.

SCHAEFER, D. and SALVATO, L. (1986) *Masters of Light*, Berkeley, University of California Press.

> Virtually a continuation of Higham, this consists of interviews with fifteen cinematographers who have come to the fore since the 1960s (Wexler, Kovacs, Almendros, Willis, etc.).

YOUNG, F. and PETZOLD, P. (1972) *The Work Of The Motion Picture Cameraman*, London, Focal Press.

> An exhaustive, very clear, practical guide to techniques and conventions from the cameraman best known for his work on the visually splendid *Lawrence of Arabia* (and, *inter alia*, several other David Lean films). Young's chapter on camera techniques, for example, suggests several alternatives for shooting two-shots to the conventional method I've outlined.

Writers

Curiously, screenwriters seem less inclined to expound their craft at book length, or be subjected to extensive interviews, than directors or cameramen; consequently I have included shorter pieces and discussions of the screenplay not necessarily written by practising film writers.

ANDERSON, L. (1981) *About John Ford*, London, Plexus.

> Includes fascinating letters to the author from Dudley Nichols, Frank S. Nugent and Nunnally Johnson.

BOBKER, L. R. (1969) *Elements of Film*, London, Harcourt, Brace and World.

> Fifty pages on story and script, including analysis of extracts.

BENNETT, A. (1985) *The Writer in Disguise*, London, Faber and Faber.

> Five television plays (one directed by, and here given a fine polemical introduction by, Lindsay Anderson) preceded by Alan Bennett's diary extracts relating to their production.

CLARKE, T. E. B. (1974) *This is where I came in*, London, Michael Joseph.

> Undemanding memoirs from the writer of some of the best Ealing comedies.

COFFEE, L. (1973) *Storyline, Recollections of a Hollywood Screenwriter*, London, Cassell.

> Ms Coffee had a lengthy and successful career in Hollywood; her recollections are prim and trite.

CORLISS, R. (1975) *Talking Pictures, Screenwriters of Hollywood*, London, David and Charles.

> Mr Corliss makes a case for the writer as *auteur*, and although I find it unpersuasive his essays on the significant work of nearly forty writers, together with their credits, is valuable.

FROUG, W. (1972) *The Screenwriter looks at the Screenwriter*, Bloomington, Indiana University Press.

GESSNER, R. (1970) *The Moving Image*, New York, Dutton.

> A very intelligent analysis of the screenplay. An English edition was published by Cassell soon after the American one, but – an indication of its value, perhaps – I loaned my copy to an English writer of radio, television and feature films several years ago and have never seen it since.

GOLDMAN, W. (1984) *Adventures in the Screen Trade*, London, Macdonald.
Contains useful advice, some insight, and a fair amount of bile, all rather badly written in a loud, colloquial voice – bestseller material, obviously.

HOCHMAN, S. (Ed) (1982) *From Quasimodo to Scarlett O'Hara*, London, Ungar.
I include this anthology from the 'National Board of Review', 1920–1940, because it includes an article by Dudley Nichols, 'The Making of a Scenario', 1939, but there are also articles by Cocteau, Lang and Hitchcock on directing.

KAEL, P. (1971) *The Citizen Kane Book*, London, Secker and Warburg.
Shooting Script, Cutting continuity, and Kael's controversial attempt to rehabilitate Herman J. Mankiewicz as *auteur-manqué*.

KUREISHI, H. (1988) *Sammy and Rosie Get Laid*, London, Faber and Faber.
This, rather than the slightly better *My Beautiful Laundrette*, because of Kureishi's Diary, which unwittingly offers insights into the limitations of so many contemporary English films: the writer appears to know virtually nothing about the art, and the ignorance comes through in shafts of arrogant condescension, for example, 'The cinema cannot replace the novel or autobiography as the precise and serious medium of the age while it is still too intent on charming its audience!'. A day later he informs us 'that serious writers don't venture into the cinema', as if he's never heard of Pinter or Faulkner, or Pasternak, or Cocteau, or Mailer, or Marquez, or Pasolini, or Eco . . .

PIKE, F. (Ed) (1982) *Ah! Mischief, The Writer and Television*, London, Faber and Faber.
Essays by seven television writers.

PIRIE, D. (1981) *Anatomy of the Movies*, London, Windward.
Includes an essay on screenwriting by David Thompson, and essays by two screenwriters, Robert Towne and Lorenzo Semple Jr.

STEMPEL, T. (1980) *Screenwriter, The Life and Times of Nunnally Johnson*, London, A. S. Barnes.
Johnson, who became a powerful producer and an uninteresting director, was a prolific and fine writer who couldn't understand why directors wanted to alter the tone of his scripts sometimes. Like Goldman, *op. cit.*, his preference was for those directors who represented his intentions, filmed the script and contributed nothing to the art of the film. Stempel tries to make a case for these mediocrities.

WAKE, S. and HAYDEN, N. (Eds) (1972) *The Bonnie & Clyde Book*, London, Lorrimer.
Includes the screenplay, a number of interviews, and a selection of reviews of this influential film, together with a piece by David Newman and Robert Benton on how they came to write the screenplay (one influence was Godard's *Breathless*), the treatment which they sent to Truffaut and his helpfulness, and then the involvements of Arthur Penn and Warren Beatty.

Some Histories of Film

DICKINSON, T. (1971) *A Discovery of Cinema*, Oxford, Oxford University Press.

A 'thesis' account of the 'three phases' and 'four factors' of film. Thorald Dickinson's best-known film as director was *Gaslight*. He also made *Secret People* (see 'Conditions of Filming' section above). Latterly he taught at the Slade, and was the first Professor of Film in Britain, at the University of London.

GRIFFITH, R. and MAYER, A. (1971) *The Movies*, London, Spring Books.

KNIGHT, A. (1957) *The Liveliest Art*, Basingstoke, Macmillan.

LLOYD, A. (Ed) (1979–1983) *The Movie*, London, Orbis Publishing.

Thirteen volumes, issued in 158 weekly parts.

MAST, G. (1980) *A Short History of the Movies*, London, Bobbs-Merrill.

SHIPMAN, D. (1982 and 1984) *The Story of Cinema*, 2 volumes, London, Hodder & Stoughton.

A number of general histories seem reasonably comprehensive in range, but reflect their authors tastes, sometimes disablingly. These volumes exemplify this danger. Shipman's antipathies pepper the pages indiscriminately, and there are nearly 1300 quite large pages, printed in double columns!

WRIGHT, B. (1974) *The Long View*, London, Secker and Warburg.

Again, a personal view, but less bulky and much more substantial than Shipman's. Wright directed some fine documentaries, including *Song of Ceylon*, and clearly enjoys, as well as understands, films. However, the most useful introductory history of film is probably Gerald Mast's.

Early Films

BARNOUW, E. (1981) *The Magician and the Cinema*, Oxford, Oxford University Press.

BROOKS, L. (1982) *Lulu in Hollywood*, London, Hamish Hamilton.

BROWN, K. (1973) *Adventures with D. W. Griffith*, London, Secker and Warburg.

BROWNLOW, K. (1968) *The Parade's Gone By...*, London, Secker and Warburg.

BROWNLOW, K. (1979) *Hollywood, The Pioneers*, London, Collins.

BROWNLOW, K. (1979) *The War, the West, and the Wilderness*, London, Secker and Warburg.

CERAM, C. W. (1965) *Archaeology of the Cinema*, London, Thames and Hudson.

DARDIS, T. (1979) *Keaton, The Man Who Wouldn't Lie Down*, London, André Deutsch.

FELL, J. L. (1974) *Film and the Narrative Tradition*, Tulsa, University of Oklahoma Press, (reprinted, 1986, Berkeley, University of California).

GISH, L. (1988) *The Movies, Mr Griffith and Me*, London, Columbus Books.

HENDERSON, R. M. (1971) *D. W. Griffith: The Years at Biograph*, London, Secker and Warburg.

KING, N. (1984) *Abel Gance*, London, BFI.

LAHUE, K. C. (1970) *Winners of the West: The Sagebrush Heroes of the Silent Screen*, London, A. S. Barnes.

LOW, R. (1948–1985) *The History of the British Film*, 1896–1939 (seven volumes), London, George Allen and Unwin.

O'LEARY, L. (1965) *The silent cinema*, London, Dutton Vista.

RAMSAYE, T. (1986) *A Million and One Nights*, Touchstone (a reprint of the 1926 classic, biased towards Edison, but still valuable).

RHEUBAN, J. (1983) *Harry Langdon, The Comedian as Metteur-en-Scène*, New York, Associated University Presses.

SLIDE, A. (1973) *The Griffith Actresses*, London, A. S. Barnes.

SOBEL, R. and FRANCIS, D. (1977) *Chaplin, Genesis of a Clown*, London, Quartet.

SPEARS, J. (1971) *Hollywood: the Golden Era*, London, A. S. Barnes.

WAGENKNECHT, E. (1962) *The Movies in the Age of Innocence*, Tulsa, University of Oklahoma.

WENDEN, D. J. (1974) *The Birth of the Movies*, London, Macdonald.

WILLIAMS, M. (1980) *Griffith, First Artist of the Movies*, Oxford, Oxford University Press.

WOLTERS, N. E. B. (1985) *Bungalow Town, Theatre and Film Colony*, A Shoreham Book.

Issues: Race, Gender, Politics, Truth, etc.

BAZIN, A. (1981) *French Cinema of the Occupation and Resistance, The Birth of a Critical Esthetic*, London, Ungar.

BISKIND, P. (1984) *Seeing is Believing, How Hollywood Taught us to stop Worrying and love the Fifties*, London, Pluto Press.

CEPLAIR, L. and ENGLUND, S. (1983) *The Inquisition in Hollywood, Politics in the film community, 1930–1960*, Berkeley, University of California Press.

CRIPPS, T. (1977) *Slow Fade to Black, The Negro in American Film, 1900–1942*, New York, Oxford University Press.

CROWTHER, B. (1984) *Hollywood Faction, Reality and myth in the movies*, London, Columbus Books.

FRASER, J. (1974) *Violence in the Arts*, Cambridge, Cambridge University Press.

FRENCH, P. (1973) *Westerns, Aspects of a Movie Genre*, London, Secker and Warburg.

GEORGAKAS, D. and RUBENSTEIN, L. (Eds) (1985) *Art Politics Cinema, The Cineaste Interviews*, London, Pluto Press.

GOLDSTEIN, R. M. and ZORNOW, E. (1980) *The Screen Image of Youth: Movies About Children and Adolescents*, London, The Scarecrow Press.
Contains synopses of hundreds of films, in fifteen main thematic categories; many, but certainly not all, of these films would be suitable for showing to children. An eclectic and very useful book.

ISAKSSON, F. and FURHAMMAR, L. (1971) *Politics and Film*, London, Studio Vista.

KRACAUER, S. (1947) *From Caligari to Hitler, A Psychological History of the German Film*, Princeton, Princeton University.
Seminal investigation of Expressionist cinema.

MELLEN, J. (1974) *Women and their Sexuality in the New Film*, London, Davis-Poynter.

MICHALCZYK, J. J. (1984) *Costa-Gavras: The Political Fiction Film*, London, Associated University Presses.

ROSEN, M. (1975) *Popcorn Venus, Women, Movies and the American Dream*, London, Peter Owen.

SARF, W. M. (1983) *God Bless You, Buffalo Bill: A Layman's Guide to History and the Western Film*, New York, Associated University Presses.

TRUMBO, D. (1972) *Additional Dialogue: Letters of Dalton Trumbo, 1942–1962*, (Edited by Helen Manfull), London, Bantam.
The letters deal mainly with Trumbo's period as a blacklisted screenwriter in the period dealt with by Ceplair and Englund above.

Criticism and Theory

Entries from Directors Talking Section above, particularly Eisenstein, Kuleshov and Pudovkin are not repeated here.

Anthologies, etc.

ALTMAN, R. (Ed) (1981) *Genre: The Muscial*, London, Routledge and Kegan Paul/BFI.

CAUGHIE, J. (Ed) (1981) *Theories of Authorship*, London, Routledge and Kegan Paul/BFI.

COOK, P. (Ed), (1985) *The Cinema Book*, London, BFI.

ELLIS, J. (Ed) (1977) *Screen Reader 1, Cinema/Ideology/Politics*, SEFT.

GLEDHILL, C. (Ed) (1987) *Home is Where the Heart Is, Studies in Melodrama and the Woman's Film*, London, BFI.

HAMMOND, P. (Ed) (1978) *The Shadow and its Shadow, Surrealist Writings on Cinema*, London, BFI.

HILLIER, J. (Ed) (1986) *Cahiers du Cinema, The 1960s*, London, Routledge and Kegan Paul/BFI.

MAST, G. and COHEN, M. (Eds) (1974) *Film Theory and Criticism*, Oxford, Oxford University Press.

NICHOLS, B. (Ed) (1976) *Movies and Methods*, Berkeley, University of California Press.

ROUD, R. (Ed) (1980) *Cinema, A Critical Dictionary, The Major Film-Makers*, London, Secker and Warburg.

SILVER, A. and WARD, E. (Eds) (1980) *Film Noir*, London, Secker and Warburg.

WILSON, D. (Ed) (1982) *Sight and Sound, A Fiftieth Anniversary Selection*, London, Faber and Faber.

Language and Art

ANDREW, J. D. (1976) *The Major Film Theories, An Introduction*, Oxford, Oxford University Press.

ARMES, R. (1976) *The Ambiguous Image, Narrative Style in Modern European Cinema*, London, Secker and Warburg.

ARNHEIM, R. (1958) *Film as Art*, London, Faber and Faber.

BAZIN, A. (1967 and 1971) *What is Cinema?* (2 volumes, translated by Hugh Gray), Berkeley, University of California Press.

BORDWELL, D. and THOMPSON, K. (1980) *Film Art, An Introduction*, London, Addison-Wesley Publishing Co.

BURCH, N. (1973) *Theory of Film Practice* (translated by Helen R. Lane, with introduction by Annette Michelson), London, Secker and Warburg.

BURCH, N. (1979) *To the Distant Observer, Form and meaning in the Japanese cinema* (revised and edited by Annette Michelson), London, Scolar Press.

HARCOURT, P. (1974) *Six European Directors, Essays on the Meaning of Film Style*, Harmondsworth, Penguin.

HEATH, S. (1981) *Questions of Cinema*, Indiana University Press, Bloomington.

KRACAUER, S. (1960) *Theory of Film, The Redemption of Physical Reality*, Oxford, Oxford University Press.

LINDGREN, E. (1963, second edition) *The Art of the Film*, London, Allen and Unwin.

METZ, C. (1974) *Film Language, A Semiotics of the Cinema*, Oxford, Oxford University Press.

PERKINS, V. F. (1972) *Film as Film, Understanding and Judging Movies*, Penguin.

SPOTTISWOODE, R. (1935) *A Grammar of the Film*, London, Faber and Faber.

STEPHENSON, R. and DEBRIX, J. R. (1965) *The Cinema as Art*, Harmondsworth, Penguin.

TYLER, P. (1971) *Magic and Myth of the Movies*, London, Secker and Warburg.

WOLLEN, P. (1969) *Signs and Meanings in the Cinema*, London, Secker and Warburg/BFI.

WOOD, R. (1976) *Personal Views, Explorations in Film*, London, Gordon Fraser.

Director and Film-centred Criticism

Directors are listed alphabetically, authors alphabetically within each group.

BENDAZZI, G. (1987) *The Films of Woody Allen*, London, Ravette.

BRODE, D. (1986) *Woody Allen, his Films and Career*, London, Columbus.

JACOBS, D. (1982) *The Magic of Woody Allen*, London, Robson Books.

SIMON, J. (1973) *Ingmar Bergman Directs*, New York, Davis-Poynter.

ARANDA, F. (1975) *Luis Buñuel: A Critical Biography*, London, Secker and Warburg.

KYROU, A. (1963) *Luis Buñuel*, Simon and Schuster.

WOOD, R. and WALKER, M. (1970) *Claude Chabrol*, London, Studio Vista.

MILNE, T. (1971) *The Cinema of Carl Dreyer*, London, Zwemmer.

THOMPSON, K. (1981) *Eisenstein's Ivan the Terrible, A Neoformalist Analysis*, Princeton, Princeton University Press.

ANDERSON, L. (1981) *About John Ford*, London, Plexus.

GALLAGHER, T. (1986) *John Ford, the man and his films*, Berkeley, University of California Press.

MCBRIDE, J. and WILMINGTON, M. (1974) *John Ford*, London, Secker and Warburg.

SARRIS, A. (1976) *The John Ford Movie Mystery*, London, Secker and Warburg.

SINCLAIR, A. (1979) *John Ford*, London, Allen and Unwin.

PLACE, J. A. (1974) *The Western Films of John Ford*, New York, Citadel Press.

PLACE, J. A. (1979) *The Non-Western Films of John Ford*, New York, Citadel Press.

(NB *Screen Reader 1* and *Movies and Methods* both reprint the influential, if somewhat one-eyed, reading of *Young Mr Lincoln* by the editors of *Cahiers du Cinema*, the former including the supplementary pieces from *Screen*; *Theories of Authorship* only uses the conclusion to the *Cahiers* effort, but has a large section devoted to other readings of his work; also worth mentioning, a John Ford issue of the *Velvet Light Trap*, (August 1971), Dan Ford's *The Unquiet Man*, (1982), William Kimber, and Robert Parrish's *Growing Up In Hollywood*, (1976), Bodley Head. The best critical studies are Anderson's and Gallagher's).

HARDY, P. (1970) *Samuel Fuller*, London, Studio Vista.

KING, N. (1984) *Abel Gance*, London, BFI.

BROWN, R. S. (Ed) (1972) *Focus on Godard*, London, Prentice-Hall.

CAMERON, I. (Ed) (1967) *The Films of Jean-Luc Godard*, London, Studio Vista.

ROUD, R. (1967) *Godard*, London, Secker and Warburg.

WOOD, R. (1968) *Howard Hawks*, London, Secker and Warburg.

TAYLOR, J. R. (1978) *Hitch, The Life and Works of Alfred Hitchcock*, London, Faber and Faber.

WOOD, R. (1965) *Hitchcock's Films*, London, Zwemmer.

RICHIE, D. (1984) *The Films of Akira Kurosawa* (revised edition with additional material by Joan Mellen), Berkeley, University of California Press.

SICILIANO, E. (1987) *Pasolini* (translated by John Shepley), London, Bloomsbury.

WOOD, R. (1972) *The Apu Trilogy*, London, November Books.

BAZIN, A. (1974) *Jean Renoir* (Edited by Truffaut), London, W. H. Allen.

DURGNAT, R. (1975) *Jean Renoir*, London, Studio Vista.

SESONSKE, A. (1980) *Jean Renoir, the French Films, 1924–1939*, Harvard, Harvard University Press.

GUARNER, J. L. (1970) *Roberto Rossellini*, London, Studio Vista.

ROUD, R. (1971) *Jean-Marie Straub*, London, Secker and Warburg.

LE FANU, M. (1987) *The Cinema of Andrei Tarkovsky*, London, BFI.

ALLEN, D. (1974) *Francois Truffaut*, London, Secker and Warburg.

INSDORF, A. (1981) *Francois Truffaut*, Basingstoke, Papermac.

PETRIE, G. (1970) *The Cinema of Francois Truffaut*, London, Zwemmer.

SALLES GOMES, P. E. (1972) *Jean Vigo*, London, Secker and Warburg.

SMITH, J. M. (1972) *Jean Vigo*, London, November Books.

BAZIN, A. (1978) *Orson Welles, A Critical View*, London, Elm Tree Books.

CARRINGER, R. L. (1985) *The Making of Citizen Kane*, London, John Murray.

MCBRIDE, J. (1972) *Orson Welles*, London, Secker and Warburg.

Narrative Arts

ABBS, P. (Ed) (1987) *Living Powers, The Arts in Education*, Lewes, Falmer Press.

ABBS, P. (1989) *A is for Aesthetic*, Lewes, Falmer Press.

ABBS, P. (Ed) (1989) *The Symbolic Order*, Lewes, Falmer Press.

ALTER, R. (1975) *Partial Magic, The Novel as a Self-Conscious Genre*, Berkeley, University of California Press.

ANDREW, D. (1984) *Film in the Aura of Art*, Princeton, Princeton University Press.

BAKHTIN, M. M. (1985) *The Dialogic Imagination*, Austin, University of Texas Press.

BARTHES, R. (1973) *Mythologies*, London, Paladin.

BARTHES, R. (1977) *Image–Music–Text*, London, Fontana.

BEJA, M. (1979) *Film & Literature*, New York, Longman.

BLUESTONE, G. (1973) *Novels into Film, The Metamorphosis of Fiction into Cinema* (original edition, 1957), Berkeley, University of California Press.

CHATMAN, S. (1978) *Story and Discourse, Narrative Structure in Fiction and Film*, New York, Cornell University Press.

COHEN, K. (1979) *Film and Fiction: The Dynamics of Exchange*, Yale, Yale University Press.

DELLA VOLPE (1978) *Critique of Taste*, London, New Left Books.

ECO, U. (1979) *A Theory of Semiotics*, Bloomington, Indiana University Press.

ECO, U. (1987) *Travels in Hyper-Reality*, London, Picador.

EIDSVIK, C. (1978) *Cineliteracy, Film Among the Arts*, University of Georgia Press.

FELL, J. L. (1986) *Film and the Narrative Tradition*, Berkeley, University of California Press.

FOWLER, A. (1986) *Kinds of Literature, An Introduction to the Theory of Genres and Modes*, Oxford, Clarendon Press.

FRYE, N. (1957) *Anatomy of Criticism*, Princeton, Princeton University Press.

GENNETTE, G. (1982) *Figures of Literary Discourse*, Oxford, Basil Blackwell.

GENNETTE, G. (1986) *Narrative Discourse*, Oxford, Basil Blackwell.

HARBISON, R. (1988) *Pharaoh's Dream, The Secret Life of Stories*, London, Secker and Warburg.

KRISTEVA, J. (1984) *Desire in Language, A Semiotic Approach to Literature and Art*, Oxford, Basil Blackwell.

LODGE, D. (1986) *Working with Structuralism*, London, Ark Paperbacks.

McCONNELL, F. (1979) *Storytelling and Mythmaking, Images from Film and Literature*, Oxford, Oxford University Press.

McFARLANE, B. (1983) *Words and Images, Australian Novels into Film*, Melbourne, Heinemann Australia.

MUKAŘOVSKÝ, J. (1978) *Structure, Sign, and Function*, Yale, Yale University Press.

NICOLL, A. (1972) *Film and Theatre*, London, Arno Press, (reprint of 1936 edition).

RANELAGH, E. L. (1979) *The Past We Share, The Near Eastern Ancestry of Western Folk Literature*, London, Quartet Books.

RENTSCHLER, E. (Ed) (1986) *German Film and Literature, Adaptations and Transformations*, London, Methuen.

SONTAG, S. (1967) *Against Interpretation*, London, Eyre and Spottiswoode.

STEINER, G. (1989) *Real Presences. Is there anything in what we say?*, London, Faber and Faber.

Some of the books in this section don't touch directly on Film, while some of those that do (Barthes, Della Volpe and Mukařoský, for example) seem to have a tangential interest, or little grasp of the art; what I do perceive as useful, however, is a freedom within semiotics, narrative and genre studies to move across the fields of the arts, as well as a freedom, in Barthes and Eco, to treat film, literature and manifestations of popular culture as readily as their more overtly scholarly pursuits. If such freedom can be brought into contact with the level of responsiveness to the experience of the particular work of art which Dudley Andrew attempts, bringing theory and criticism back to that most vulnerable realm of the personal, against which what really matters ultimately must be tested and discovered, and, finally, if it can be set intimately beside the creative disciplines that enable us to think *in* and *with* art, rather than just *about* it, then the model I proposed in my concluding chapter would begin to be embodied.

Index

Abbs, Peter *ix–xi*
A Bout de Soufle 78–9
abstract/abstraction 4, 82
Abyss, The 119
Acres, Birt 9, 133
acting 9, 41, 46, 53, 55–8, 68, 126
actions(s) 65, 100
  parallel 47
actors 9, 46, 51, 52, 78, 92n11
  non-professional 56, 57, 90
  in sitcoms 123, 128
aesthetic(s) *ix*, 1, 7, 47, 83, 99, 126, 132, 156
  education *x*
  of gameshows: simplicity 105
  of pop-videos/commercials 116, 118, 121–2,
    128
  technology factor in 48
  see also Blind Date; cinematic structure; film;
    News; simplicity; sound; television
agenda, News 108–9, 110, 112, 113, 114
Ah, Wilderness (1935) 123
Akerman, Chantal 111
Alex in Wonderland (1970) 142
Allen, David (1965) 5
Allen, Woody 72–3, 142
  (1983) 93
Almendros, Nestor 116, 146
Alter, Robert (1975) 114–15
Amadeus (1985) 73
ambience, creative exploitation of 69
American
  film 56, 133
  postmodernism 134
Anderson, Lindsay 2, 57, 116, 133
  (1981) 42, 96
Anderson, Perry 133

Andrei Rublev (1966) 62
Andy Hardy films 123
angled shots 25–7
angles, high/low 44
animation 117, 118, 119
Anna Karenina 121
anonymity 95, 97
Antonioni, Michelangelo 2, 82
Apocalypse Now (1979) 79
Apted, Michael 116
archetypes, study of 115
arc lighting 81
Aristotle 18, 19, 100–1, 104
art *xi*, 6, 10, 114–16, 18, 85, 110
  'bad' 99, 107, 122
  collaborative 98–9
  film 2, 32, 133, 134, 142
  forms 98–9
  see also borrowings; film as; language; pop-
    video; speech; television
artifice and realism *x-xi*
artificial lighting 90
artist(s) 8, 97
artistic convention/work *x*
artistic effect 52
artistic expression 15–16
artistic quality 6, 7
arts, the *x*, 7, 15–16, 45, 92, 149
arts
  see also education; narrative; popular; teacher
Astruc, Alexandre 9
atmosphere/atmospheric 44, 74, 106, 146
audibility 66
audience 8, 46–7, 50, 52, 107, 113, 120
  involvement 68, 69, 72, 87, 123, 126
August 1914 45

aural language: separate from vision 49, 65
auteur, the 137–40, 159
auteurism 136, 138–40, 141–2
auteurist criticism 7
author/authorship 7, 112, 129
avant-garde film-makers 27

back-projection 114
Bad Company (1972) 45
Bakhtin, M. M. (1985) 101
Balcon, Michael 133
Ball of Fire (1942) 67
Bantock, G. H. (1981) 99
Barth, John 62
Barthes, Roland 91
  (1973) 166
  (1977) 17, 166
Bazalgette, C. (1986, 1989) 1
Bazin, André 81, 86, 88
  (1967) 89
BCU
  see big close-up
Beauty no. 2 (1965) 96
Beckett, Samuel 58, 68
Beckett, Sister Wendy (1989) 104
Beirut — The Last Home Movie (1988) 57
Benton, Robert 45
Bergan, R. and Karney, R. (1988) 83
Berger, John 114
  (1965) 1, 2
  (1969) 110
  (1980) 44
Berger, T. 45
Bergman, Ingmar 2, 32, 100, 115
Berkoff, Stephen 57
Berlin 15
Berlin Alexanderplatz 100
BFI
  see British Film Institute
Big (1988) 74
big close-up (BCU) 25
Big Heat, The (1953) 145
Birds, The (1963) 40–1
Bitzer, Billy 46
Blackadder 62
black and white/colour: lighting 78
Blackmail (1929) 70, 73
Blade Runner 119
Blind Date x, 100–8
Blood Meridian (1989) 45
Bloomsbury Foreign Film Guide 83
Blow Out 145
Bob and Carol and Ted and Alice (1969) 142

Bogdanovitch, Peter 67
borrowing(s) by commercials/arts 119, 136
Boudu sauve des eaux (1932) 142, 143
Boyle, Danny 85
Boys from the Black Stuff 41
Brandt, Bill 81
Brazil 119
Breathless 160
Bresson, Robert 57, 85, 88, 102, 158
  (1967) 73–4
Bringing up Baby (1938) 67
British Film Institute (BFI) 8, 151
  (1964, 1966) 4, 5
  (1978) 6
Brown, Clarence 81, 123
Brown, K. (1973) 46, 47
Buñuel, Luis 2, 133, 144, 148
Burch, N. (1979) 39
Butler, I. (1971) 8, 10

Cabinet of Dr. Caligari, The (1919) 82
Cahiers du Cinema, The 1960s 136, 164, 165
Calvino, Italo 62
camera *x*, 21, 34, 43, 84–5
  as creative/sensitive instrument *ix*, 9, 15, 35, 36
  handheld 90, 113
  -man/men 46, 158
  movements *xi*, 27–8, 38, 45, 57, 83, 90, 96, 124
  and narrative 31, 39–40
  positions 22–42, 46, 47, 49, 54, 124
  static 27–8, 85
  techniques 10, 27, 37, 51, 55, 56–8, 159
  -work 46, 106, 114, 117, 124–6, 127, 158–9
  see also dialogue; multiple; plot; rhythm; single;
    video
Carringer, R. L. 60
Carry On Films 133
cartoons, strip 43, 44
Cassirer, Ernst (1972) 112
Cathy Come Home (1966) 51, 57
Chabrol, Claude 116
Chaplin, Charles 58
character(s) 59, 68, 69, 90
Chaucer, G. 65
Child of God (1973) 45
children 1, 3, 5, 146
  films suitable for 163
Chronicle of Anna Magdalena Bach, The (1968) 27–8
Circus, The 89
cinema, 45, 51, 129, 142, 143
  see also children
cinematographers 158–9
Citizen Kane (1941) 81

Citizen Kane Book, The (1971) 59–60
classical narratives 100
cliché 97
close-up (CU) **36–40**, 44, 46, 85, 124, 126, 147
  and dialogue 67
  and editing 54
  and long shot 22–3, 86, 87
  medium (MCU) 25
  multiple cameras 51–2
Coca Cola advertisements 120–1, 128
collaboration/collaborative 64, 98, 99, 112, 115, 148
Collingwood, R. G. 99
colour, 9, 48, 90, 106, 141, 143
  and tinting/lighting 44, 78, 79, 121
Come Back to the 5 and Dime, Jimmy Dean, Jimmy Dean (1982) 79
comedy 44, 89, 108–9
comic-based films 97
commercial(s) 27, 115–16, 117, **118–22**, 128–9
  enterprises, TV/cinema as 91, 99
communication/communicating *ix*, 6, 8, 17
competition *see* gameshows
composition 9, 14–15, 56, 82, 117
computer software 1
Conrad, Joseph 45
constraints 27, 63, 113
construction 108
  see also editing
contemporary, the 133–4, 136
continuity 41, 44, 51, 59, 72, 117
  editing 39, 43, 53–5, 70, 79, 80, 82, 84–5, 89
  and news broadcasting 113, 114
  see also eye-line; mismatching
control 102, 112
convention(s) *x*, 17–42, 46, 96, 109, 113, 146
  basic 42, 107
  and commercials 119–20, 121
  and expressiveness 15–16
  formulaic 22, 95, 132
  and language of film 50, 129
  narrative 85–6
  see also auteurism; objective validity; structural
Cool Hand Luke (1967) 30
Coover, Robert 115
Coppola, Francis Ford 79, 116
Coutard, Raoul and Godard, Jean-Luc 78–9
Crabbe, George 45
Crane, Stephen 45
creativity/creative *x*, 48, 73, 97, 99, 112, 129, 149
  in camerawork *ix*, 15, 92n11, 114
  directors' 59, 63, 92n11
  and speech/dialogue 66, 67

criticism 7, 40, 114–15
  and theory 155–8, 163–6
Crucible, The 62
Cruel Sea, The (1954) 56
CU
  see close-up
cubism and film 44
Culpepper Cattle Company, The (1972) 45
culture 3, 5, 44, 108, 129, 131, 133–4, 137
  mass 127
  see also film; popular
curriculum, place of film on *ix*, *x*, 8, 149
cut 34, 72, 85
  cross- 65, 66
cut-ins 52
cutting 21, 31, 86, 87, 90, 120, 127
  continuity 59, 60
  to parallel action 47
  rhythm(s) 57, 74, 96

Dance on 4 57
Daniels, William 81
Days of Heaven (1978) 146, 158
Days of Hope 51
Dead Men Don't Wear Plaid (1983) 56
Defence of the Realm (1985) 69, 145
deep-field composition 82
deep focus 43, 53, 79, 80–2, 86
De Mille, Cecil B. 51–2, 54
De Palma, Brian 145
depth of field 77, 81
description: film/novel 44
Dial M for Murder (1954) 49
dialogue 9–10, 40, 41, 44, 48, 59, 68, 146
  and camerawork 33, 34, 35
  emphasis on 53, 129, 141
  styles 43, 64–9
Diary of a Chambermaid (1946) 144
Dickens, Charles 44
  (1854) 149, 150n11
Dickenson, Thorold 161
directional/direction 21, 39, 40
  change 42
  continuity 41
director(s) 46, 62–4, 67, 79, 96, 144, 146, 155–8, 165–6
  and *auteurism* 7, 112–13, 138–9
  function of 54, 60, 63
  and script/scenario 59, 63–4
  see also European; Russian
discipline 27, 29, 114
discussion, classroom: film in *ix*, *x*, 4, 5
documentaries 108, 127–8, 133, 161

documentary 3, 15, 43, 57, 78, 113, 114
  style 51, 88, 90
Dos Passos, John 45
Down and Out in Beverley Hills (1986) 140–4
drama 44
  live/TV 51, 129
dramatic
  intensity, communicating 147
  narrative, continuous 79
  order 51, 52
dramatization of novels 61
Dreyer, Carl 146
Drums Along the Mohawk (1939) 89–90
Drury, David 69
dubbing 75
  over- 48
Duel (1972) 21
Duning, George 117
duration 52, 54, 118
  of shot 21, 27, 38
Dziga-Vertov, 88, 155

Ealing Studios 133
EastEnders 57, 65, 66, 70, 74
Eastman, George 43
Eco, Umberto 62
  (1979, 1987) 167
editing 3, 37, 38, 44, 45, 49, 80, 126, 147
  commercials 120, 121
  construction through 42, 56, 79, 82–3
  and multiple cameras 51, 52
  news broadcasts 109, 111
  pop-videos 117
  students' work in 112
  during transmission: TV drama 52, 54
  video 35, 54, 117
  see also continuity; tape-to-tape
education 102, 135, 137
  arts *x*, 4, 115
  film in *ix*, *x*, **1–10**, 86, 131, 132, 149
  narrative arts in 105–6, 134
8½ 142
Eisenstein, Sergei 3, 56, 57, 155–6
  (1949) 44
Eliot, T. S. 102
  (1946) 98
ELS
  See extreme long shot
emotion(s) 56, 72, 129
emotional aspects of film/TV 66, 68, 86, 108, 109, 114, 117
English film 131, 134, 135–7
  and American 133

and television 133
English skills: use of film in 5
English, teaching of 5
entertainment 43, 99
  see also popular
environment and film 3, 14, 49, 68, 80, 83
establishing shots 37, 52
ethics 110
European directors 138
evaluation 91–2
excess in film/TV language 17–18
  see also 'real-life'
expression 13–14, 15, 29, 40, 44, 149
expressionism/Expressionist cinema 82, 163
expressive art, film as 5
expressive devices 45
expressive innovations 56
expressiveness 15–16, 29, 47
exteriors 46, 78
extreme long shot (ELS) 25
eye-line matching 39, 40

Face to Face 89
Fanny och Alexander 100
Fassbinder R. W. 100
Fauchois, Rénè 142, 143
Faulkner, William 45
Fawlty Towers 67, 74, 124–6, 127, 128
Feldman, Edward 144
Fell, J. L. (1986) 44
Fellini, Federico 2, 142
feminists' approach to media 7
fiction, classifications of 97, 100
Fifth Queen, The 62
film
  academic base for 7
  aesthetic field of *ix*, *xi*, 5, 9–10, **43–53**, 86
  art 8, 75, 127–8, 129, 131, 137
  art of 54, 148
  as art 12, 14, 29, 45, 50, 75, 91, 132, 148, 149
    'hybrid' 43–7
  as art form *ix*, *x*, 3, 9, 15–16, 27
  black and white 90
  as collaborative enterprise 99, 115, 148
  and culture 2–3, 5, 129, 133
  in curriculum *ix*, 131, 149
  early/beginning of 11–16, 44, 46, 47, 49, 58, 161–2
  in education *ix*, *x*, 1–10, 75, 131, 134, 149
  emulsions 76, 78
  language of 9–10, 68, 107, 129, 149
  and literature/literacy *x–xi*, 8–9, 45, 131
  magazine capacity, effect of 52, 85

-maker(s) 63, 95

-making *x*, 9–10, 14, 27, 54, 57, 64, 129, 154

and narrative arts 87, **131–50**

noir genre 78, 81

as scientific achievement 12

teaching *x*, 4, 5, 127–8, 151

technology/technique 8, 12, 42, 54, 56, 69–70, 78, 81, 96

and television 2, 13, 40, 50, 51, 52–3, 55, 86, 92n11, **95–129**

and theatre/stage 46, 47–8, 49, 51, 52, 53, 123

theory/theorists 7, 15

understanding through education and research study 137, 140, 148

and video 8, 69–70

see also American; art film; comic-based; commercial; constraints; environment; media studies; novel; pop-videos; realism; remakes; speed

'filmic' qualities 46, 49, 51, 84–5

filming

conditions of 154

'wild' 38

filtration 121

Fleischer, Richard 146

focus 77–8

see also deep; depth of field; pulling

Ford, Ford Madox 62

Ford, John 41–2, 57–9, 82, 89–90, 102, 137, 146, 148

and camera 158

cutting rhythms 74

influence of 138

lighting 78, 81

sound 71

Foreign Correspondent (1940) 67

form and meaning 110, 112, 115

formalist position: criticism 19

Forman, Milos 2, 73

Four Hours in My Lai (1988) 57

Four Men and a Prayer (1938) 82

frame(s) 39, 40, 44, 46, 79, 122

framing 34

Freund, Karl 15

Friendly Persuasion (1956) 146

Front Page, The (1931) 66

Frye, Northrop (1973) 97

Fuller, Samuel 2, 90, 138

Further Education, film in 4

Gallipoli (1981) 146

Gance, Abel 133, 162

Garnham, N. (1981) 1

Gaslight 161

gameshows/quizzes 51, 100, 101, 102, 104

generic forms/types 97, 98, 129

genres, television and language *x*, 7, 62, **95–130**, **137–40**, 167

see also Blind Date

German cinema/expressionism 81, 82, 133

Gilliam, Terry 62–3

Godard, Jean-Luc 2, 81, 85, 88, 90, 199–1, 160

use of sound 72, 73–4

'Golden Age' of TV: 1960s 50, 51

graphics 111, 112, 117, 119

Grapes of Wrath, The (1940) 81, 90

Great Escape, The (1963) 56

Grierson, John 3

Griffith D. W. 28, 46, 56, 57, 58, 158, 161, 162

influence of 86, 138

techniques 39, 44, 46, 47, 54, 86, 121

Güney, Yilmaz 139

Guns in the Afternoon (1961) 26–7

Hall, S. and Whannel, P. (1964) 4

Hamlet 157

Hammer Films 133

Hawks, Howard 66, 67, 68, 69, 142

Health (1980) 68

Hecht, Ben

and Hawks, Howard 67

and Hitchcock, Alfred 67

and MacArthur, Charles 66

and Wellman, William 67

Heimat 100

Henderson, R. M. 47

(1971) 46

Hen House, The (1989) 85

Hepworth, Cecil 133

mimetic, high/low 97, 100

High Noon (1952) 56

Hill Street Blues 147

His Girl Friday (1940) 66

historical

development/research 47–8, 140

/period reconstructions, dramatic 61, 62

history of film 75, 121, 161

Hitchcock, Alfred 29, 42, 45, 49, 70–1, 90, 133

The Birds 40–1

and Hecht, Ben 67

and long take 85–6, 87, 88, 96

Psycho 73

Hollywood 31, 73, 78, 79, 81, 82, 38

horror films 79, 81

Hopkins, Gerard Manley 64

Hopkins, John 50

human behaviour/meaning *x*, 45
Human Desire (1954) 144
humour 62, 74, 123
Hurricane, The (1937) 82
Huston, John 156

ideology 4, 6, 89, 99, 152, 153
Ignatieff Michael, 108
illusion 4, 12, 14, 19, 50, 80, 85
images(s) 6, 8, 12, 39–40, 44, 86, 117, 127
 -analysis 7
 and sound 50, 70, 73, 74
imaginative development 114
Imie, Tony 51
immediacy, 5, 51, 110
improvization 58, 68, 88, 90
incandescent lighting 81
Indiana Jones 119
individuality and creativity 99
information *x*, 151
Informer, The (1935) 57–8, 78
innovation 116, 119
interior filming 46 78–9
Interiors (1978) 72, 73
interpretation 21, 35, 36, 61
intertitles 59
interview(s), filming 35, 38, 108
Ipcress File, The (1965) 18, 19, 145
Italian cinema 57, 133
Ivan the Terrible (1944) 62

Jabberwocky 62
Japanese cinema/directors 39, 133, 138
Jarman, Derek 116, 117, 121
Jarre, Maurice 146
Jaws (1975) 73
Jennings, Humphrey 133
Johnson, Nunnally 159, 160
journalism and film 44
Jules et Jim 142
Juno and the Paycock (1930) 71, 74

Kael, Pauline (1974) 59–60
Kennedy, K. (1972) 5
Kierkegaard, S. (1964) 104, 105
King, Allan 113
Knight's Tale, The 65
Korda, Sir Alexander 133
Kramer versus Kramer 158
Kubrick, Stanley 133
Kuleshov, Lev 56, 115
 (1920) 55–6
 (1987) 48, 55–6, 57, 58, 63
Kurosawa, Akira 2, 21, 45, 133, 144, 166

La Chienne (1932) 144
La Guerre est Finie 82
Lancelot of the Lake 74
Lang, Fritz 2, 72, 144
language of film-making 5, 9–10, 17–18, 43, 67,
 129, 138
 acquisition 90–1
 and art 65, 67, 97, 129, 131–2, 164–5
 aural/visual 48–9, 65
 common 95, 97, 129
 genres and television **95–130**
 see also commercials; conventions; poetry;
 teaching
La Règle du Jeu (1939) 81
L'Argent (1983) 74, 102
La Ronde (1950) 87–8, 96
Last Days of Pompeii (1898) 44
Last Laugh, The 15
Last Wave, The (1977) 146
Last Year at Malibu 142
Lawrence, D. H. 65, 129
Lean, David 133
learning 104, 106
Leavis, F. R. *x*, 115
 (1975) 98
 (1976) 96–7
 and Thompson, D. (1933) *ix*, 3, 99
Le Bete Humaine (1938) 144
L'Eclisse 82
Le Fanu, Mark (1987) 84
Le Journal d'une Femme de Chambre 144
lenses 26, 77, 78, 81, 82, 90
Le Prince, Louis 9, 11–12, 13–14, 15, 17–18, 21,
 133
Les Bas-Fonds (1936) 144
Les Carabiniers (1963) 81, 85
Le Signe du Lion (1959) 140
Lifeboat (1944) 49
Life of Brian 62
light 76–7, 78, 79, 82
lighting, 9, 43, 56, 75–9, 82–3, 90, 121
 in multiple camera technique 59, 92n11
 in TV programmes 106, 123, 126
 see also arc; artificial; black and white;
 cinematography; colour; incandescent
Lindsay, V. (1916) 15
listening 68, 70
literacy *x–xi* 133–4
literature 5, 44, 45, 47, 63, 131, 133–4, 135
Little Big Man (1970) 45
live
 performance 50, 51, 86
 television 43, 50, 51, 52, 54, 79

Loach, Ken 51
location 46, 51, 74, 114, 146
London Films 133
Long Goodbye, The (1973) 68
long shot (LS) 21, 22–3, 25, 39, 40, 86, 90
  and cinema position 34
  and deep focus 80
  and multiple cameras 51
  and television 114, 126
  see also cartoon; extreme; master shot
long take, 43–94, 95
  and chronological movement 84–5
  and deep focus 53, 79
  and meaning 87, 96
  static 89, 90
Long Voyage Home, The (1940) 78, 81
Losey, Joseph 133
Lower Depths, The 144
Lowndes, D (1968) 5
LS
  See long shot
Lubitsch, Ernest 138
Lumière brothers, 9, 12, 29, 43, 80
Lynch, David 116
Lyne, Adrian 116

M (1931) 72, 73
McBride, J. and Wilmington, M. (1974) 24–5, 42n3
MacCabe, C. (1988) 50, 92n10
McCarthy, Cormac 45
McLaren, Norman 117
magic lantern 43
Major Dundee (1965) 45
Malick, Terence 146
Malle, Louis 36
Mankiewicz, H. J. 59, 60
Marker, Chris 2
Marshall, Penny 74, 116
Mary Barton 61
Mary of Scotland (1936) 82
mass-production 133
master-scene 61
mastershot(s) 37, 79, 106
Maysles brothers 113
Mazursky, Paul 142–4
meaning *x*, 6, 91, 95–6, 102, 114–15, 129
media **5–7**, 8, 43, 112
  mass, 3, 98–9
  studies *ix*, *x*, 1, 2, 6, 7, 9, 86
medium/language/art, 131–2
medium close-up, shot/reverse shot in, 35–6
medium shot, 25, 34, 38, 39, 86, 87, 106

Méliès, Georges 9, 43
melodrama 43, 45, 56
Melville, Herman 45
Menges, Chris 51, 116
Menzel, Jiri 2
Mercer, David 50
Metamorphosis (1989) 57
Milestone, Lewis 66
Milton, John 45, 64
mime, experiments with 48
Mishima (1986) 79
mismatching 39
mixing 68
Mizoguchi, Kenji 133
modernism 101, 134
monitoring 127
Monkey Business (1952) 67
montage 3, 44, 54, 55–6, 57, 63, 85
  versus long take 82–3, 86
Monty Python Team 62–3
mood 34–5, 41–2 106, 111, 117, 119, 146
motivation 55
Mouchette (1967) 57
MS/MCU
  see medium shot/medium close-up
multiculturalism 134
multiple cameras, using 43, 51–2, 54, 58, 59, 67, 79
  and realism 53, 57
  and TV 51, 55, 92n11, 127
multiple sound, recording 68
  see Altman
Munsterberg, H. (1916) 15
Murnau, F. W. 15, 57
music 1, 9, 27, 41–2, 44, 73, 111, 146
  in commercials 119, 120
  continuity function 72
  in pop-videos 117, 118
  see also popular
music hall, influence of 44
My Darling Clementine (1946) 145
My Dinner with André 36

narration 57, 111
narrative 45, 47, 65, 77, 79, 84–5, 97, 128
  art(s) 116, **131–50**, 166–8
  awareness 112
  of commercials 53, 119, 121–2
  context 31
  continuity 32, 38, 53–5, 79, 80
  development 87
  film 9, 42, 53, 54, 61, 113, 146, 148
  forms 115, 129

of gameshows/*Blind Date* 101, 102, 104, 105–6
improvization 88
of news broadcasts 108, 109–10
patterns 115
of pop-videos 32 116 117 118
narrative sequence **17–42**
skills 120
structure 61
study/studies 95, 149, 167
types 128
texture 73
see also camera; conventions; dramatic
narratives 44, 68, 100, 109, 128–9
Nashville (1975) 68
National Curriculum, film possibilities in 8
National Museum of Photography, Film and
    Television (Bradford) 11
Neighbours 57
noe-realism, Italian 133
News, study of *x* **108–14**, 127–8
News at Ten 57
news editor as author 112
Newsnight (BBC2) 110
Newsom Report (1963) *ix*, 3–4
newspapers 5, 111, 112
newsreaders, function/roles of 111
New York Stories (1989) 34
1984 119
1960s film 2–3, 50, 51
Nostalgia (1983) 57, 83, 84, 86, 87, 100
Nothing Sacred (1937) 67
Notorious (1946) 67, 120
novel(s) 43, 50–1, 61, 62, 84, 115, 134
    and film: similarities, 44, 47, 148
Nykvist, Sven 116

'objective validity', 112
Odyssey, The 128
off-screen sound 74
One From the Heart (1982) 79
180 degree rule 29–33, 38, 39, 40, 41, 124
O'Neill, Eugene 123
Ophuls, Max 87–8, 96
oral tradition 75
Osborne, John 50
over-the-shoulder shot 35, 36, 37
    see also point-of-view
Ozu, Yasujiro 36, 49, 88, 133

paired shots 35–6
Palmer, Frank (1971) 90–1
panning 38, 114
    see also interview filming

Paradine Case, The (1947) 67
parallel action 47
parallel plotting 46
Paris, Texas 100
Pasolini, Pier Paulo 143
Paul, R. W. 9, 44, 133
Peckinpah, Sam 42, 25
peepshow, 13
Penn, Arthur 45
Pennebaker, Don 113
perception and 180 degree rule, 32, 38
performance 56, 57, 58, 83, 141, 146
    arts; and film 75
    and multiple camera shooting 52, 53 79, 92n11
    and television 86
periodicals/journals/magazines 151
personal
    expression, film as, 13–14
    project, film as 144
perspective, using 40–1
photography 1, 13, 14, 44, 146
Picnic at Hanging Rock (1975) 147
Pierrot le Fou 82
Pinter, Harold 68
pitch, varying 66
planning: work with students 112
play(s) 44, 46, 134
plot 21, 102, 106, 108, 110, 145
    camera- 124
    and story 18–19, 23, 100–1
    see also parallel; shooting scripts; sub-plots
Poe, Edgar Allan 45
poetic language 67, 96–7
    see also commercials
poetry 96–7, 98
    narrative
Point Blank (1967) 145
point-of-view (POV)/over-the-shoulder 36, 37,
    39, 40–1
Popeye (1980) 68
popular
    arts 98–9, 137
    culture 8, 167
    entertainment *x*, 137, 138
    (pop) music 1, 115–16
    taste 104
pop-videos 32, 91, 96, 115–18, 128
postmodernism/modernism 134
post-structuralism 114
post-synchronization 70, 71, 75
Potter, Dennis 50
POV
    see point-of-view

Powell, Michael 133
preparation 27
Price of Coal, The 51
primary
  education 134
  schools 8, 116, 151
Prizzi's Honour 156
producer, control by 63-4
programmes, TV 50-1
project work in classroom: film in *ix*
Psycho (1960) 45, 73
Pudovkin, Vsevolod 3
pulling focus 78, 80
pupils, lower ability: and film 4

Quiet Man, The (1952) 23

radio 1, 5, 13, 75, 123
Ran (1985) 45
Ray, Nicholas 138
Ray, Satyajit 2
reaction shots 37, 38, 106
reading; film/literature 91, 134
realism 45, 49, 53, 54, 56, 57, 71
  in dialogue 67
  and early film 43, 46
  and illusion *x–xi* 19
  in live performance 52, 79
  and long take 89-90
  and narrative 53, 97
  and news broadcasting 110
  in shooting script 60
  theories of 81
  see also documentary style; lighting
reality 43, 51, 53, 54, 57, 65, 80
  illusion of 50, 68, 69, 85
  and news broadcasts 108, 110, 111
'real life' 17, 18
Rear Window (1954) 49
receptivity 91
  see also audience
recording 50, 68
Reed, Carol, 133
reflection 98, 149
Reitz, Edgar 100
rehearsal 58, 90
remakes of films 96, 144
Renoir, Jean 3, 74, 81, 142, 144
  (1974) 143, 148
repetition 27, 35, 104, 109, 117, 118
representation/reality conflict 53
research, historical 47-8, 140
Resnais, Alain, 2, 49, 82
resources 8, 9, 47, 79

rhythm 27, 38
  see also cutting; duration; music; repetition;
    sound; time
Richards, Dick 45
Richards, I. A. 99
Rio Bravo (1959) 67, 142
Rio Grande (1950) 41-2, 71-2, 73
Roaring Twenties, The (1939) 139
Rohmer, Eric 140
roles, overlapping 64
romance(s) 97, 100, 101
Rope (1948) 49, 67, 85-6, 87, 96
Rosenberg, Stuart 30
Rossellini, Roberto 166
Rowell, Arthur 85
Roxie Hart (1942) 67
Russell, Ken 115
Russian
  cinema 133
  directors 56, 138
  Formalist critics 19

Sacrifice, The 83-4
Sarris, Andrew 138
Scarface (1932) 145
Scarlet Street (1946) 144
scenario 58, 63
scene/episode 86
  see also master
school(s), film in curriculum of *ix*
  see also primary; secondary
Schrader, Paul 79
science fiction 45
Scorsese, Martin 34-5, 116, 133
screen direction: 180 degree rule 32
Screen Education (1977/78) 6, 10
screen plays, published 59, 72, 93n27, 159
screen-writer(s) 63, 159-60
script(s) 43, 58-64 93n27, 123, 126, 129, 154
  improvising 90
scripting exercises 60-2, 68, 149
scriptwriters 62-3, 129
Seale, John, 146
secondary education 4, 134
Secondary Schools Teachers' Packs 151
Secret People 154, 161
selection/selectivity 15-16, 54, 61
self/subject/audience relationship, 113
semiotics 114, 131, 166, 167
sequence 20-2, 32, 38, 47, 52, 54, 149
  analysis, 148
  editing 37, 83
  see also narrative

sequencing 21, 38, 46
Sergeant York 141–2
series/serials 66, 128
seriousness/triviality 136
Serpico (1973) 145
Seasonske, Alexander (1980) 143
set(s) 123, 126, 146
setting 34
Seven Samurai (1954) 21, 62
Shakespeare, William 44, 45, 64, 65, 108–9
Shane (1953) 145
Shklovsky, V. B. 19
shooting 56
   procedure 127
   script 59–60, 61, 63, 154
shot/reverse shot, 33–6, 38, 39, 40, 54, 84, 85
   pairs 66, 79 124
shot pattern/duration 38
shots 47, 50, 54, 56, 59, 83, 147, 149
   in *Fawlty Towers* 124–6, 127
   see also angled; close-up; establishing; master;
      medium; long; paired; POV; reaction;
      single; three; two
silence, use of 73
silent film period 44, 47, 49, 59
   see also film, early
simplicity 102, 104, 105
simultaneity, 44, 50
single camera 27–8, 37, 54, 67, 86
single shot 42, 43, 48
sitcoms
   see situation comedy
situation comedy (sitcoms) 51, 123–7, 128
skills 5, 129
Skolimowski, Jerzy 133
snapshots to long take, from **43–93**
soap operas 65, 100, 128
social dimensions 4, 5, 121
society 6, 7
Solzhenitsyn, A. 45
Some Like It Hot (1959) 56
Song of Ceylon 161
Sontag, Susan (1967) 144
sound 9, 27, 43, 49, **69–75**, 147, 148
   background, use of 68, 69, 70
   in commercials 120
   and image 50, 70, 73, 74
   and pop-videos 117
   in 'silent' period 44
   in sitcoms 123
   synchronized 44, 48–9
   of voices 34
   see also music

space 18, 29, 89, 100
spatial
   continuities 83
   relation(s) 89
   unity 89
spectator 110
   see also audience; collaboration; viewer
speech 66, 68, 99, 128
speed/mood 34–5, 76–7, 147, 148
Spellbound (1945) 67
Spielberg, Stephen 133
   (1984) 21–2
spontaneity 52, 58, 68, 127
stage
   see film; theatre
Stagecoach (1939) 41, 82, 93n27
stereotyping 56, 116
still, back-projected 114
still image: pop-video 117
story/stories 18–19, 23, 26–7, 100–1, 105, 108,
   134
storyboard/storyboarding 21, 28, 29, 39, 40, 47,
   149
Straub, Jean-Marie 28
structural conventions 119–20, 132
structuralism 7, 114
structure 41, 102, 104, 105
students, working with x, **19–28**, 40, 47, 48, 75,
   82, 90–2, 106, 129
   acting 57
   commercials 121
   dialogue 67, 68
   lighting 79
   news broadcasting 112–14
   pop-video 117, 118
   scripting exercises 61–2
   sound 74
studio 46, 51, 79, 139
study 91–2, 128–9, 148
style(s) 113, 116, 117, 129
subject/self/audience relationship 113
subjective quality 46–7
subject matter 110, 112, 113, 115, 138
sub-plots 128
Super-8 40, 71, 118, 121
surrealist film 133
suspense 65, 73, 120
syllabus, film in 131, 134, 135
synchronization 44, 48–9, 75
   post- 70, 71

take
   see long

tape, video 77
tape recordings 68
tape-to-tape editing 117
Tarkovsky, Andrei 57, 83–4, 87, 95–6, 100, 102
Tashlin, Frank 138
teachers *x*, 149
Teachers' Packs 151
teaching, film **3–10**, 127–8, 151, 152–3
technique 15–16, 42, 129
technology 12, 53, 105, 115, 153–4
television (TV) 29
86, 99, 123, 127, 128
   aesthetic quality *ix–x*, *xi*, 50, 52–3, 86, 128
   and/as art 6–7, 8, 50, 99–100, 102, 107
     'bad' 138
   camera techniques 27, 37, 51, 55
   development of 13
   in education *ix*, *x*, 1, **3–10**, 149, 152–3
   films on 2, 40, 45, 100
   genres and language **95–130**
   interview/dialogue technique 35, 38–9, 108
   and language 10, 17, 128, **95–130**
   'live' 43, 50, 86
   as narrative 107
   novel dramatizations 61
   as reality 50, 111
   serials 66
   sound 50
   undervaluing potential *x*, 53, 105, 107
   see also commercials; film; news; sitcoms
Tempest, The 121
temporal continuities 83
temporal movement 84–5
Teorema (1968) 143
theatre 42, 44, 49, 50–1, 123, 124, 129
   see also film
theatrical
   devices 84
   format 90
   structure 46, 47
theme/topic work in English 5
theory/theories 1, 6, 7, 15, 115
   see also criticism
They Were Expendable (1945) 57
Thing, The (1951) 67
Third Man, The (1949) 80
This Sporting Life (1963) 57
Thompson, D. *ix*
   (1964) 4
thought, contemporary 115
thought and language 97–8
three-shot, using 40, 41
thriller, the: realism 45

Throne of Blood (1957) 21, 45
time 29, 44, 83, 86, 100, 105–6
   passage of 84–5, 121–2
Time Bandits 62
time-lapse photography 122
timing 120, 126
tinting 121
Tokyo Story (1953) 36, 49
Toland, Gregg 81
   and Ford, J. 82
Tolstoy, L. 121
tone 22
Touch of Evil (1958) 28, 86–7
Toute Une Nuit (1982) 111
tracking shot 86, 88
tradition 29, 134
Traffik 121
Train Entering a Station, A (1985) 80–1
trivia, appeal of 105
Truffaut, Francois 2, 142
   (1969) 85, 86
TV
   see television
Twentieth Century (1934) 67
two-dimensionality 82
Two Rode Together (1961) 90
two-shot 37, 38, 41, 54, 106, 114, 159
   and close-up: dialogue 67
   with multiple cameras 52
'typage' 56

UFA: Germany 78, 81
Ulmer, Edgar 138
unconventionality/excess 18
Une Femme Mariée 82
university students: short films 116

value
   judgment criteria 96, 97
   and meaning 102
Vampyr (1931) 146
variety 38–9
vaudeville: influence on film 44
verbal arts: and film 75, 131–50
Vertov, Dziga 9
video 8, 9, 12, 13, 69–70, 127, 149
   aesthetic quality *ix–x*, *xi*
   camera 29, 48, 75–7, 79
   editing 54, 112, 117, 121
   in education 1, 152–3
   sets, distribution of 127
   sound 48, 71
   students working with 40, 67

tape 77
  see also film; pop-
Vidor, K. 138
viewer 95, 113
  see also audience; spectator
Violent Saturday (1955) 146
vision/sound 50
visual arts 75
visual language 49, 65
Vivre sa vie (1962) 88, 90
voice(s) 34, 72
voice-over 57

Wagonmaster (1950) 146
Wallis, Hal 139
Walsh, Raoul 138, 139
Warhol, Andy 96
Watson, R. (1987) 127, 130n17
Webb, E. (1987) 8, 10
Wedding A (1978) 68
Weekend (1967) 88
Weir, Peter 145, 146–7
Wellman, William 67, 138
Welles, Orson 82, 86–7
Wenders, Wim 100
What's Up, Doc? (1972) 67
Wheare Report (1950) 3

Wild Bunch, The (1969) 45
Wilde, Alan (1981) 134
Williams, Billy 116
Williams, R. (1962) 4
  (1974) 108, 130n12
Willie and Phil 142
Willis, Gordon 116
Window, The (1949) 145
Without Reservations (1946) 56
Witness (1985) 140, 144–9
  see also plot
Woman of Affairs, A (1928) 81–2
Wood, Robin (1976) 141–2
Wollen, P. (1969) 43
Wright, B. 161
writers, film 51, 60, 136, 159–60
  see also screen; script
writing as concept of film 68
Wuthering Heights (1939) 81
Wyler, Williams 81, 146

Year of Living Dangerously, The (1982) 146
Yol 139

Zelig (1983) 56
Zsigmond, Vilmos 116